REBUILDI
SCOTLAN

1945-1975

REBUILDING SCOTLAND

SCOTLAND

THE POSTWAR VISION 1945-1975

EDITED BY MILES GLENDINNING

TUCKWELL PRESS

Previous pages:
GLASGOW'S HOUSING CRUSADE
Councillor David Gibson, the Corporation's Housing Committee
Convener, inspects the Scotstoun House multi-storey
development along with the Lord Provost, Dame Jean Roberts,
during construction in 1963. [Outram]

First published in 1997 by
Tuckwell Press Ltd
The Mill House
Phantassie
East Linton
East Lothian
EH40 3DG

ISBN 0 898410 33 X

British Library Cataloguing -in-Publication Data
A cataloguerecord for this book is available
on request from the British Library

Book design by Mark Blackadder

The Editor and Publishers wish to acknowledge the support of:

RCAHMS

ROYAL FINE ART
COMMISSION *for* SCOTLAND

Printed in Spain by GraphyCems

CONTENTS

MM: Contributions to RFACS 1993 'Minds Meeting' seminars

VR: Contributions to DOCOMOMO Scottish Conference 1992 ('Visions Revisited')

GENERAL ACKNOWLEDGEMENTS

The material in this book was compiled under the aegis of DOCOMOMO Scottish National Group. The editor would like to thank the other members of the group committee (at the time of preparation: Claudia Boelling, Suzanne Ewing, Ranald MacInnes, David Page, Sally Stewart, Paul Stirton, Diane M Watters, David Whitham) for help at various stages in this process. The 'Visions Revisited' conference was mainly organised by Ranald MacInnes and Paul Stirton, and the 'Minds Meeting' seminars were organised by Suzanne Ewing (with Charles Prosser of RFACS).

In addition to the help given by individual contributors in checking their own papers, the editor also thanks those who read through the manuscript of Part One, including Isi Metzstein, James Morris and Robert Steedman, Aidan Matthew, John and Margaret Richards. Others who helped in the preparation of the book, in various ways, include: Kirsteen Borland, Alec Buchanan Campbell, Sam Bunton Junior, Ian Campbell, Kate Comfort, Mrs Sadie Gibson, Andrew Gilmour, Sir Robert Grieve, Alison, Kitty and Sally Horsey, Juliet Kinchin, Derek Lyddon, Richard J McCarron, Charles McKean, Aonghus Mackechnie, Stefan Muthesius, Miles Oglethorpe, Charles Prosser, Ron Simpson, Geoffrey Stell, Margaret Tierney, and the staff of the National Monuments Record, the RCAHMS Photographic Department, and the Glasgow City Archive (formerly Strathclyde Regional Archives).

PICTURE ACKNOWLEDGEMENTS

Academy Publications: 3.1; Copcutt 1963 article
Architects' Journal: 1.27, 1.32, 3.38
Rowand Anderson Partnership: 1.61, 4.23, 4.26, 4.27
Baxter, Clark & Paul: 1.59, 4.13
Boswell, Mitchell & Johnston: 1.71
L C H Bunton: 3.24
S Bunton Jnr: 3.26
Mary Cosh: 1.15
Cumbernauld Development Corporation: 1.50, 1.51, 1.52, 2.1, 3.2-3.8, 4.45, 4.46
A Daniels: 2.13
Edinburgh District Council: 2.23
Fife Regional Council: 1.44
GEC: 1.35, 4.65
Mrs S Gibson: 1.39, 2.7
Gillespie, Kidd & Coia: 1.53, 1.68, 2.12, 3.56, 3.57, 3.62-3.68, 4.7, 4.42, 4.48
Glasgow District Council: 1.40, 1.47, 2.10, 3.27-3.29, 4.51, 4.58
Gordon & Dey: 1.7
Gray's School: 4.12
HLM Architects: 4.68
Holmes Partnership: 4.49
Hurd Rolland: 1.14, 4.17
Hector Innes: 4.2
R McCarron: 4.70
J Mackintosh: 1.46, 2.30, 4.36, 4.47
Matheson Gleave: 4.40
Aidan Matthew: 1.25, 1.28
B L C Moira: 4.39
Morris & Steedman: 3.39-3.45, 3.48, 4.16

Outram: Front Cover, 1.38, 1.45, 1.75, 2.22

Planair: 3.9

RCAHMS: 1.6, 1.8, 1.9, 1.11, 1.17, 1.26, 1.34, 1.36,
1.37, 1.41, 1.49, 1.55-1.57, 1.62, 1.72–1.74, 2.8,
2.14, 2.18, 2.31, 3.10, 3.13, 3.17, 3.25, 3.30,
3.59–3.61, 3.71, 3.73, 3.76, 3.77, 4.4, 4.11, 4.21,
4.24, 4.32, 4.37, 4.38, 4.43, 4.50, 4.53, 4.55, 4.56,
4.66, 4.67

Reiach & Hall: 4.22, 4.34

RMJM: 1.29, 1.33, 1.54, 3.49–3.54, 4.5, 4.8, 4.25,
4.29–4.31, 4.69

Pat Rogan: 2.19

Royal Incorporation of Architects in Scotland: 1.1,
1.10, 1.13, 1.18, 1.30. 1.31, 1.64, 1.65, 2.3, 3.11,
3.14, 3.15, 3.18, 3.19, 3.21-3.23, 3.55, 3.72, 3.75,
4.9, 4.15, 4.20, 4.28, 4.33, 4.35, 4.54, 4.71

The Scotsman: 2.5, 2.20, 2.21, 2.24, 3.20

Scottish National Portrait Gallery: 3.12

Scottish Office Environment Department: 1.5

Scottish Power: 4.41

Scottish Special Housing Association: 1.20, 2.6, 2.15

Scott Wilson Kirkpatrick: 2.26–2.29

St Andrews University: 4.10

Strathclyde Regional Archive: 1.21, 2.4, 4.52, 4.59,
4.60

D C Thomson: 1.43, 2.9, 2.17

UKAEA: 4.14

Warnett Kennedy: 1.19

Sir Anthony Wheeler: 1.22, 1.58, 1.60, 1.67,
3.31–3.37, 4.6

Sir W Whitfield: 3.70

G F Wilson: 1.42

Wylie Shanks: 4.61, 4.62

Raymond Young: 1.69

NOTES ON CONTRIBUTORS

MARK BAINES
Architect, Lecturer in architecture and architectural history and year master at Mackintosh School of Architecture.

GEOFFREY COPCUTT
Group Leader (Central Area), Cumbernauld Development Corporation Architects' Department, late 1950s/early 1960s; subsequently worked in Craigavon New Town (Ireland).

RONNIE CRAMOND
Senior Administrator (Principal, Assistant Secretary, Under Secretary) in the Department of Health for Scotland/Scottish Development Department, 1957–77.

MILES GLENDINNING
Head of Topographical and Threatened Buildings Surveys, RCAHMS. Committee member, DOCO-MOMO Scottish National Group. Honorary Fellow, Department of Social Policy, University of Edinburgh.

PROFESSOR HUBERT–JAN HENKET
Co–Founder of DOCOMOMO International, and Chairman, Netherlands DOCOMOMO Working Party. Architect, and Professor at Eindhoven University.

RT. HON. DR. J. DICKSON MABON
MP for Greenock, 1955-83. 1964-7: Joint Parliamentary Under-Secretary of State (Minister in charge of the Scottish Development Department). Subsequently Minister of State at the Scottish Office and the Department of Energy.

JAMES P. McCAFFERTY
Partner, Scott Wilson Kirkpatrick, Consulting Engineers. Worked on motorway and other road schemes in 1960s, including Glasgow Inner Ring Road. Subsequently involved in projects in Scotland, England, Middle East, Hong Kong and Nigeria.

PROFESSOR CHARLES McKEAN
Professor of Architecture, Dundee University. Secretary, Royal Incorporation of Architects in Scotland, 1979-95; author of *The Scottish Thirties*, and numerous RIAS Guides (as Series Editor).

PROFESSOR ANDREW MacMILLAN
Professor of Architecture and Head of the Mackintosh School of Architecture, Glasgow, 1973-1994. Former partner in Gillespie, Kidd & Coia, architects.

PROFESSOR ISI METZSTEIN
Formerly Forbes Professor of Architecture, University of Edinburgh; has also taught widely elsewhere, e.g. at Mackintosh School, Architectural Association (London) and St Louis, Missouri. Former partner in Gillespie, Kidd & Coia, architects.

PROFESSOR PATRICK NUTTGENS
Formerly Professor of Architecture, University of York (since 1986, Hon. Professor) and Director of Leeds Polytechnic, 1969-86.

DAVID PAGE
Partner in Page and Park, architects; commentator on contemporary architecture and lecturer in architectural theory at the University of Strathclyde. Member of the Royal Fine Art Commission for Scotland.

JOHN RICHARDS

Architect (John Richards Associates). Partner in
Robert Matthew, Johnson-Marshall & Partners, 1964-
86 (Chairman, 1983-6). Former Deputy Chairman,
Scottish Homes.

PROFESSOR CHARLES ROBERTSON

Professor of Architecture, University of Strathclyde.
Formerly Chief Executive of the National Building
Agency. Was the job architect for Basil Spence &
Partners' Hutchesontown/ Gorbals Area 'C' develop-
ment.

PATRICK ROGAN

Councillor for Holyrood Ward, Edinburgh
Corporation, 1954-73; Bailie, 1966-9. Police Judge,
1975-84. Chairman of the Corporation's Housing
Committee, 1962-5.

ROBERT STEEDMAN

Partner, Morris & Steedman, architects and landscape
architects. Governor, Edinburgh College of Art.
Secretary, Royal Scottish Academy, 1983-91.

PROFESSOR DAVID WALKER

Hon. Professor of Architectural History, St Andrews
University; formerly (to 1993) Chief Inspector of
Historic Buildings, Scottish Development
Department/Historic Scotland.

SIR ANTHONY WHEELER

Consultant (before 1986, Partner), Wheeler &
Sproson, architects and town planners. President of
the Royal Scottish Academy, 1983-90.

SIR WILLIAM WHITFIELD

Senior Partner, Whitfield Partners, architects, and former Professor of Architecture, Victoria University of
Manchester.

PROLOGUE

The early postwar period of Scottish history – the years between approximately 1945 and 1975 – witnessed a national reconstruction drive of unprecedented vigour. So colossal and audacious were its utopian visions that we, today, have difficulty in even grasping, let alone inhabiting them. The reaction to this disparity of values during the past twenty years, for the most part, has been violent condemnation. (Figs. 1.1, 1.2) Yet this is sure to change, as is demonstrated by the precedent of nineteenth-century architecture, and its equally tempestuous passage through the cycle of opinion. That was a century of the most violent transformation, a period which brought Scotland the most shocking social and visual dislocations in its wake. And these inspired, at the time,

comprehensive denunciations from all sides, from ordinary people and intelligentsia alike. Yet, once fresh changes had dimmed memories, the condemnations gradually fell silent, and were replaced by more measured appraisals, and then by nostalgic praise: in the 1960s and 70s the word 'tenement' changed, within a few years, from a symbol of the harsh modernity of industrial capitalism to an emblem of 'traditional' urban community.

This volume has been motivated by the belief that we are now, in the 1990s, just reaching a position where we can begin building up a historical perspective on the postwar era of reconstruction. On the one hand, this is arguably historically a closed subject: no longer

1.1 Hutchesontown/Gorbals Area 'C' (Basil Spence, built 1960-6): 1958 perspective of proposed blocks.

1.2 'Blowdown' of Hutchesontown 'C' on 12 September 1993.

do 'crusading' councillors call for the maximum output of new tower blocks, or 'utopian' Modern architects demand the definition of scientific standards of mass provision – although the hyper-urbanist concepts of some contemporary international architecture point to the possible revival of Modernist concerns such as 'density' and 'urbanity'. And some major Modern buildings are now in decay, even being demolished. But at the same time, many of those key people of the time are still around, to recall their ideals and values to us. Today's blanket anti-Modern rhetoric, which brands an entire generation as base and corrupt, is not only in itself implausibly simplistic but also, in the process, silences the potentially invaluable testimony of participants from those years – people whose experience could be of help not only to the academic historian and researcher, but also to those concerned with remedying the real practical problems which arise out of any revolutionary period of building. Only when the raucous background noise of invective finally ceases will this historical 'silence' also end, and today's real concerns about postwar buildings begin to be properly recorded and addressed.

This, then, is the aim of this volume: to begin the task of clearing away the blanket condemnations, and of dissolving the Utopia-Dystopia polarisations. It contains two main sections. The first (Part 1) presents a brief historical introduction to this period, drawn from some primary sources, but chiefly from published material: for a fuller account, readers should consult Chapters 8 and 9 of *A History of Scottish Architecture* (Edinburgh, 1996, by M. Glendinning, A MacKechnie,

R MacInnes). The second section (Parts 2, 3, 4) is the more important, as it contains a selection of direct testimonies from the years 1945 to 1975, in the form of a series of lectures and papers by key figures from that time. For arguably, in a controversial subject such as this, the most accessible way of beginning a reassessment is to listen to the voices and concerns of those who were actually involved.

As is well known, these years, in Scottish architecture, were dominated by Modernism. But the book also encompasses other prominent architectural movements of the time – including those tendencies, carried over from the '30s, which were most usually referred to at the time as 'Traditional' or 'Traditionalist'. And it also encompasses *all* kinds of buildings during that period, the everyday alongside the architecturally elevated.

While its architectural and building-type scope is wide, its approach to the sociology of architecture and building provision is more selective. In this area we begin by the sweeping claim, that all historical investigations of buildings ask two main types of questions. The first is the subject of this book: the provision of the buildings in the first place. Here the fundamental questions are: why, by whom, how? In other words: What was the purpose of the building? Who was the patron? And how did the designer and constructor address these demands? In practice, as we will see in the following pages, answers to these questions tend to merge into more complex formulations encompassing groups of ideas: examples of such formulations are 'functionalism', 'housing crusade', or 'package-deal building'.

The second type of question looks into what happened after the buildings were completed: their use, experience – all the things which nowadays seem most immediate in the case of buildings over 20 years old. This vast area, which requires a different range of historical expertise from the investigation of provision – expertise concerned especially with questions of habitation, building repair and management – is not addressed directly or systematically in the present volume. It is, however, frequently touched on in passing, not least because there are significant areas of overlap, notably the question of how the providers thought their buildings would be used. However, we must remind ourselves that our own present-day orthodoxy of 'user participation' in design and provision – however much rooted in the Modern concern for definition of 'user needs' – is, in its full-blown form, only a recent phenomenon, falling largely outwith the chronological scope of this book. The intention here is not to reiterate yet again the values of our own time, but to begin the rediscovery and reassessment of the values of the great postwar rebuilding drive, and to draw attention to key built realisations of those ideals.

These early postwar buildings, like their nineteenth-century predecessors, are monuments to a revolution in all aspects of building. Some evoke the era's sheer energy, the vast quantity and often huge scale of building; and some are exemplars of its constructional and technical daring. Others, by contrast, testify to the fact that architecture, as an art, flourished undiminished during these years. This was a period of complexity, in its often tempestuous debates and ideas, and yet also of simplicity – of consensual confidence in progress and rationality, however variously defined.

The contents of this volume are derived largely from activities organised, or co-organised, by the newly founded Scottish National Group of DOCOMOMO – an international working party which, as its acronym indicates, is dedicated to the 'Documentation and Conservation of the Modern Movement'. Professor Hubert-Jan Henket's contribution (included in Part Two of this book) explains in more detail about the organisation's purpose and multi-national structure. In mapping out an initial strategy, DOCOMOMO decided to begin by organising a conference, to put the reassessment of postwar architecture firmly on the public agenda. This conference, 'Visions Revisited', sponsored by Historic Scotland and by the Royal Incorporation of Architects in Scotland (RIAS), took place in October 1992 at the University of Glasgow, and brought together testimonies from key contemporary actors from the 60s, with contributions from younger historians and an audience of professionals and interested lay people.

'Visions Revisited' was followed up with two events during 1993, arranged in collaboration with other national organisations. A seminar series, organised along with the Royal Fine Art Commission for Scotland, elaborated the idea of first-hand testimonies, by setting several key Modern designers in conversation with present-day critics and historians. In other words, a two-pronged approach: direct recollection of the past; and engagement of the past with present-day values. The RIAS Festival Exhibition, for which DOCOMOMO acted as curators and authors, took public debate a stage further, by identifying sixty key monuments of historical and architectural importance, and – to encourage debate and research – putting them on public display through the medium of original drawings, photographs and models. These events will, it is hoped, lead on to successively more focused initiatives in the future, including the preparation of a formal register of monuments of significance (derived from the original 'sixty' list) for the use of ICOMOS and Historic Scotland; and, of course, the publication of the present book.

In the interests of comprehensibility, this book has merged the 1992 and 1993 lectures into a single series, arranged thematically under two basic section headings. The first group of lecture papers, 'Patronage and Building' (Part Two of the book), views buildings above all in their political and social context: in other words, in the framework of an archaeology of building provision. The other group of papers (Part Three), 'Architects' Architecture', focuses on one particular way of visualising buildings – as works of architecture – and on the description of this process chiefly through the words of designers themselves; and it rounds off the series of papers by reproducing the wide-ranging discussion which ended the 'Visions Revisited' conference. In order to retain the immediacy of the original lectures, we have not, in this book, converted the papers into academic footnoted texts. Part Four presents, with slight modifications, the list of sixty key buildings prepared for the RIAS 1993 exhibition.

All in all, this volume should be seen not as any kind of definitive history of Modern architecture in Scotland, but rather, as the first step in the opening up of the subject – a presentation of contemporary testimonies and preliminary present-day accounts, intended to lay down markers for future detailed research.

PART ONE
1945-75: AN ARCHITECTURAL INTRODUCTION
Miles Glendinning

'Above all, there was a belief in the inevitability and desirability of progress. Inventions, once made, could not be de-invented. Art had gone through a revolution since Mondrian and Stravinsky which could not be ignored. All the lines of all the graphs were going up: population, health, the economy, and expectations of an egalitarian and well-ordered society.' John Richards, 1985 (1)

PRELUDE TO REVOLUTION: THE INTERWAR AND WARTIME EXPERIENCE

To trace the roots of the ideas which drove Scotland's post–1945 reconstruction, we actually have to begin before the First World War. Prior to 1914, Scottish national identity, and nationalistic pride, had been bound up with the global capitalist and colonialist adventure of the British empire: Scotland was proud to be the 'imperial partner'. But this confident conception of a martial Presbyterian nation was dealt a heavy blow in the trenches of the Western Front. From that point on, a new pattern of economy and society began to emerge, in which State intervention, guided increasingly by ideals of social welfare, would provide the central dynamic.

During the interwar period of transition, a great variety of initiatives was attempted. In the social housing field, for instance, the 1917 Ballantyne Commission Report's denunciation of speculative housing and demand for municipal control was exploited by Glasgow Corporation through a direct building campaign, while Edinburgh attempted a policy of municipal support for private building. The capital, indeed, saw something of an economic recovery during these years, but the deep 1930s slump elsewhere in the country prompted the beginnings of Government-sponsored industrial development programmes. That these would increasingly be linked with social building as part of planned 'development' was indicated by the Government's 1937 foundation of the Scottish Special (Areas) Housing Association (SSHA), a State housebuilding organisation dedicated to provision in depressed areas. (2)

The architectural response to these transformations was similarly measured and gradual, avoiding the Modernist upheavals of countries such as Germany or Russia. (3) Two contrasting architectural traditions had become dominant at the turn of the century – a Glasgow-based tendency of forward-looking Beaux-Arts rationalism, led by J J Burnet, who characterised the architect as 'the poet of modern necessity', (4) and an Edinburgh-based tendency, led by Rowand Anderson, Geddes and Lorimer, which reacted against aggressive modernity by evoking the ideal of an archaising Scottish wholeness. These broadly continued into the 1920s and '30s, with the addition of decorative elements drawn from Continental and US 'Art Deco' Modernism. (5) The culmination of this phase was the dignified, axial, yet also popular Art Deco design of the 1938 Glasgow Empire Exhibition, superintended by Burnet's interwar partner Thomas S Tait. (6) (Figs. 1.3, 1.4)

1.4 Opposite. Night view from 1938 Glasgow Empire Exhibition brochure: at left, T S Tait's Tower of Empire; at centre, Basil Spence's ICI Pavilion.

Among the younger generation, some, such as Basil Spence and William H Kininmonth, continued in a playfully eclectic Art Deco vein almost up to the war. (7) In Glasgow, the young Jack Coia powerfully energised both the teaching and the practice of the Glasgow Beaux-Arts tradition. (8) However, the mid and late '30s also saw the first stirrings of broader architectural change, in the form of a new polarisation around the question of the nature and degree of modernity. On the one hand, there was a 'Traditionalist' grouping springing from the Andersonian utopianism of golden-age Scots wholeness, and led by the Saltire Society, Lord Bute and Sir John Stirling-Maxwell. They demanded a 'deeper' or 'sane' modernism, a 'sound modern tradition in building design' inspired by (although no longer literally based on) 16th and 17th century Scots architecture. The aim was a 'national awakening' which would expunge cosmopolitanism and class divisions and help restore an organic unity of the nation. (9) Ideas, and rhetoric, such as this, were popular in various

forms all over Europe in the '30s, not just in the totalitarian states: we need only cite the Swedish 'People's Home' movement, with its demands for mass social reorganisation. (10) Architectural expressions of these ideas varied from a harled, steep-roofed geometry for houses to a cubic, austere classicism for public buildings. Two of the most distinguished examples of the latter were begun in the late '30s, left as partly-assembled steel skeletons during the war, and finished in the 50s: Reginald Fairlie's National Library of Scotland (1938-55) and David Carr's Kirkcaldy Town House (1937-56).

In strong contrast to this Traditionalism, younger designers of the late '30s such as Robert Matthew, in Edinburgh, and Warnett Kennedy, in Glasgow, also aspired to the aim of social progress, but believed that this should be achieved by a stepping up of rationalist, or 'Functionalist' Modernism, in areas such as housing design and, above all, town and country planning. (11) While these two widely contrasting views exemplified the open-endedness of the ideal of modernity in architecture – an open-endedness which would lead to further controversies in the 1960s and '70s – it should be noted that Scotland, during the interwar years, saw no built realisations of mainstream 'International Modernism', as exemplified, and institutionalised, by the Congrès Internationaux d'Architecture Moderne (CIAM).

The nation survived World War II with relatively light material damage, excepting the devastation of Clydebank in 1941. (Fig. 1.5) But the climate of 'war effort' gave an urgent boost to the demands of the late '30s for national reconstruction through centralised planning. The reshaping of the idea of the nation, which had been in progress throughout the interwar years, was now reinforced to the point where laissez-faire Scots imperialism could be portrayed as anti-patriotic: William Power wrote in 1941 that Victorian Scotland, 'if it was not a mere "knuckle-bone of England", was an appendage and playground of an Imperial economic system, and its organisation on anything like a national basis was out of the question', whereas now 'national planning is no longer a Utopian fantasy. It is an urgent and admitted necessity, to which the State has implicitly pledged itself'. (12)

1.3 Thomas S. Tait's St Andrew's House, 1936-9 (centre of devolved Scottish government administration) portrayed on the cover of J A Bowie's 1939 book, *The Future of Scotland* – a key text advocating modernisation of the Scottish economy and diversification away from heavy industry.

In fact, despite Power's rhetoric, this new strategy, like that of imperialist Scotland before it, rested on a combination of cultural/social autonomy with a continuing consensus between Scotland and England concerning the overall direction of state policy. (13) Coordinated by the Scottish Office, especially by the Department of Health for Scotland (DHS: responsible for housing and planning as well as health), the overriding aim of the 1940s and '50s was to combine social regeneration with industrial diversification, (14) balancing the needs of the industrial Lowlands for regeneration with those of the Highlands for the stemming of depopulation. (15) Some of the programmes, such as a daring new hydro-electric programme in the Highlands, would command wide consensus support, while others would prove more contentious, such as the project to force over-crowded Glasgow to 'overspill' her excess population into 'new towns'. But all would be united by the wartime spirit of mobilisation and 'planning'. Even the substantial prewar efforts at reform were now branded inadequate: a 'tormented, dolorous and dole-ridden' era

of 'ineptitude' (16) As Alan Reiach and Robert Hurd wrote in 1941: 'Here is a new Scotland to be built.' (17)

THE TWILIGHT OF TRADITIONALISM

In the early postwar years, the bulk of actual building, especially in the East, was still substantially influenced by Traditionalist ideas carried over from the late 1930s. Many architects remained determined to resist international cosmopolitanism, and to maintain – in contrast to CIAM Functionalism – some distinctions between honorific buildings and more utilitarian types. This experience was mirrored in several other countries around 1950; in the Netherlands, former International Modernist J J P Oud wrote in 1947: 'I have no belief in the application of the form of labourer-dwellings and factories to office-buildings, town halls, and churches!' (18) In some cases, architects simply perpetuated the existing stylistic recipes of the late 30s – a cubic classicism for public buildings, a pitched-roof, harled style for religious or domestic

PLANNING

OUR NEW

HOMES

REPORT BY THE SCOTTISH HOUSING ADVISORY COMMITTEE ON THE DESIGN, PLANNING AND FURNISHING OF NEW HOUSES

Publication prepared for the Committee by the Department of Health for Scotland

EDINBURGH: HIS MAJESTY'S STATIONERY OFFICE. 1944

Price 3s. 0d. net

"THE policy of waging war until victory would be incomplete, and indeed spoiled, if it were not accompanied by a policy of food, work and homes in the period following the victory for the men and women who fought and won."

The Prime Minister: 9th November 1943.

Frontispiece

1.5 Title page and frontispiece of the Scottish Housing Advisory Committee's 1944 prescription for postwar housing design and furnishing, *Planning Our New Homes* (the Westwood Report). The frontispiece shows central Clydebank immediately following the two air raids of March 1941.

structures, and a dynamic 'Streamform' for 'modern' building types. But alongside this, some designers tried to take the war into the Modern camp, by devising alternative, Traditionalist solutions for that central concern of state reconstruction, the drive to provide new housing and 'communities'.

Of the prominent architects who continued with an interwar-style eclecticism, perhaps the most versatile, covering a full range of building types with subtly differentiated styles, was Spence's former partner, W H Kininmonth (of Rowand Anderson, Kininmonth and Paul). In public buildings, his work continued a late 1930s formality, while avoiding overbearing scale: for example, at Pollock Halls university residences in Edinburgh (1952-9). (19) A small country house, Philiphaugh (1964), near Selkirk, was built as a plain harled classical block with high piended roof and elaborately pedimented doorway. For a University examination halls building in Chambers Street, directly opposite Old College (1954), Kininmonth avoided modernism in favour of a more vertical, monumental classicism, while building at the same time the extravagantly modernist Renfrew Airport Terminal, fronted by a soaring bowstring arch – a building resembling nothing so much as one of the 'streamform' pavilions at the 1939 New York World's Fair. (20) The official buildings designed by Government architect Stewart Sim also reflected the Traditionalist philosophy of differentiation of building types by style, including the almost neo-classical Fountainbridge Telephone Exchange, Edinburgh (1948-50), and the severely Lorimerian detached pavilions of the Carstairs State Institution, a high-security national mental hospital built in 1956-8. (Fig. 1.6)

In a broad overview of early postwar building types dominated by Traditionalism, there was also much continuity with the 1930s. The renowned Glasgow Beaux-Arts institutional architect E G Wylie, appointed in 1937 to the post of Senior Co-ordinating Architect to the state-sponsored Scottish Industrial Estates company, ensured consistency in the horizontally-styled industrial developments under his oversight, and a similar manner was adopted in some social buildings such as Thomas S Cordiner's Notre Dame School, Glasgow (designed 1939, built 1949-53), and Lourdes School (1951-7). In urban commercial buildings in the East, a severe classicism was also perpetuated: for example, in W N W Ramsay's Edinburgh University Medical School (1951), or in Esme Gordon's work. (Fig. 1.7) The new projects of the Church of Scotland were also, on the whole, modestly Traditionalist, in a somewhat domestic manner, as at Kininmonth's Drylaw (1956) or Ian G Lindsay & Partners' Livingston Station and Colinton Mains churches (1949 and 1954). By contrast, Catholic churches in the West, where the 1950s saw a massive building drive in the many new parishes, kept up and even accentuated their honorific status, with brick monumentality on the exterior and marble adornment inside. Approaches ranged from a fairly conservative

1.6 Montrose House, Glasgow: a notable example of Traditionalist government architecture. (Stewart Sim, 1951-3)

1.7 Electricity Board office and showroom, George Street, Edinburgh (Gordon & Dey, 1960-4, with sculpture by Tom Whalen).

neo-Romanesque, as at Alexander McAnally's St Teresa of Lisieux, Glasgow (1956-8), to the triangular 'Gothic' elements of Jack Coia's monumental St Lawrence, Greenock (1951-4) and Cordiner's A-framed Immaculate Conception church, Glasgow (1955-6). (Figs. 1.8, 1.9) A more unusual offshoot of the continuing Catholic emphasis on hierarchical decorativeness in churches was the remarkable Italian Chapel on Lambholm, Orkney: a conversion of two Nissen huts designed and executed by Domenico Chiocchetti and other Italian prisoners of war in 1943-5: highlights of the scheme were the elaborate Gothic facade and the sanctuary, featuring an altar painting based on Nicolo Barabina's Madonna of the Olives.

One of the largest religious projects of those years to consciously evoke 'traditional' imagery – in the context, however, not of Scotland but of England – was Basil Spence's winning design in the 1951 competition for a new Anglican Cathedral at Coventry (built 1954-62). We will discuss below the racy Modernity adopted by Spence in exhibition design. Here, by contrast, he put his theatrical skills to use in creating a

stone-faced image of 'permanence': 'Although it was fashionable to design glass boxes and cubes, I went the other way.' (21) The building's focus, above the altar, was a giant tapestry by Graham Sutherland, while at the other end, a huge glass window and overhanging external canopy attempted to integrate the ruins of the old cathedral within the sequence of spaces. Inside and out, there was a proliferation of commemorative features, such as stained glass windows or sculptural detail: the Gothic detailing Spence had originally planned was eventually replaced by more abstract symbols, but there remained generalised evocations of 'English tradition', notably in the 'Perpendicular' connotations of the huge entrance window and of the column and vault pattern. A detailed factual account of the cathedral's conception and planning is contained in Campbell's books. (22) Charles Robertson's paper in this book recalls the organisation and work of Spence's office (based in both London and Edinburgh) in the late 50s and early 60s. (Fig. 1.10)

Alongside these efforts in public and religious architecture, there were also Traditionalist attempts to tackle the wider issues of housing and replanning, bringing to bear 'organic' or 'national' concepts of Community that were rather different to those of their modernist contemporaries, and fairly closely related to the turn-of-century ideas of Geddes. (23) In 1948, for example, Frank Mears published a report on the replanning of Central and South East Scotland Plan, which advocated the use of nucleated towns, similar

1.9 Immaculate Conception Church, Glasgow, built in 1955-6 to the designs of Thomas Cordiner: 1987 view prior to demolition. The triangular theme represented the Holy Trinity.

1.10 Coventry Cathedral: early design by Basil Spence, 1951, looking from ruined old cathedral through porch to altar.

to old small burghs, as the main framework of development. (24) The scope of Mears's Traditionalist vision extended equally to the small-scale and intense: he designed the Royal Scots memorial in Edinburgh (erected 1951-2) as a curved line of monoliths evoking 'something of the simple dignity of an ancient stone circle.' (25) The climax of Traditionalist planning was a bold series of power stations in the Highlands, commissioned by the North of Scotland Hydro-Electric Board (set up in 1943), which carried on the 1930s trend of cubic, austere classicism, here intensified with the use of much rock-faced rubble. H O Tarbolton designed the Sloy (1946-50) and Tummel-Garry (1947-53) schemes, while subsequent stations were the work of James Shearer and Annand. Describing the Fasnakyle station (1952), in contrast to Modernist excitement at the display of industrial power, Shearer emphasised its concealment beneath the serenity of elevated landscape and architecture, hailing 'the stillness of the place, over which only the clouds now move . . . no visitor walking about in the quiet forecourt at Fasnakyle has any inkling that he is crossing three eight-feet diameter pipes containing water with an explosive pressure of four hundred and fifty feet of head.' (26) (Figs. 1.11, 1.12, 1.13)

Urban replanning schemes by Traditionalists varied from those mainly comprising preservation to new developments or infill in a more openly 'contemporary' manner. The latter were increasingly influenced by a new conception of Scottish 'Vernacular', a kind of picturesque urban pattern of enclosed-space design, mainly inspired by simple old buildings in the countryside or small burghs. These visual preferences were bolstered by socio-architectural definitions of small-burgh community: for example, in 1951, St Andrews preservationist Ronald Cant exalted Scots medieval towns as paragons of 'functional . . . human community'. (27) The bogeyman was the same as it had been in an influential Traditionalist call for burgh preservation in 1936 by Lord Bute: namely, the new municipal housing schemes, whose sanitary openness was seen as alienating and fragmenting. (28) In 1961, burgh preservation activist Moultrie R Kelsall claimed that a child reared in 'a village where there is ample witness to the past in stone and lime is likely to have a much deeper sense of social continuity – of being part of a mature, yet still developing community – than a child brought up in a typical housing scheme, raw, rootless, and lacking any individuality.' (29) The Royal Mile in Edinburgh also saw a rejuvenation of Geddes-like conservative surgery at the hands of the key Traditionalist architect, Robert Hurd, in a programme designed to restore the Canongate's 'couthy, intimate quality': the programme comprised Tolbooth Area Redevelopment (1953-8), Morocco Land (1956-7), and Chessel's Court (1958-66). (30) The postwar work of Ian Lindsay

1.12 NOSHEB's Achanalt Power Station, Conon Valley scheme (Shearer & Annand, from 1951). In Shearer's words, 'The station is built hard against a great vertical cliff on two sides and has a massive simplicity . . . the few window openings are in exposed aggregate concrete blocks of simple heavy section . . . the random rubble is taken from the site. The whole quality of the building in conception, massing and material seems to spring naturally from its location. It comes nearest perhaps of all the power stations in the Conon Valley to having a really dynamic character.' (*The Builder*, 4-5-1956)

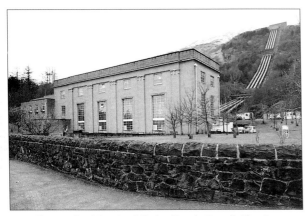

1.11 The North of Scotland Hydro-Electric Board's Sloy Power Station (H.O. Tarbolton, 1946-50).

(Opposite) 1.8 St Lawrence's Church, Greenock (Gillespie, Kidd & Coia, 1951-4).

1.13 Unrealised proposal by Leslie Grahame Thomson, 1949, for NOSHEB Central Control, Research and Headquarters Buildings, Pitlochry, in a towered Lorimerian manner.

1.14 View of Robert Hurd & Partners' Chessels Court redevelopment, Edinburgh, when newly completed in 1966.

included not only oversight of a nationwide programme of historic-buildings 'listing' for the government (an extension of pioneering 'burgh lists' of 1936 carried out for Lord Bute), but also active involvement in burgh preservation, especially for the National Trust for Scotland's new 'Little Houses' programme. Of Lindsay's individual restorations, the most noteworthy was that of Iona Abbey (1939-56). (Figs. 1.14, 1.15, 1.16, 1.17)

SETTING THE 'STANDARDS': MODERNIST EXPERIMENTS IN THE 1940s AND EARLY 50s

The war's centralised planning and industrialised production chimed in with Modernist Functionalism's central tenets, and emboldened its advocates. Previous movements, such as the Beaux-Arts, or Geddesian utopianism, had tried to fuse aesthetic with social or rationalistic aims, but CIAM-style Functionalism made this integration far more hard-hitting, by binding it into a simple, unidirectional logic, which governed both its ends and its means.

The overall task was seen as that of facilitating the march of Progress, in both material betterment and the development of social community. (31) Most Modern architects held that this aim would be achieved by a rational, linear process, in which universal 'standards', defined by research into the 'needs' of a newly-defined group in architecture – the users, or occupants of buildings – would be embodied in mass provision for all. The older use of ornament and symmetry to denote degree of stateliness was abandoned in favour of the free disposition of unadorned shapes in open space. Within Modernism, the freedom of 'form' implicit in this new spatial openness was always in tension with the discipline imposed by the movement's rectilinear austerity, and its insistence on close links with social or rational ideals.

Within the architectural profession, Modern Functionalism's stress on the public and the collective seemed to build on, and bring to a culmination, earlier Beaux-Arts and Arts and Crafts tendencies. Organisationally, it emphasised the public architectural office organised on the collectivist 'team' or 'group' system, and closely collaborating with sociologists, engineers and a host of other groups: in Robert Matthew's words, 'women and men from many schools, possibly other countries, and . . . with members of other Departments directly representing education, housing and other social services'. Even its most prestigious private practices would soon begin to imitate many attributes of this new, complex professional ideal of public architecture. Potentially, public architecture 'for the first time since the fifth century B.C. . . . has become popular architecture – in the strict sense, by the people, for the people'. (32) But these democratising tendencies were combined with the creation of an international super-elite of architects and canonical works. In relation to the Continental or American 'pioneers', Scotland was at first seen as a recipient of influence. In the more complex relations of late Modernism in the 60s, Scotland would also become a contributor to this international Modern canon: in one single week at the end of September 1968, for example, Cumbernauld New Town was visited by 18 French architects and planners, 13 Danish engineers, 23 Dutch members of the International Society of City and Regional Planners, the City Architect and Deputy City Engineer of Auckland, New Zealand, and a US party comprising members of Urban American Incorporated. (33)

1.15 Ian G Lindsay seen on Duniquaich (overlooking Inveraray Castle and burgh) in the mid 1960s.

1.16 Iona Abbey, restored by Ian Lindsay in 1939-56.

1.17 Baker Street, Stirling: improvement and infill scheme from 1953 (initial design from 1940) by Sir Frank Mears & Partners.

In the 1940s, however, all that lay in the future. For the moment, the main concern of Modernist designers was with the researching and propagation of their ideas; and here a trio of architects who had first made their mark in the very different climate of 1930s Edinburgh – namely, Robert Matthew, Alan Reiach and Basil Spence – began to set the pace.

The most immediate and arresting way in which the general public was made aware of Modern ideas was through the medium of public exhibitions. Here, Basil Spence played a prominent part, combining propaganda of Modernist rationalism with a continuation of his old pictorial eclecticism. In some smaller commissions, such as the redecoration of his own Edinburgh house in 1946 (where a brightly-papered Modern living room stood alongside an even more startlingly coloured 'Adam-inspired' classical dining-room), or the building of the massive seating shelters along the terraces on the north side of Princes Street Gardens, he remained faithful to more classical patterns. (34) But in his specialist exhibition work, he adopted an exuberant and forceful modernity.

Alongside a number of less important shows (e.g. 'Enterprise Scotland' or 'Britain can Make It'), Spence's two key exhibition works of the early post-war years were the 'Sea and Ships' pavilion at the 1951 South Bank exhibition in London, and – his set-piece - the Exhibition of Industrial Power in Glasgow during the same year. (35)

The Glasgow exhibition, which comprised a series of enclosed spaces constructed entirely within the Kelvin Hall, was based on a combination of symmetry and grandeur in the main setpieces (such as Thomas Whalen's 'Coal Cliff' relief) with curving vistas in between. In this, he was doubtless influenced by recent examples of dramatic interior design, including Art Deco cinemas or the spectacular structures at the 1939 New York World's Fair, such as the 'Democracity' pavilion. Like Mackintosh, Spence relied heavily on contrasts of light and dark space; also remarkable, from a 1990s perspective, was the anticipation of recent 'tableau-vivant' techniques. (36) T Warnett Kennedy, former Modern propagandist and partner of Jack Coia in the late 30s, also began to specialise in

1.18 Thomas Whalen's 'Coal Cliff' relief in the 1951 Exhibition of Industrial Power, Glasgow: 'large, dark, and rather like a cave carving'. (Spence)

exhibition design after the war, with an increasing penchant for science-fiction futurism. For the 1946 'Britain Can Make It' exhibition he designed a model of an atom-powered interplanetary spaceship, and for a 1947 exhibition of the Society of Aircraft Constructors he designed a display of plywood tubing 'somewhat reminiscent of flying saucers.' In 1952, however, Kennedy emigrated to Canada and embarked on a distinguished second career as an urban theorist and alderman in Vancouver, B.C. (37) (Figs. 1.18, 1.19)

While Spence reigned supreme in the world of spectacle, a different force was becoming dominant in that central area of Modernist substance: the researching and definition of rationalist 'standards' under the aegis of the State, and, increasingly, under the oversight of Robert Matthew. Rising to become the Department of Health's Deputy Chief Architect in 1943, and, in 1945 (succeeding G D Macniven) Chief Architect and Planning Officer, Matthew took decisive steps to set up an integrated structure for oversight across Scotland, by State designers, of the emergent discipline of regional planning. On his move away in 1946 to spend seven years as Architect to the London County Council – where he masterminded the building of the Royal Festival Hall (1948-51) and established his younger architects as world leaders in Modernist housing design – he was succeeded at DHS by Robert Gardner-Medwin and (subsequently) by T A Jeffryes. Matthew's return to Edinburgh in 1953, establishing his own private practice, would herald a final and decisive breakthrough in the fortunes of the Modern Movement in Scotland.

In Matthew's view, the integration of architecture and planning advocated by Modernists of the 1930s-40s would make it possible to coordinate micro-level aims - the design, construction and mass-production of the Modern dwelling, with all mod. cons. – with the macro-issue of 'community planning': the conception of self-contained residential areas with optimal light, air and greenery, set within wider schemes of town and country planning. (38) Matthew's friend and former fellow-student Alan Reiach played a key role in the preparation of the Government's most authoritative wartime statement of housing design aims: the Westwood Committee Report (*Planning our New*

Homes: published 1944). It was equally important to Matthew to begin establishing cross-disciplinary research programmes. On a visit to Stockholm's Southern Hospital as DHS Chief Architect, in 1945, he was 'amazed at the extent of study and analysis (including full-scale prototype theatres) that had taken place before work had been started, involving close collaboration between architects, doctors and nurses', and became determined that these methods should also be applied to Scotland. (39) This philosophy was, for example, applied in DHS's design (1951-3) of the country's first health centre, at Sighthill, Edinburgh.

Owing to wartime and postwar shortages of conventional building materials, there was also much experimentation in housing construction in the 1940s, focusing on single and two-storey dwellings in metal, timber or concrete. One of the most tireless innovators at this time was the Glasgow architect Sam Bunton, whose office was an inexhaustible source of exotic prefabrication proposals, couched in millenarian rhetoric of reconstruction: his friend Warnett Kennedy recalled that 'Sam could read the telephone directory and make it sound like a religious announcement!' (40) A later paper in this book provides more detailed information on Bunton's career and often extravagant ideas. In the same years, Glasgow Corporation's direct labour organisation embarked on the first of its many headstrong ventures: the building of a 'foamslag' (power-station waste) precasting factory for concrete-

1.19 'The New Health Service' exhibition, Edinburgh, 1948; designed for the Department of Health for Scotland by T Warnett Kennedy.

panel 2-storey flats; it proved grossly uneconomic and had to be closed down after only four years' operation. The mania for 'systems' extended also to primary schools: several were built using plastic wall panels (e.g. Hyvot's Bank and Drylaw, Edinburgh, 1953-4) or aluminium (the first of these being Ballingry, 1948). Systems for larger buildings were associated mainly with the heavier methods of the '50s, such as no-fines or blockwork. (Figs. 1.20, 1.21)

But while all these programmes made a major contribution to output in the materials-starved '40s and early '50s, and did so by well-researched constructional methods of impeccable Modernity, their often utilitarian appearance and sprawling layouts attracted much criticism. 'Unrepentant traditionalists' such as Steel Maitland attacked them as 'bleak and joyless', (41) while many Modernists found them technically admirable, but visually and socially reprehensible. Among the rare exceptions was Vale of Leven Hospital, designed by J L Gleave during his time as a partner in Keppie, Henderson & Gleave, and the first new postwar hospital built by the Scottish national health service (1952-5). Here a brick-built service

spine was flanked by prefabricated two-storey ward units built in a lightweight concrete system devised by Gleave. The traditional pavilion layout was retained, but there was a new stress on flexibility in the units' modular planning (something which anticipated trends of the '60s), and the subdivision of wards into smaller and more private rooms. (42)

In the field of 'community planning', Bunton at first also made considerable impact, through his energy in preparing a Modern rebuilding plan for Clydebank following the massive bombing raids of 1941. Following the passing of comprehensive town and country planning legislation in 1947, the Secretary of State proclaimed that the nation now stood at a 'crossroads' as decisive as the 18th-century beginning of industrialisation. This time, however, 'we have learned the need for direction if we are to avoid a new age of industrial squalor'. (43) Of the town plans which followed the Act, perhaps the most arresting was W Dobson Chapman and C F Riley's *Granite City* (1952). This was based not on a demand for reconstruction and clearance, as in the Central Belt, but on the assumption that Aberdeen was already a fortunate community and,

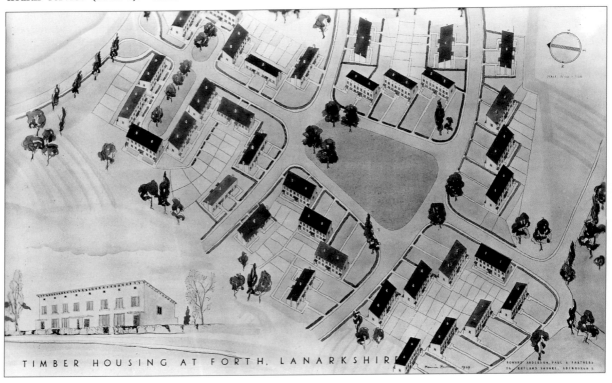

TIMBER HOUSING AT FORTH, LANARKSHIRE

1.20 Timber housing, Forth, Lanarkshire (Rowand Anderson, Paul & Partners, 1939). Designed by Kininmonth and Spence.

with improvement and beautification, could become an 'ideal city'. (44) A more ambitious formula of fully-fledged regional planning, including green belts and 'overspill' of population to planned new towns, was set out by the Clyde Valley Regional Plan, prepared in 1943-6 under the direction of Patrick Abercrombie and Matthew. Here the planners' agenda was now leading them into increasingly open conflict with established municipal housing interests, led by Glasgow Corporation. The first new town, East Kilbride, was designated in 1947 – in the face of fierce opposition from the city – and there began two decades of inter-mittent conflict between Glasgow and the planners. (45) The papers in this volume by Dickson Mabon, Ronnie Cramond and Pat Rogan recall the tensions of the time between, and within, both central and local government over the issue of housing output versus planning.

By the late 1940s, there were already the beginnings of a counter-trend: a weakening of the ideal of the archi-tect-planner. The 1947 Act's nationalisation of land development value was stirring up public unease, and in 1949 Matthew's DHS successor, Gardner-Medwin, questioned whether architect-planners, in setting up regional planning, had not 'invented a monster machine destined to overpower us'; their 'creative planning' might be turned by others into 'mechanistic' application of rules. (46) Here we see the beginning of the split between the architect 'designer' and the 'development control' planner, so prominent today.

SALTIRE HOMES: HOUSING DESIGN IN THE 1950s

The vast aspirations, but uneven results of Modernist ideals at the level of regional planning contrasted with the smaller scale achievements which, by the early 50s, were actually beginning to be realised in individual housing projects. Of these, the most closely related to the Traditionalist ideas discussed already were small-scale housing schemes comprising mainly new build-ings. In such projects, often singled out for the presti-gious Saltire Society housing design awards, relatively 'traditional' materials and enclosed space were com-bined with a shift towards more Modern ideas – a ten-dency advocated most articulately by Alan Reiach, author (with Robert Hurd) of the polemical book, *Building Scotland* (1941), and admirer of the fusion of modernity and tradition in contemporary Danish archi-tecture. Reiach himself designed an influential small group of flats and shops at Whitemoss, East Kilbride (from 1949), and East Kilbride New Town's own archi-tects soon took up the same theme on a large scale. By 1952, with 500 dwellings completed, East Kilbride had begun to dominate the Saltire Awards. In that year, the judges singled out a group at the Murray development, designed by the new town's former chief architect, D P Reay, for its 'welcome air of vitality and freshness . . . soft colours contrasting with gaily coloured entrance doors', and commended Reiach's Whitemoss group for its 'sim-ple excellence...a valuable contribution to the Scottish tradition of the present day.' (47) (Figs. 1.22, 1.23)

1.21 Prototype block of Swedish Timber Houses, Balornock, Glasgow: fourth day of timber erection, November 1945. Glasgow took 200 of a consignment organised and designed by Robert Matthew in 1945 – the beginning of his preoccupation with building in timber.

1.22 Royal Fine Art Commission for Scotland field trip to Iona, 1968. From left to right: Alan Reiach, Eden Coia, Jack Coia, Robin Philipson. Photograph taken by Sir Anthony Wheeler.

In the East, the most celebrated example of this tendency was Basil Spence's fishermen's housing scheme at Dunbar (1949-52), a calculatedly picturesque group of small infill blocks with rubble and harl walling and forestair-like balconies. Younger architects developed similar solutions, including the Lerwick infill schemes of Richard and Betty Moira of Edinburgh, (48) and the Fife redevelopments of H Anthony Wheeler. Wheeler put his Glasgow Beaux-Arts training to work in the very different conditions of the East, in a series of complex Modernist interventions in numerous Fife burghs, including Leslie (The Bowery: 1953-6), Burntisland (Somerville Street, 1955-7), Dysart (1958-71), Pittenweem (1962) and Old Buckhaven (1964-73): he also designed some innovative

redevelopment work in West Lothian, at Blackburn (1968) and Broxburn (1968-70). Wheeler's principles were to juxtapose predominantly enclosed space with elements of Modernist spatial 'drama', especially in the remodelling of previously derelict backlands. In his paper included in this volume, Wheeler explains in more detail the principles which guided the planning of his Dysart scheme.

The move towards freely-flowing Modernist housing layouts was assisted by an apparent sharp decline in the popularity of separate gardens and in private gardening as a means of community-building after the war. In Lerwick, it was reported in 1952 that many gardens in housing schemes were 'disgraceful, with stones,

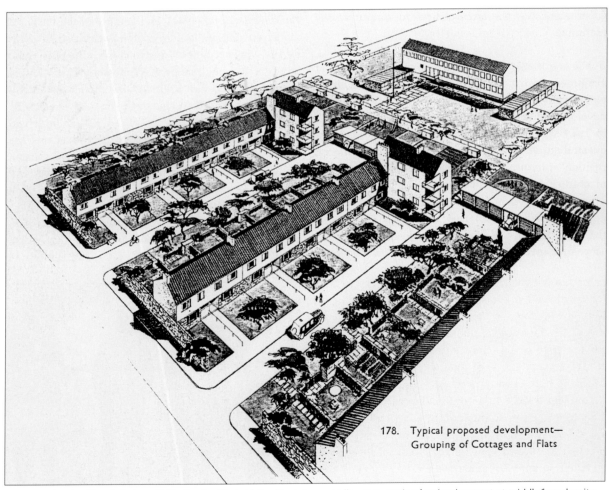

178. Typical proposed development—
Grouping of Cottages and Flats

1.23 Drawing by Alan Reiach, c.1946, for the Clyde Valley Plan's Leven Valley case-study of redevelopment at middle/low density. This pattern of two-storey cottages and three-storey flats, influenced in some respects by Danish and Swedish precedents (e.g. in the informally disposed group in the background), presaged the initial phases of housing within East Kilbride New Town.

rubbish and a wealth of . . . objectionable weeds'. (49) Now a landscape architect, tasked to design collective spaces, often became an essential part of the 'community planning' team: Jane Wood wrote of planting's 'rightful contribution to the three-dimensional composition of the landscape' in housing areas. (50) Scottish Office housing minister J Nixon Browne declared in 1955 that 'we have much to learn from Scandinavian countries on how to blend our housing schemes into the natural background . . . by making good use of colour and the natural contours, and by careful pre-planning.' (51) The great mass of housing during the '40s and '50s, in reflection of postwar natalist policies, comprised 'family' dwellings in cottages or low flats: rural designs built on a large scale included the cottages of Argyll County Council (architect: W R Tocher), with their huge triangular gables and overhanging eaves, built most notably at Dunbeg Village, near Oban (1957-61).

A new type, the single-storey old people's terraced house, gained in popularity, with numbers being built in Glasgow and Aberdeen. As pressures for urban output built up during the '50s, however, the proportion of flats began to rise too, especially in Glasgow, where Green Belt pressure by the planners led to the building of many thousands of dwellings in 3- and 4-storey suburban tenements. (Fig. 1.24)

THE TOWER ARTISTICALLY CONSIDERED: MODERNISM ASCENDANT

After his return from London in 1953, although no longer himself employed by a public authority, Robert Matthew set about the task of consolidating and extending the status of public architecture, by yoking private architectural firms and academia more firmly to its central aims of planned social provision. Modernist philosophy, as we have already noted, was dominated by a belief in rationally-determined social Progress. The replacement of the old hierarchical and fragmented ways by mass provision of 'comprehensive' environments constituted both a social ideal, of planned Community, and a method of achieving it. In 1953, Matthew declared that the architect's task was 'to lay the foundations not only of a new architecture, but of a new society'. (52) (Fig. 1.25)

Throughout the 1950s, Matthew sought to combine international Modern Functionalism with elements of the equally utopian Andersonian tradition of a 'social' and 'national' Scottish architecture. His pronouncements of the mid '50s were full of calls for the revitalisation of Scottish architecture, for a halt to the 'drift south', and for Scotland to 'look at herself in the glass and emulate other small countries like Switzerland,

1.24 Dunbeg Village, near Oban, built 1957-61 (W R Tocher, County Architect): one of the largest of the County Council's schemes of standard cottages, with tall roofs and massive, triangular gables.

1.25 Robert Matthew, 1940s photograph.

Sweden and Denmark in quality of building, industrial design and environment.' (53) In 1957, he told the Edinburgh Architectural Association: 'Remembering that small countries are outstandingly the leaders in architectural thought to-day, let us take heart from our own past – a small group of young men in the eighteenth century made Edinburgh for a time the focus of the world!' (54) Like Reiach and the modernising Traditionalists, Matthew upheld a modified version of Andersonian 'golden age' thinking, in which Vernacular and small burgh buildings were seen as the thread of visual and social continuity, against the grandiloquent 'imported style' of classicism. (55) (Fig. 1.26) Despite the Modern Movement's vehement rejection of the style-based hierarchies of the 19th century, there remained subtle elements of pre-Modern building-type differentiations: a rectilinear, open-space monumentality for large urban or industrial projects, a more irregular, enclosed-space intimacy for small-scale or small-town work. The overt ranking of buildings by status, with public monuments at the top, had gone. But there persisted, despite Modern architecture's insistence on homogeneous provision for all, a kind of division between elevated and mundane solutions.

The novelties and ambiguities of Modern Functionalism were encapsulated in one building type in particular: the multi-storey block. 'Tower blocks'

showed that Functionalism's insistence on the integration of visual beauty with solidity and utility (the three elements in Vitruvius's definition of architecture: *venustas, firmitas, utilitas*), in no way precluded the creation of arresting forms, or spaces. The free-standing Modern high block, with mod.cons. (such as lifts or central heating) incorporated as a matter of course, was a gesture of clear divergence from even modernising Traditionalism. (Fig. 1.27)

To Matthew, the formal task of Modernism was above all to express the free flowing of space, outside and, preferably, inside buildings: and this applied to the most prestigious as much as to the most mundane projects. To the Traditionalists who had applauded Walter N W Ramsay's monumental classical plan for the redevelopment of the north side of George Square in 1951, Matthew's rupture of the square's south-east corner only nine years later with a boldly open-planned University redevelopment, including the 15-storey Arts Tower (1960-3), seemed 'an insolent, even cruel win' for Modernism (although the proposal for a high block here was in fact inherited from an earlier plan by Spence). (56) (Fig. 1.28, 1.29)

Tower-building was equally seen as a possible option within the previously low-status field of massed working-class housing construction. Within the 1944

1.26 Robert Matthew's interpretation of urban 'vernacular': Burtons shop, Hawick High Street, designed c.1956.

1.27 The high building as 'landmark': illustration of a Swedish point block near Stockholm in the *Architects' Journal*, 1952.

Westwood Committee, there had been a spilt between a majority, spurred on by Reiach, who tentatively suggested building of 6-10 storey blocks of dwellings in cities, and a Garden City faction led by Jean Mann. She opposed them on the socio-moral grounds that they would harm family life and cause a fall in the birth rate, and would prevent what she, in now rather old-fashioned terms, saw as the proper segregation of 'the classes'; it would be better to have 'the essential elements for family living, combined with relatively primitive accommodation.' (57)   In a pioneering (unbuilt) 1935 redevelopment project, Matthew had taken a very different view of the aim of provision for all, by arguing that use of Modern high blocks was bound up with achievement of Modern living standards: mod. cons. inside, more light penetration and greenery outside. We will see below that tower blocks were eventually built in very large numbers – with controversial effects on the eventual public estimation of the success of Modern architecture.

MODERN BUILDING PROGRAMMES

Let us, now, trace the patterns and variations of Scottish Modernism in the period of its initial ascendancy in the '50s and early '60s, as expressed in the work of Matthew and his contemporaries in a selection of key building programmes. Paradoxically, the building type where CIAM Modernity was expressed most flamboyantly was the traditionally most prestigious field: the great public building. Dominating the skyline of Hamilton, for instance, was a vast new civic acropolis, which proclaimed the power and ambitiousness of Lanark County Council, Scotland's largest county authority. The 17-storey, glass-walled office tower and adjoining buildings, including a circular council chamber and raised forecourt plaza, were designed (1960-4) within the office of the County Architect, D.G. Bannerman. (58) An even more structurally daring Modernist design was built to celebrate the attainment of burgh status by the new town of East Kilbride: the Dollan Baths, constructed in 1964-8 to the designs of A. Buchanan Campbell. (59)   The

1.29 Queens College, Dundee: perspective of Matthew's extension scheme (1958-61).

1.28 Early drawing (c.1958) by Robert Matthew of his proposed George Square redevelopment scheme, Edinburgh.

Beaux-Arts instincts acquired by Campbell at Glasgow School of Art had been reinforced in the '30s by the influence of Jack Coia. Now, commissioned to design a municipal swimming pool for a 'young and proud council' determined not to build a mere 'box', Campbell decided to roof the structure with a sweeping, 324-foot wide parabolic arch. His original intention, inspired by examples such as Burnet, Tait & Partners' arched entrance to the South Bank Exhibition, London (1950), had been to use glued laminated timber, but transport problems prevented this. The eventual concrete structure, inspired by the 'freedom' of Nervi's designs, was planted on massive diagonal struts. (60)

But the Modernity and prestige of Functionalist rectilinear architecture was not the preserve of public monuments such as Hamilton. Instead, its practical and visual clarity, and the variety of its solutions, was applied across a wide range of secular public architecture: in building for education, for example. (Figs. 1.30, 1.31) In a Glasgow city-centre project of 1960-4 to build new Stow Colleges of Distributive Trades, and Building and Printing, Wylie, Shanks & Underwood designed tall slabs with boldly modelled roof structures, travertine-clad gables, and sheer glass curtain walls. (61) A competition for a new Paisley Technical College was won in 1957 by Alison and Hutchison and Partners of Edinburgh with a free-flowing layout of flat-roofed blocks, including a 9-storey slab, around a series of terraced and partly enclosed spaces. Gardner-Medwin, who was assessor, praised its 'warmth and humanity' and predicted that 'Paisley will have an

example of modern architecture and town planning which visitors may travel many miles to see'; Alison and Hutchison subsequently became specialists in higher education and hospital design. (62)

If, in the broadly defined field of public buildings, it was relatively straightforward to apply rectilinear CIAM Modern principles, a slightly different situation prevailed in the types which were previously considered more utilitarian: transport, public utilities, industry. We saw above that Kininmonth's solution to the task of building an airport terminal was a theatrical concrete structure with bowstring arch portico. Robert Matthew's first commission on his return home, Turnhouse Airport Terminal (built 1954-6; demolished 1995) was a studiedly unostentatious mahogany-clad group; and Kincardine Power Station (1954-60), prototype of a series of giant coal-burning stations, was treated by Matthew as a test-case for the fusion of architectural and engineering approaches: the design, flanked by slender 400ft. chimneys, comprised a steel-framed structure by Redpath Brown with light cladding of aluminium and glass. (63) (Figs. 1.32, 1.33, 1.34) The ambitious new 'super-collieries' designed by Egon Riss, Scottish Chief Production Architect of the National Coal Board, aimed to convey a new, modern image of 'contemporary . . . industrial design' with a 'dignity and elegance conspicuously absent from the...untidy-looking pit-heads of the past.' (64) The new 'monumentality' of designs such as Killoch (1953), Seafield (1965) and Monktonhall (1965) was achieved by a deliberate 'functional' asymmetry in the overall layout, combined with a rigorous

1.30 Belmont Hall of Residence, Dundee University, 1963-5, by Gauldie Hardie Wright & Needham: drawing by Sinclair Gauldie.

1.31 Refectory interior, Belmont Hall: 1965 drawing by Gauldie.

1.32 Turnhouse Airport, seen on completion in 1956. Matthew's first commission after his return home, an elegant and spatially ingenious group in timber and rubble, was hailed by Michael Laird as 'the matrix of a new Scottish vernacular in the modern movement.'

exclusion of picturesque or variegated detailing. One of Riss's former colleagues recalled that a junior architect once began drawing the elevation of an administration block with the windows grouped in pairs. 'Now whenever anyone was doing that sort of thing, through some sixth sense Riss always seemed to know. And on this occasion, straight away he came in, and

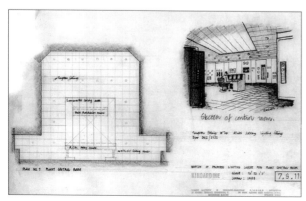

1.33 Kincardine Power Station (1958-60): 1958 sketch and plan of control room.

1.34 Longannet power station (RMJM, 1965-6); aerial view.

snapped, "No! You're messing around with the spacing! You know what I want. I want window-window-window, each one the same, fourteen times!"' (65) (Figs. 1.36, 1.37)

'COMPREHENSIVE' REPLANNING

Within Modern architecture, the designing of individual projects such as these was always seen in the potential context of overarching 'comprehensive' schemes of town and regional planning. Here the 1950s saw a growing concentration on inner-urban problems: and the central position of Glasgow within the housing-planning debate ensured that the greatest attention in these redevelopment debates would be claimed by its Hutchesontown/Gorbals area, whose showpieces were two sections allocated to Matthew (Area B, built 1958-64) and Spence (built 1960-6; demolished 1993). Both chose solutions dominated by tall blocks. Spence's section was built in the form of two massively monumental slab blocks, with inset communal balconies romantically intended to evoke tenement drying-greens: Charles Robertson's paper in this volume recalls the process of designing this extraordinary scheme. Matthew's project architect, Ian Arnott, recalled that 'Glasgow was certainly keen – it was probably Jury's influence – to get prominent *Scottish* architects involved the Gorbals.' (66) Matthew's layout was a rectilinear grid of 18-storey towers and lower blocks aligned, typically of CIAM practice, on a north-south axis (to optimise daylight and sunlight exposure), disregarding the existing street alignments. Internally, the towers (originally designed for the Leith Fort competition in Edinburgh, 1957) were planned by Arnott with an ingenious staggered cross section inspired by a scheme by J R Bakema; externally, 'Matthew's philosophy was to keep things simple – he didn't like filigree details and individualistic touches.' (67) Matthew's design sparked off a clash with older, sanitary notions of working-class housing provision, when Glasgow Corporation's Medical Officer of Health, Dr William A Horne, resisted the inclusion of internal, mechanically-ventilated bathrooms: 'Matthew tried to persuade him that God's fresh air could come in through ventilation pipes as well as windows, but he stuck his ground. He was only finally defeated when he was incautious enough to remark that Professor Matthew didn't want bathroom windows because they would spoil his pretty elevations – to which Matthew's response was, "I can design bathroom windows as well as any other windows!"' (68) (Fig. 1.38)

How, if at all could the Modern prescription of boldly comprehensive rebuilding be applied to small burghs? One solution seemed to be to use rectilinear building forms, but to retain the enclosed type of layout. Percy Johnson-Marshall's Edinburgh civic design course

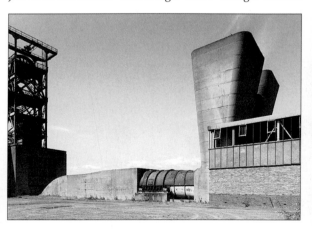

1.37 Kinneil Colliery, fan house.

(opposite) 1.36 Rothes Colliery (designed by Fife Coal Co./Egon Riss; completed 1957), photographed in 1993 prior to its demolition. The colliery was built in association with Glenrothes New Town, but had to be closed within a few years, owing to an unexpected geological fault.

1.35 Hunterston 'A' nuclear power station (1957-64, GEC and Simon-Carves Ltd.): view of control room.

addressed this issue in 1961, with a project for the central area redevelopment of Dunbar: one student (C.V. Storm), for instance, proposed to retain all the existing historic facades around the High Street, but to clear a large belt of open space behind and redevelop the harbour area beyond with medium-height blocks around courtyards: a tall slab block, standing just behind Spence's cottages, would provide a strong vertical landmark. (69) In a redevelopment of Dalkeith Town Centre (1962-4), R J Naismith (of Sir Frank Mears & Partners) departed from Mears's old Lorimerian formulas, and instead disposed heavy, flat-roofed blocks faced with precast aggregate slabs on a right-angled, yet still quite enclosed layout.

THE CONTROVERSY OF MASS BUILDING

In the early 1960s, the success of Matthew and others in establishing high blocks and Modern architecture as a credible vehicle for postwar reconstruction began to have unexpected results, as those patterns began to be taken up and reproduced in large numbers by the groups with real political power in the rebuilding drive. Massed reproduction was, of course, an integral part of the Functionalist recipe, but that did not make its actual reality any more palatable to the designer-innovators. It was above all the large-scale building of multi-storey blocks in Glasgow from 1960 by the 'crusading' Housing Committee Convener, David Gibson, that brought to a head this first Modernist crisis of confidence. Gibson seized on multi-storey tower and slab blocks as a way to cut through the Clyde Valley Plan's pressure to curb the City's own building and force overspill, and began to build them on any available site within the city. (70) Among the largest scheme was a 27/31 storey group of tower and slab blocks built by the City's direct labour organisation at Red Road, Balornock (1962-9), designed by Sam Bunton on highly unorthodox constructional lines: steel-framing with timber-framed asbestos cladding. Why did these, and similar, blocks attract criticism from the Modern design establishment? They *looked* 'Modern', and included as a matter of course advanced amenities:

1.38 Hutchesontown/Gorbals Area B (RMJM, 1958-64) seen under construction in 1961.

1.39 David Gibson and his wife Sadie, c.1930. [Mrs S Gibson]

central heating, lifts, and communal waste disposal collection. Indeed, their opportunistic construction on any available site maximised the output of new, self-contained dwellings with mod. cons., a campaign whose impact is shown by the more recent laments about loss of 'tenement community'. Between 1961 and 1971, the proportion of Glasgow households enjoying exclusive use of hot and cold water, a fixed bath, and inside WC rose from 59% to 75%. The main accusation against them was, rather, their conflict with 'comprehensive' planning, and the fact that many of them were designed by contractors as 'package-deals' (design and build). (Figs. 1.39, 1.40, 1.41)

1.40 Glasgow Corporation Housing Committee (David Gibson, Convener, third from right), seen in 1961.

The quantitative success of the tower-block designs of contractors such as Crudens provided an answer to a question posed by Matthew in 1957: did, or could, architects 'lead the building industry?' (71) In a subject as emotive and politically charged as housing, architects could only exert any oversight over design if they were prepared to pragmatically adapt Modern principles of research-based definition of 'needs', to accommodate forcefully-expressed client 'wants'. By the mid 1960s, with the mutually hostile package deal and direct labour multi-storey drives in progress, and moves by the planners to reassert themselves, there was, in Glasgow alone, a seemingly chaotic picture of competition by different groups. This diversity was a sign not of the weakness, but of the strength of the reconstruction drive in the '60s – as was the

1.41 Ardler multi-storey development, Dundee: a massive 'Zeilenbau' development designed and built (in 1964-6) by Crudens. Its six 17-storey slab blocks each contained almost 300 dwellings; several blocks have recently been demolished.

flourishing in Modern housing of regional variations, such as the North-East's fascination with multi-hued precast ('Fyfestone') facing blocks, and the lavish communal facilities of the slab blocks in the Aberdeen central redevelopment areas (e.g. Gallowgate, by George McI Keith, City Architect, 1964-6). In the later papers by Mabon, Cramond and Rogan, this diversity of patrons and solutions is fully explored.

If one were adopting a hostile anti-Modern perspective, it might seem a fitting *reductio ad absurdum* of the Functionalist logic of standards and mass provision, to label package-deal high blocks as their climax. But the criticism of these blocks at the time as crude and not properly Modern had, itself, another 'modern' aspect: it formed part of the incessant division of labour within 20th-century architecture, the cycle of criticism and creation of ever more complicated professional groupings. But this takes us on to Late Modernism, and to a more general questioning not just of 'debased' offshoots but of Functionalism itself.

COMPLEXITY AND CONTRADICTION: LATE MODERNISM

The increasing perception of prosperity in the early 1960s led to calls for a redefinition of the planned welfare state. What was demanded was not fewer experts, but larger numbers of more sophisticated experts. The 1964-70 Wilson Government's endorsement of a technocratic ideology coincided with the climax of the Scottish Office's building of a devolved structure of regional planning – now (from 1962) under the aegis of a new department of infrastructure: the Scottish Development Department (SDD) (72) The Scottish Office minister in charge of the SDD after Labour's election victory in 1964 was J. Dickson Mabon, whose paper is included later in this volume. The North had

1.42 Building for the affluent society: interior of living-room in slab block, Woodside Area 'B' development, Glasgow (built from 1970; Boswell, Mitchell & Johnston), seen newly completed in the early 1970s.

already experienced a glimpse into this heady world since 1955, when the burgh of Thurso, steered by its go-ahead Provost, John Sinclair, prepared a bold planning strategy to handle the influx of population and prosperity brought by the Dounreay experimental nuclear plant. The burgh's consultant planner was H A Rendel Govan (Mears's former partner, and a vehement Traditionalist), and the architect for its large new housing schemes and inner redevelopments was H Sinclair Macdonald. (73)

Among architects, while some exulted at the triumphs of modernisation, the moment of equilibrium was fleeting. The moment mass provision began actually to be realised, so the questioning of the 'clinical sterility' of CIAM Modernism began. (74) Among possible alternatives, the open pursuit of the 'national', or of Traditionalist ideas, now seemed to be ruled out. For example, the crowstepped and classical winner of a

1960 competition for Midlothian County Buildings, Edinburgh (by G Reid & J S Forbes) was not built: eventually, in 1968, a Robert Matthew Johnson-Marshall design was built instead, which acknowledged its Old Town setting with a rubble base and timber-framed fenestration above. Any attempts to express 'national' associations would now have to be indirect. The main emphasis was now on developing Modernity, to make it more sophisticated and complex. It is an excessive exercise of hindsight to say that the moment of Modernism's triumph was also the moment it began to break up. But at any rate, there seemed little conception any more of a unified 'great tradition'. Interationally speaking, from around 1960, Modernism became an affair of pluralist strands, each developing and heightening what, within Functionalism, had been integrated elements: the social, the rationalistic, and the aesthetic or 'formal'. (75)

1.43 Communal warm-air drying cupboard, Hillside Court, Menzieshill multi-storey development, Dundee, seen in 1964: one of the up-to-date amenities taken for granted in Modern multi-storey blocks.

Some architects responded to the growing perceptions of affluence and social change by a simple call for more of the same. For example, Sam Bunton, in 1958, claimed that savings from rationalisation of construction had been 'reinvested' to get 'luxury standards' of equipment in his newly-completed St Cuthbert's School, Hamilton: 'The pupils will have the benefit of "all mod cons" in the shape of heated classrooms with desks fitted for typewriters, cupboards with sliding glass fronts, thermostatically heated water, towelmasters and liquid soap containers . . . the girls' commercial room has all the attributes and facilities of the general office in a modern multi-storey office block.' (76) Demands to reflect affluence were naturally focused on housing, that central arena of the spread of individualised or self-contained living. Even as many Labour authorities bolstered their policies of massed output and low rents, some architects began to demand acknowledgement of higher living standards and the spread of mod. cons.: the RIAS magazine *Prospect* advocated, in 1956, that tenants should pay for improved services (77); and Edinburgh's City Architect, Alexander Steele, argued that 'the traditional open fire ought to be abandoned as soon as possible, in favour of systems which will provide whole house warming under the absolute control of the tenant'. (78) (Figs. 1.42, 1.43)

1.44 Early proposal for the Forth Road Bridge, in a heavy Art Deco style: illustration on front cover of *Fife Looks Ahead* report, 1946.

1.45 The Forth Road Bridge as built: North Tower, raising climbing structure: view of jacking corner, October 1960.

In the field of area redevelopment, some responded to the demands of the motor vehicle for parking and roads by maintaining, or even expanding Functionalist tabula-rasa formulas. As late as 1965, it was argued that the proposal to redevelop Laurieston/Gorbals in Glasgow with 23-storey slab blocks and expressways would create an area of 'high amenity'. (79) An accelerated road-building drive included the Scottish Office's construction of the long-awaited Forth Road Bridge (1958-64, Mott Hay & Anderson/Sir Giles Scott, Son & Partners), whose design was widely admired across the world as the herald of a new era of lightness in spun-cable suspension bridge design. (Figs. 1.46, 1.47) And it took in Scotland's first motorway ring road, the Glasgow Inner Ring Road, begun in 1965 under engineers Scott Wilson Kirkpatrick, and consultant architect W Holford. (80) In James P McCafferty's essay in this book, the planning and implementation of this massive project are outlined. (Fig. 1.47)

At the same time, there were more architecturally elevated responses to the new ideas of the consumer society. Critics in various countries reacted by proposing, for instance, the aestheticisation of the everyday, or (with the French Situationists, founded 1957) the futuristic exploitation of ever-expanding technology to heighten social flexibility, through such devices as 'mobile' architecture of spaceframe with flexible infill - an aestheticisation of communication. (81) In Scotland, the writings of John L Paterson questioned the orthodox Modern city pattern and called for a new kind of classless urban 'vernacular' that would intensify 'urban reality': when working on Matthew's Hutchesontown 'B' project in Glasgow, he was able to implement a pioneering proposal to put street lights on top of the high blocks, with the aim of turning night-time life in the scheme into 'theatre.' (82)

THE ARCHITECTURE OF RATIONALIST ECONOMY

Among the early 1960s attempts to modify mainstream Functionalism and give expression to a more affluent and variegated society, there were some who tried to express technological advances and affluent society through greater rationalism. This had two

1.46 Forth Road Bridge: northward view in March 1961.

1.47 Glasgow Inner Ring Road: view by Alexander Duncan Bell of Kingston Bridge (Glasgow *Highway Plan*).

main aspects, sometimes overlapping: rationalism in the design of buildings, and rationalism in the building process. Matthew was, on the whole, a supporter of this tendency: in 1967, he spoke to the Royal Scottish Society of Arts of his hopes for the further systematisation of architecture as a 'rational discipline of design' which would move some way 'from an Art to a Science'. (83) And, as we will see shortly, his own firm, Robert Matthew Johnson-Marshall, became a bastion of this idea during the 1960s. But in those years, Matthew himself became more detached from the day-to-day work of RMJM, and increasingly involved with international architectural politics: in 1961-5 he was President of the International Union of Architects, in 1962-4 President of the Royal Institute of British Architects, and in 1965-8 he founded and presided over the Commonwealth Association of Architects. (Fig. 1.48) In 1965, for instance, within a single five-week period he chaired the inauguration of the CAA, in Malta, and visited the United States, Paris (as President of the International Union of Architects), and Greece (for the Third International Symposium on Ekistics). The previous year he had visited China, and met Khrushchev in Moscow. (84)

The most consistent building strategy of the '60s based on concepts of scientific organisation of processes in building use, including an integrated user-research element, was the hospital programme. Here, the old ideas of dispersal and ventilation were superseded by a multi-storey Modern type of deep-plan block – the 'racetrack plan' – containing central services ringed by a loop of small, relatively private rooms. A small prototype block of subdivided wards was built at Greenock in 1951-2, under the auspices of the Nuffield Investigation, while the Radiotherapeutic Institute designed by John Holt's team in Edinburgh also had 1- and 4-bed rooms, to create 'a hotel atmosphere' and a 'human approach'. (Holt) (85) The first fully-fledged racetrack multi-storey block in Scotland was built by Gillespie, Kidd & Coia at Bellshill Maternity Hospital (1959-62), followed by a user-study prototype under Scottish Office oversight at Falkirk Royal Infirmary (1963-6), and, finally, by a fully-fledged programme: this included both high-density inner redevelopments (e.g, at Glasgow's Western Infirmary, 1965-74, by Keppie, Henderson & Partners), and new suburban developments (e.g. Gartnavel General Hospital, Glasgow, 1968-73 by Keppie Henderson, or Ninewells Hospital, Dundee, 1961-74, by RMJM). (86) (Fig. 1.49)

Another 1960s attempt to give rationalistic expression to 1960s affluence emphasised a somewhat understated construction, preferably not in wet but in dry

1.48 Robert Matthew seen in discussion with Nigerian government officials and architects at the 1969 Lagos conference of the Commonwealth Association of Architects: Matthew was the founder and first president of the CAA.

construction, whether in panel or skeleton form. The most spectacular example of the latter was the tetrahedron space-frame construction of Edinburgh Royal Botanic Garden's new Plant Exhibition Houses, built in 1965-7 to the designs of MPBW Scotland (team leader George A H Pearce, in consultation with the engineer L R Creasy). (87) A doctrine of rationalist economy was developed especially within Matthew's firm, where John Richards and others devised a restrained architecture of low ranges faced in precise dry-cladding. (88) From Richards's perspective, a building like the Queen's College tower in Dundee seemed too calculatedly picturesque: 'Things which bothered me, like cladding the whole of a 12-storey tower in random rubble, didn't seem to bother Robert at all!' (89) The first of this new series of rationalistic RMJM projects was the lightweight steel-framed structure built in a mere 18 months as the first stage of the new University of Stirling (1966-7) – an academic new town, set in spectacular parkland, which was itself one of the key projects of Scottish Modernist community-building. (90) At the Royal Commonwealth Pool (1965-70), this theme was developed in a more monumental manner, in the design of a great public building which presented a calculatedly modest face to the street. (91) In his paper later in this book, Richards recollects this project in greater detail. Architects were, however, less successful in attempts to apply scientific rationalism to mass building programmes. In housing, for example, 'package-deal' contractors continued to dominate throughout the '60s, rebuffing architectural advocacy of supposedly more flexible 'open systems'.

1.49 Inverclyde Royal Hospital, Greenock, 1977-9, by Boswell, Mitchell & Johnston: the most grandiose of the new racetrack ward multi-storey hospitals.

LATE MODERNIST 'COMMUNITY' BUILDING: THE SOCIAL AND POETIC VISIONS

If the advocates of heightened rationalism built on, rather than rejected, the basic tenets of CIAM Functionalism, the other main grouping within Scottish late Modernism represented a genuine departure from CIAM, and developed the most open-ended tendencies of Modernism – tendencies which would eventually, at the end of the decade, lead to a rejection of Modernism altogether. It encompassed on the one hand people who built on the earlier Modern concern with 'community' and the 'social', and, on the other, people who followed Corbusier into a new formal, 'poetic' emphasis.

In the next pages, we will trace the two architectural concepts of 'community planning' which embodied these ideas most closely. The first was that of 'Megastructure': the idea of an artificial landscape governed by communication, in which many different uses could be flexibly incorporated. One obvious precedent was Corbusier's Unité d'Habitation in Marseille. G A MacNab remarked in 1952 (92) that the Unité was 'not a block of flats to be categorised as "working-class", "middle-class" or "luxury", but a vertical neighbourhood unit of independent homes.' The mature vision of Megastructure was not, however, a clear vertical slab of this sort, but a more complex mound-like agglomeration. The second new prominent pattern was equally intense: the designing of residential areas in 'low rise high density' forms such as 'patio' or 'courtyard' housing.

A vital element in this movement for greater complexity in housing or urban design was a swing against layouts of separate multi-storey blocks, which was beginning in the late '50s among some Scottish Modern architects. Shaw-Stewart, Baikie & Perry's competition-winning entry for Edinburgh's Leith Fort redevelopment competition (1957; built 1960-66) included point blocks (with Kahn-like jutting service towers and industrial-aesthetic precast cladding) at one end of the site, but in combination with a large 'deck-access' block and a dense grouping of patio houses. (93) The research & development frameworks set up by Matthew played a key role in propagating these heightened ideas of the 'social' within Scotland – as well as, of course, helping create new, more complex user-centred discourses of architecture to occupy the growing numbers of young graduates. In 1967, he himself criticised the pursuit of 'finite and monumental solutions' when 'the functional problem in hand' instead demanded 'open-endedness'. (94) In the evolution of the megastructure pattern, the most important individual project was the Central Area of Cumbernauld New Town. (Fig. 1.50, 1.51) Cumbernauld's planning, as a whole, reacted against the fairly low density and separate residential units of East Kilbride: the initial town plan, drawn up by L Hugh Wilson, Chief Architect and Planning Officer (until 1962; thereafter, D R Leaker) envisaged a single cellular urban mass clustered around a dominant, hilltop town centre. In its segregation of traffic, wooded landscaping, and town centre with vertical transport integration, there was some resemblance to the previous paragon of new town planning, Sweden's Vällingby (built from 1952). However, Cumbernauld's urban fabric was to be rather more tightly compressed, and its Centre far more monumental in scale: in 1967 the American Institute of Architects, singling out the town

as a world-beating example of 'community architecture', declared that 'the dreams of the 1920s and 1930s are being built on a hill near Glasgow'. (95) (Fig. 1.52)

Phase 1 of the Centre's design was entrusted to Geoffrey Copcutt, a stylish and exuberant figure, habitually clad in a thick tartan suit, who gave the lie to any idea that Modernism was an architecture of anonymous grey apparatchiks. (96) By 1959, it had been decided that the Centre would be multi-level, and in November 1962, Copcutt's conception was revealed in all its audacity: a linear, stepped, multi-function structure set on an elevated ridge, with vehicle access ways (including a fast dual carriageway road) passing right through, and pedestrian access routes entering the complex at right angles. (97) Later in the book, we reprint both a contemporary description, and a more recent recollection, of his design – both of which texts fuse megastructural imagery with a Futurist rhetoric of technological consumerism. The main structure was of reinforced concrete with waffle-slab floors, but rising through this was a structurally separate series of concrete columns supporting, at the very top, a range of penthouses. But only the first phase of the Centre was built largely to Copcutt's designs (in 1963-7): after

1.50 1964 perspective of Cumbernauld Town Centre by M. Evans, emphasising the complex's daring multi-level planning concept.

1.51 1967 aerial view of Cumbernauld Town Centre Phase One (almost complete), and (in background) Bison point blocks and terraces in the Seafar and Ravenswood areas.

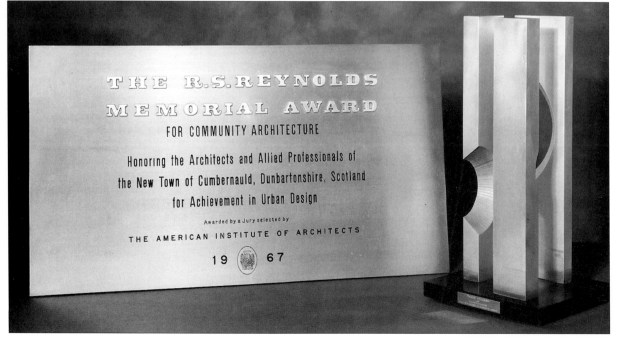

1.52 R S Reynolds Memorial Award for Community Architecture, awarded to Cumbernauld New Town in 1967 by the American Institute of Architects (in preference to Tapiola and Stockholm). The award comprised a plaque and accompanying sculpture 'Three Columns' (by Roy Gussow).

that, he was promoted to a more administrative job, and the later stages were built in a highly simplified manner. The reason for this was a conflict between the visionary brilliance of his designs and the pragmatic needs of building.

Where Cumbernauld Town Centre was a spectacular 'one-off', other designers were evolving consistent building programmes influenced by the same ideas of agglomerative social complexity. An ingenious sectional planning concept was developed by the firm of Gillespie, Kidd & Coia, which had been joined since the war by some younger Modernist designers, notably Isi Metzstein (in 1945, as an apprentice) and Andrew MacMillan (in 1954), and, from then until the mid 1960s, had been run as an 'atelier' dedicated to the evolution of new socio-architectural and aesthetic ideas. From 1958, the firm began a series of educational commissions which rejected the older type of layout with long corridors and thin wings in favour of a denser arrangement, with double-banked teaching or residential accommodation flanking communal spaces in the middle. The most significant of these Modernist

1.53 St Peter's College, Cardross (Gillespie, Kidd & Coia, 1959-66): 1966 view of ramp to rear of sanctuary.

sectional buildings was a seminary, St Peter's College at Cardross (1959-66), the showpiece of the Archdiocese of Glasgow's bold postwar building programme. Here a cluster of new accommodation and teaching buildings, designed by Isi Metzstein, was built in a 'U' shape around an existing Baronial house in a steep woodland setting. The papers by Isi Metzstein and Mark Baines later in this volume analyse the architectural forms, and explain the patronage context, of Gillespie, Kidd & Coia's remarkable sectional planned complexes; Diane Watters's recent account provides both a detailed description of the Cardross project, and an overview of the Church's building programme in the context of Modern architecture and liturgical reform. (98) (Fig. 1.53)

In educational designs by other architects, elements of agglomerative social planning began to creep in: for example, in the social core and radiating wings of James Stirling's university residences complex at St Andrews (1964-7). Stirling's blocks, while homogeneous in colour, were externally articulated in a studiedly harsh, crystalline manner, with striking juxtapositions of concrete and glazing: the surface-ribbed precast concrete panels were prefabricated in Edinburgh and transported to the site. The subsequent popularisation of the megastructure idea (Figs. 1.54, 1.55) simplified and narrowed it into a new kind of introverted urban commercial complex: only in the 'plug-in' structures of North Sea oil platforms did the idea find a late and dramatic realisation.

In the case of the other main innovative 1960s type of dense community layout – namely, 'low rise high density' – the key prototypes were not collective groups, but some small private houses of the late '50s. Here the dominant tendency was towards open-planned interiors influenced by contemporary American practice. Examples included Peter Womersley's timber-framed designs (e.g. High Sunderland, 1956-7, for textile designer Bernat Klein, or Port Murray, Maidens, 1960-3); Alan Reiach's own house at Winton Loan, Edinburgh, 1962-4; and the early work of Morris & Steedman (beginning with Avisfield, Edinburgh, 1956-7). (Fig. 1.56) A more detailed account of Morris & Steedman's pioneering houses is provided in the papers by Steedman and

1.54 Edinburgh University Comprehensive Development Area (planned from 1962): model prepared by Percy Johnson-Marshall, envisaging a megastructural redevelopment of the whole University area.

1.55 St James Centre, Edinburgh (Ian Burke & Martin, 1964-72), a simplified megastructural project, seen under construction in 1972.

Page in this volume. By contrast to this open-plan interpretation of Modernity, Frank Perry's design for a house at Newlands, East Lothian (1960-1) comprised an agglomeration of gabled wings and separate spaces, with enclosed court beside it. (99)

1.56 Alan Reiach's own house, Winton Loan, Edinburgh (1962-4): view of dining room and living room.

In the field of social housing, these ideas began to interact with the concepts of enclosed urban layouts pioneered by Spence and Wheeler. The most coherent and large-scale realisation was achieved by the designers of Cumbernauld New Town Development Corporation: a 'carpet' of low-rise housing, punctuated by sparing tower blocks, and carefully related by landscaping to the town's hilltop setting. Wheeler & Sproson made a calculatedly more urban intervention in Cumbernauld's satellite development at Abronhill, in the form of a formal pedestrian axis, approached by a flying bridge between 'portal' towers of flats and flanked by 4-storey ranges intended by Wheeler to recall Glasgow tenements. (Figs. 1.57, 1.58) However, the subsequent new towns, Livingston and Irvine, reacted against this relative density. Their embrace of the Motor Age led to a different sort of grid, tending more towards rationalist ideas and open-space planning: not a megastructure grid but a loose grid of roads. In Livingston, for example, the car was the 'primary determinant', and similar patterns were found at

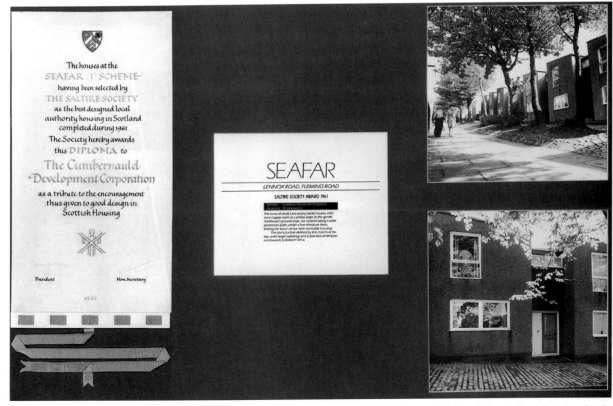

1.57 Display panel prepared by Cumbernauld New Town architects for the Saltire Society award (1961) for Seafar 1 housing development. Up until the Development Corporation's winding-up in 1996, its many Saltire awards were displayed on the walls of the prefabricated entrance wing of Cumbernauld House (CDC's headquarters).

Erskine, an unofficial New Town sponsored by Renfrew County Council and begun in 1968. (100) In other places, the dense and low carpet patterns were maintained, gradually evolving towards the Vernacular of the '70s, with monopitch rooms gradually steepening, but still remaining faithful to a dense, late-Modernist nervously aggregated layout: for instance, in Baxter Clark & Paul's projects at East Street, St Monans and St Peter's Street, Peterhead (1968); or, in the private sector and on a suburban site, Roland Wedgwood's Craigmount Avenue North scheme, Edinburgh, 1968. Other schemes prefigured a different, simpler and more consciously 'traditional' type of '70s Vernacular: for example, Wheeler & Sproson's two-storey terraces at Stirling Road, Milnathort (completed 1967). (Figs. 1.59, 1.60)

The tendency towards visual monumentality evinced in patterns of social agglomeration such as Megastructure was heightened further by some architects of the late '50s and early '60s, who followed Le

Corbusier's postwar adoption of a more uninhibitedly poetic and personalised approach to Modern design. Within Rowand Anderson, Kininmonth & Paul, the arrival of younger designers was followed by bold designs such as the Scottish Provident headquarters,

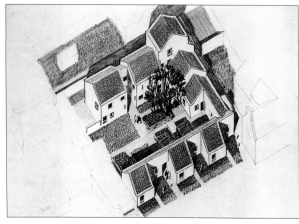

1.59 East Street housing scheme, St Monans (Baxter, Clark & Paul, 1968-70): aerial perspective. A transitional pattern between Late Modernism and the Vernacular of the 1970s.

1.58 Abronhill 4 development, Cumbernauld, by Wheeler & Sproson (1968-70). The formal, axial layout was designed to reflect the Glasgow tenements in which the tenants had previously lived.

Edinburgh (1961-9), with its sharply-contrasted solids and voids: a small Glasgow office building by Gillespie, Kidd & Coia (1968-70) was rather more muted and contextual. (Figs. 1.61, 1.62) Peter Womersley now began a systematic pursuit of 'sculptural' form, in a series of monumental concrete designs for public buildings. At Roxburgh County Buildings, a tall tower gave an air of civic dignity (1966-8); a small studio for Bernat Klein at High Sunderland (1969-72) was articulated by deep, horizontal edge

beams; and at the Nuffield Transplantation Surgery Unit, Edinburgh (1963-8), medical requirements for isolation and sterility were combined with bold visual interpenetration. (Figs. 1.63, 1.64, 1.65, 1.66) Some Modernists were distrustful of this 'new phase of stylism': for instance Frank Fielden in 1964 bemoaned its preoccupation with 'form and fashion', which he attributed to the failure to convince the public of the necessity for 'austerity' and 'science'. (101) Proposals by Womersley for the extension of Edinburgh College

1.60 Stirling Road, Milnathort: housing development by Wheeler & Sproson (completed 1967). The plain terraced design was envisaged by Wheeler as a return to 'tradition'.

1.62 BOAC Office, Buchanan Street, Glasgow, by Gillespie, Kidd & Coia (1970).

1.61 Scottish Provident Association offices, Edinburgh: Rowand Anderson, Kininmonth & Paul, 1961-9: view when newly completed.

1.63 Boldly prismatic concrete forms at Gala Fairydean football stadium, Galashiels. (1963-5: Peter Womersley, with Ove Arup)

of Art, with ferociously articulated facades, took the sculptural tendency to an extreme, and were turned down; in the event, a more sober and massive design in red sandstone by Wheeler and Sproson, intended by the architects to create a 'quiet academic precinct', was built instead (1972).

Alongside these efforts in secular buildings, others were exploiting the more obvious potential for 'poetic' design offered by religious architecture, where the emphasis on worshipper-centred plans (especially in the Catholic Church, around the time of the Second Vatican Council) encouraged a growing stress on more

1.64 Model by Peter Womersley (1964) of proposed Nuffield Transplantation Surgery Unit, Edinburgh (built 1965-8).

1.65 Nuffield Unit: 1968 view of physiological monitoring desk (from which a nurse supervised two patients' rooms by remote control).

unified, monumental forms. By the mid-60s, even the kind of solution attempted by Spence at Mortonhall Crematorium, Edinburgh (1964-7) – a cluster of spiky chapels, faced with smooth, ashlar-like blockwork – was already a little old-fashioned. By then, patterns

which were more fluid and unified in both mass and space were well-developed. Within the Kirk, it was important to avoid dark mysticism. Wheeler & Sproson's Torbain Parish Church, Kirkcaldy (1964-8), for example, exploited concealed lighting to combine

1.66 Edenside Group Practice Surgery, Kelso (1967): a rare example of Vernacular tendencies in Peter Womersley's 1960s work.

1.68 Interior of St Patrick's Church, Kilsyth (1964).

1.67 Interior of Wheeler & Sproson's Torbain Parish Church, Kirkcaldy (1964-8). [Wheeler & Sproson]

the preaching-church function with 'a sense of, not mystery, but seclusion' (102). (Fig. 1.67) Within the Catholic Church, more revolutionary changes were made at the instigation of the younger designers of Gillespie, Kidd & Coia. At St Paul's Church, Glenrothes (1956-7), the grandly hierarchical pattern of previous Coia churches was jettisoned in favour of a compressed, wedge-shaped plan with sectional top-lighting (through a roof projection) and massive walls with irregularly-placed small windows. The practice's prolific 1960s church output continued on this path of formal innovation, in a range of designs including the fortresslike, brick St Bride's, East Kilbride (1963-4), with its tall campanile (since demolished), and St Benedict Drumchapel (1965-7: demolished), its swept-up, prow-like ceiling supported on curved, laminated timber members. The innovative brilliance of these designs was widely recognised, even among designers who represented other strands of Late Modernism. (Fig. 1.68) John and Margaret Richards, for example, would 'go on long trips in the car to see Andy and Isi's latest church – those designs were absolutely phenomenal!' (103) Metzstein and MacMillan's romantic, sculptural response to the vision of a powerful client seemed, at first glance, very different from that of John Richards's team at RMJM. Where Richards aimed at a 'post-Cubist modelling of space', Coia's team 'carved building out of solids'. But there was in fact quite a lot in common: Richards held 'that a building could exist as an idea independently of your perception of it . . . as a Platonic form, even.' (104) In the discussion between John Richards and Andy MacMillan on the Commonwealth Pool, included in this volume, some of these issues are touched on.

Looking, overall, at these 'social' and 'formal' approaches within Late Modernism, we can see that they represented a substantial complication of, if not departure from, what they saw as the rigidity of the Matthew generation's integrated Functionalist formulae. But – just as the rationalist aspirations of 'systems' seemed at times to dissolve into contradictions – this, in turn, threw up new inconsistencies. Many of the buildings meant to reflect the new, complex society suffered, themselves, problems of social rejection: for example, some, but by no means all, Cumbernauld residents branded the Town Centre a draughty and

hostile environment, while Spence's Hutchesontown 'C' slabs became 'unlettable' and were dynamited in 1993. And buildings meant to celebrate Modernist conceptions of beauty were later argued, by some users, to have done so at the expense of solidity and utility: the Catholic Church, claiming structural or maintenance problems, demolished a number of Coia's most daring designs, including St Benedict's Drumchapel and the campanile of St Bride's. But before long, whether or not there was an inconsistency or shortfall in the Late Modernist ideas of the 60s would seem less and less important, as the following decade began to see a move away from Modern architecture as a whole. All these issues – the claimed contradictions within, and the attacks on, Modernist values – are addressed in detail in the DOCOMOMO conference discussion reprinted in this book.

THE REJECTION OF MODERNISM

The 1970s and '80s were the decades when the restructuring of the Scottish economy away from dependence on heavy industry was completed. This fulfilled many of the dreams of the regional planners; yet their own legitimacy, along with that of other mechanisms of State mass provision, was also now questioned. This scepticism did not take the form of a swashbuckling laissez-faire rhetoric, as in Thatcherite England – indeed, there was a gradual decline of consensus with England over social issues, with a concomitant further growth in separatist nationalism – but a more measured, consensual trend of diversification away from State monopoly provision, towards a combination of greater commercialisation and more direct user-participation. A key landmark, for instance, was the Labour government's 1977 Green Paper on the future of Scottish housing, which called for increased tenurial variety. (105)

In architecture, these tendencies rapidly gained ground. First, they cleared a space for themselves by attacking Modernism. The Modern dwelling, a product of Functionalist logic, had itself done much of the work of social privatisation. Now the tight 'need-fit' recipe of Functionalism was rejected altogether, in favour of looser groups of ideas. This transition was spotlighted, in polarised form, at a public debate on planning and participation in Edinburgh in 1969, entitled 'Where People Live'. The two main protagonists were Peter Daniel, former chief architect-planner of Livingston New Town, and the radical Episcopalian minister Richard Holloway, subsequently Bishop of Edinburgh and Primus of the Scottish Episcopal Church. Daniel's analysis remained essentially faithful to Modernist linear Progress; he advocated more sensitive and refined mechanisms of planning, which would prepare people better for 'the cost and social consequences of change' and 'avoid the tragedy of fragmentation of responsibility among those who provided facilities in new communities, and the creation of "them" and "us" situations.' To Holloway – a Glaswegian who had become deeply involved in housing activism in the 1960s, including the organisation of rent strikes in the Gorbals and the setting up of an ecumenical housing association – this kind of reformist managerialism was beside the point. The problem was not the manner of social provision, but provision itself: and the planned State provision of the 20th century now seemed just as paternalistic as the laissez-faire provision it had supplanted: 'The entrepreneur was replaced by the "expert".' The planned reconstruction of Scotland, he declaimed, had 'resulted in a crushing architectural dreariness, smothering the country in "schemes" of almost brutal ugliness' – a 'Lego architecture' which had made 'Scottish cities . . . indistinguishable from all the dreary urban wastes that stretch from Detroit to Dusseldorf.' Now, what was needed was a 'third force', a 'revolt of the amateurs, who love cities, love houses, understand the poetry of their town, and are determined that their environment will not be decided for them by either profiteer or expert.' (106) In this powerful rhetoric, we see the 'social nationalism' of Geddes and the Traditionalists in the process of transmutation into present-day 'community participation' – the two having in common a rejection of Modernist ideals of social Progress. What no-one could have predicted was that the voluntaristic 'third force', destined to replace state socialism as the most prestigious force in the shaping of the built environment, would also contain a strong element of revived laissez-faire capitalism.

1.69 Govan (Taransay Street) Treatment Area: view of Elder Street, 1970. It was here that Raymond Young founded the Govan Tenement Improvement Project, forerunner of ASSIST and prototype for the housing association-based tenement rehabilitation movement which would sweep Glasgow in the late 70s and 80s, as part of the widespread reaction against local-authority housing provision.

1.70 Brae, Shetland: 100 houses built for oil-related development by Zetland County Council from 1975. This package-deal design, by Miller Ltd., contractors, was (in contrast to the dense small-burgh pattern of Vernacular) deliberately designed to reflect the 'dispersed settlement' pattern of older Shetland dwellings.

The collapse in the status of Modernism was not immediate and evenly distributed. For example, in the mid-70s, Modernist public housing was in sharp decline, with large-scale new building of multi-storey blocks virtually confined to Aberdeen's popular programme (the last, at Jasmine Place, being completed in 1985). But the school-building drive was only just reaching its climax, following the raising of the leaving age in 1972: in Lanarkshire, for instance, this had prompted a crash programme of system-built secondary schools, and the building of numerous primary schools designed by the County Architect on an ingenious circular plan.

Perhaps the most fatal blow to Scottish Modernism occurred in June 1975, with the death of Robert Matthew. But by then, Matthew's views – which had evolved from 'vernacular' Functionalism in the '50s to a heightened rationalism in the '60s, had gone through a further change; and he had begun to give decisive backing to what would be the dominant aspect of Scottish architecture in the 1970s: the Conservation Movement. It was largely at his instigation that the growing demand for action to arrest the decay of the Edinburgh New Town was channelled, in 1970, into the formation of a powerful, State-financed organisation, the Edinburgh New Town Conservation Committee. (107) The following year, in Glasgow, a different, but equally influential type of socially-orientated conservation got under way, steered by the avant-garde architec-

tural collective ASSIST, along lines pointed to by the work of Holloway and his colleagues in the '60s: namely, the rehabilitation of working-class tenements through the agency of local housing associations. (108) Compared to all this preservationist activity, new architecture was much lower in profile during the '70s, and was dominated by an expansion of the Vernacular and low/medium-rise high-density housing tendencies of the '60s. Large swathes of Irvine New Town, and a variety of inventive small-burgh schemes by Baxter, Clark & Paul, were built in this style. In the area of public buildings and inner-urban sites, insertion of new interiors into existing shells became popular. One of the few large Vernacular public buildings was Barry Gasson, John Meunier and Brit Andreson's Burrell Collection, Glasgow (1971-83). (109) (Figs. 1.69, 1.70, 1.71, 1.72)

Only in the expansionist Postmodern architecture of the 1980s did new building become more assertive in character once again. With the rejection of the Modernist refusal to discuss 'style' separately, there was an often extravagant diversity of stylistic solutions. These ranged from the relatively international idiom of Postmodern Classicism to renewed attempts to evoke the 'national' – including Ian Begg's monumental evocations of 'Old Edinburgh' Traditionalism, and the Mackintosh Revival triggered by Gillespie, Kidd & Coia's designs for Robinson College, Cambridge (1974-80). (110) And Postmodernism also

1.71 View of the Woodside 'B' redevelopment, Glasgow (built from 1970, Boswell Mitchell & Johnston: project architect, Nori Toffolo), when newly completed. This influential Late Modern scheme combined megastructural elements (the decks and bridges), with curved excrescences suggesting Pop-Art influence: the use of bright facing brick anticipated Glasgow's Postmodern tenement revival of the '80s.

1.72 Landmark Visitor Centre, Stirling Esplanade: 1971 conversion by Johnston and Groves-Raines of the shell of an 18th-century hotel into a multi-level, flowing sequence of spaces.

abandoned Modernism's wider formulas of comprehensive or regional planning in favour of a new and more intense focus on the 'regeneration' of 'The City'. (111) Reviving some elements of Traditionalism, urban Community was now envisaged as something to be protected against, rather than constructed by means of, change and the New. In a set of recipes ultimately devised by the American theorist Jane Jacobs in the early 1960s, it was demanded that the destruction allegedly caused by Modernist formulas, now labelled 'tabula rasa' planning, must be healed by piecemeal 'interventions', and Functionalist segregation of uses must be replaced by a dense mixture of uses. (112) The most complex realisation of these ideas was the improvement of a rundown area of central Glasgow (dubbed 'The Merchant City') by a mixture of public and private initiative, including a new breed of architect-developers such as Kantel and Burrell. The same kind of formula was adapted for the large-scale improvement and stonecleaning of surviving pre-1914 tenemental areas, and later for the rehabilitation of run-down council schemes. Here the showpiece was the Crown Street Regeneration Project, in which part of the Hutchesontown CDA multi-storey redevelopment (the Area E 'Tracoba' deck blocks, built from 1968) was demolished and replanned in the form of 'traditional streets' and tenements: the conception of this project, with its evocations of user-participation and its condemnation of Modernism, is outlined by its director, Mike Galloway, in the DOCOMOMO conference discussion included in this book.

Eventually, in the early 1990s, there was the beginning of a reaction against the eclectic freedom of Postmodernism, and a demand for greater idealism – which brings us back to the context in which the present volume originated. Under the inspiration of younger designers, some Edinburgh firms founded in the Modernist era began, in the words of Neil Gillespie of Reiach and Hall, to return to 'ordering principles'. (113) Acting in parallel to this were the vigorous efforts of newer practices in Glasgow and elsewhere, such as Page & Park, Elder & Cannon and Richard Murphy. There was a growing demand that contemporary work should be informed by the experience, and inspired by the commitment, of the Modern Movement in Scotland – for an end to what Page, in

this book, calls 'the censorship of neglect'. But, at the same time, there was a clear recognition that Modern architecture's specific forms and solutions were not necessarily relevant, or acceptable, in present day conditions: there was no likelihood, in the foreseeable future, of anyone demanding the massed building of Zeilenbau slab blocks! The reaction away from what was now held to be the eclectic chaos of architectural Postmodernism was not accompanied by any significant departure from the wider cultural movement of postmodernity: the 'principles' which were now appealed to did not revive the ideals of material or social Progress held by Modern architects – although, as we have constantly seen in the preceding chapters, Modernism itself was nothing if not open-ended in many of its key values. This change of climate among architects was linked to developments in the field of historical research – which led, among other things, to the founding of Scottish DOCOMOMO in 1992. There now seemed, for the first time, to be a possibility of standing back and, at the very least, taking an overview of the dimensions and the ideals of postwar rebuilding, and especially of the Modernist revolution.

What patterns did this historical overview begin to reveal? 19th-century capitalism had unleashed a

1.73 Wester Hailes Contract 5: seven 9-storey slab blocks built from 1969 by Crudens and demolished 1993. Photographed in 1990 in semi-derelict state.

physical transformation which was just as sweeping and violent, but only its most prestigious building types had come within the scope of architecture or architects. It was in opposition to precisely that period that Modernism defined its own fundamental values, by concentrating on the design and planning of everyday, mass building, and insisting, in its philosophy, on the integration of *venustas* with *utilitas* and *firmitas*. Moreover, Modernism not only aspired to reconstruction of the country as a whole, but in the most socially emotive areas – the areas that mattered most to people in those decades – it very largely succeeded in carrying through its aims. In social housing, for instance, by the 1960s, *all* new dwellings embodied a Modernist consistency of standards, in space, mod. cons. and self-containment. And the surroundings of people's homes had also been transformed: the dirty, smog-ridden industrial environments of recent memory no longer existed.

This was a utopian legacy of awesome proportions, and one which, even after a quarter of a century of passionate debate and criticism, we are only now beginning to live with more comfortably. In part, this is because the pace of Postmodern rebuilding has broken up the apparent homogeneity of Modernist areas, and placed a greater distance between ourselves and those

1.74 Niddrie Marischal housing scheme, Edinburgh: scene during festivities preceding the abortive 'blowdown' of two Bison point blocks, September 1991. The supposedly 'badly built' blocks, which survived unscathed the detonation of over 2,000 charges of high explosive, eventually had to be smashed down by a giant battering ram.

that survive in their original state. (Figs. 1.73, 1.74) Grey slab blocks frown down with the inscrutability of prehistoric monuments, as the bustlingly variegated work of 'regeneration' goes on around them. Over the next quarter century, as the challenge of maintaining these buildings and adapting them to new uses is tackled, it will be the job of historians to begin the task of documenting both the structures themselves, and the aspirations and passions that brought them into being.

NOTES

1 J Richards, *EAA Review* 1985.
2 General historical accounts: J S Gibson, *The Thistle and the Crown*, 1985; L Paterson, *The Autonomy of Modern Scotland*, 1994, Chapter 6; A M Mackenzie, *Scotland in Modern Times*, 1941. SSHA: T Begg, *Fifty Special Years*, 1987.
3 General account: C McKean, *The Scottish Thirties*, 1987.
4 *British Architect* 1-4-1892.
5 Burnet: see e.g. D M Walker, *St Andrew's House*, 1989; *The Architectural Work of Sir John Burnet and Partners*, Geneva 1930. Anderson, Geddes, Lorimer: S McKinstry, *Rowand Anderson*, 1991; P Savage, *Lorimer and the Edinburgh Craft Designers*, 1980; I Hay: *Their Name Liveth, The Book of the Scottish National War Memorial*, 1931; H Meller, *Patrick Geddes*, 1990.
6 T S Tait, *QRIAS* 60 4-1939; R Crampsey, *The Empire Exhibition 1938*, 1988.
7 L Campbell, *JRIBA* 4-1993.
8 R W K C Rogerson, *Jack Coia*, 1986.
9 'Sound modern tradition': R Hurd, in London Scots Self-Government Committee, *The New Scotland*, 1942; 'Awakening': 4th Marquess of Bute, *A Plea for Scotland's Architectural Heritage*, 1936, 12; Sir John Stirling-Maxwell, *Shrines and Homes of Scotland*, 1937, and *QRIAS* 51 1935; G Bruce, *To Foster and Enrich*, 1986; J R Allan (ed), *Scotland 1938*, 1938, chapters by Scott-Moncrieff and Hurd; R Hurd, *Scotland under Trust*, 1939; I G Hannah, *The Story of Scotland in Stone*, 1934 (see e.g. page 1 against cosmopolitanism).
10 P Wagner, *A Sociology of Modernity*, 1994, 66.
11 See e.g. T Warnett Kennedy, *QRIAS* 57 1938; *The Scottish Architect and Builders' Journal* passim (1938-9). Matthew's Bossom flats project: *JRIBA* 1936, 393-415.
12 W Power, foreword to J Mann (ed), *Replanning Scotland*, 1941.
13 Paterson, *Autonomy*, Chapter 6.
14 J A Bowie, *The Future of Scotland*, 1939.
15 Gibson, *Thistle*, Chapters 4-6; G Pottinger,

The Secretaries of State for Scotland, 1979, Chapter 9.

16 N Fraser, in *The New Scotland*, 1; Mann, *Replanning Scotland*.

17 A Reiach, R Hurd, *Building Scotland*, 1941/4.

18 *Architectural Record* 3-1947.

19 *B* 26-5-1961, 991.

20 *B* 7-1-1955; interview with Richard Ewing.

21 L Campbell (ed), *To Build a Cathedral*, 1987, xiv.

22 *To Build a Cathedral*; L Campbell, *Coventry Cathedral*, 1996.

23 Interview with R Cant, 1991.

24 *Journal of the Town Planning Institute* 1948.

25 *B* 20-6-1952.

26 *B* 5-12-1952; P L Payne, *The Hydro*, 1988; Shearer, article in *B* 30-11-1956; The Scotsman, *The New Scotland* 1958; *B* 30-11-1956.

27 *B* 1-6-1951.

28 Bute, *Scotland's Architectural Heritage*, 16.

29 M R Kelsall, S Harris, *A Future for the Past*, 1961.

30 National Trust for Scotland *Newsletter* 14; *EAAYB* 3 1959; *B* 1-8-1952, 7-12-1951, 20-6-1952, 15-2-1952.

31 See e.g. F A Walker, *Prospect* 19 1960.

32 Matthew: *B* 8-2-1952. 'Popular architecture': *QRIAS* 8-1952.

33 *B* 4-10-1968.

34 *House and Garden* 6-1954; Princes Street: information from Kitty Cruft.

35 *B* 22-6-1956; M Banham, B Hillier (eds), *A Tonic to the Nation*, 1976, 108-9.

36 *QRIAS* 85 1951; Banham and Hillier, *Tonic*, 152-4; *Prospect* 8-1956.

37 Correspondence with T Warnett Kennedy, 1994.

38 Robert Scott Morton notes in NMRS Architects index folders, 1-1984; *QRIAS* 8-1952.

39 *Proceedings of the Scottish Society of Arts, Bulletin* 23, 1967.

40 Correspondence with Warnett Kennedy.

41 *QRIAS* 89 8-1952.

42 *ABN* 29-9-1955.

43 *QRIAS* 11-1947.

44 W D Chapman and C F Riley, *Granite City*, 1952, vii. Edinburgh: P Abercrombie, D Plumstead, *A Civic Survey and Plan for Edinburgh*, 1949.

45 P Abercrombie, R H Matthew, *The Clyde Valley Regional Plan 1946*; M Glendinning and S Muthesius, *Tower Block*, 1994, Chapter 20.

46 *QRIAS* 75 1949.

47 *QRIAS* 94, 1953.

48 Wheeler: RFACS 'Minds Meeting' lecture 1993. Lerwick: Shetland Archive, Heddell's Park file, 3-1-1957 letter R Moira to Lerwick Town Clerk.

49 Shetland Archive, Lerwick Housing Committee minutes, 28-8-1952.

50 *QRIAS* 97 1954.

51 *B* 9-1955.

52 *QRIAS* 2-1954.

53 NMRS, R Scott Morton notes, 1971; *EAAYB* 1964.

54 *B* 7-6-1957.

55 Matthew, *Town and Country Planning*, 9-1954.

56 NMRS notes by R Scott Morton, 1984; *AJ* 18-2-1960.

57 SHAC, *Planning our New Homes*, 95.

58 *Prospect* 19, 1960; *B* 4-9-1964.

59 *B* 14-6-1968.

60 Interview with A B Campbell, 1993.

61 Doak, *Prospect* 14 1959.

62 *B* 26-4-1957.

63 *Prospect* 8 1957; RMJM, *The Early Years*.

64 J McKechnie, M Macgregor, *A Short History of the Scottish Coal Industry*, 1958; *SBCEY* 1963, 105.

65 Interview with D Whitham, 1995.

66 Interview with Ian Arnott, 1987.

67 Interview with J L Paterson, 1son, 1987.

68 Interview with Ian Arnott, 1987

69 *EAAYB* 1962, 96.

70 Glendinning and Muthesius, *Tower Block*, Chapter 25.

71 *B* 7-6-1957.

72 Pottinger, *Secretaries of State*, Chapters 14-16; Gibson, *Thistle and the Crown*, Chapter 6.

73 I Sutherland, *Dounreay*, 1990, 45-50; P Johnson-Marshall, *SBCEY* 1963, 53-5.

74 Doak, *Prospect* 14, 1959.

75 Ockman, *Architecture Culture*, 181.

76 *Glasgow Observer* 14-3-1958.

77 *Prospect* 3, 1956.

78 *B* 5-4-1957.

79 *B* 30-4-1965.

80 Scott Wilson & Kirkpatrick & Partners, *Report on a Highway Plan for Glasgow*, 1965.

81 Ockman, *Architecture Culture*, 273ff.

82 J L Paterson, *Prospect* 8 1957 and 10 1958; interview with J L Paterson, 1987.

83 *Royal Scottish Society of Arts Bulletin* 23 1967.

84 NMRS, R Scott Morton notes 1984.

85 Holt, *B* 27-11-1953.

86 SHHD, *The Falkirk Ward*, 1966; Edinburgh Royal Infirmary, RMJM: E F Catford, *The Royal Infirmary of Edinburgh*, 1984.

87 DOCOMOMO fiche by D Whitham, 1994; E E Kemp, *Royal Botanic Garden . . . the New Plant Houses* (unpublished memoir), 1992.

88 J Richards, RFACS Minds Meeting seminar 1993.

89 Interview with J Richards, 1995; J Richards, RFACS Minds Meeting seminar 1993.

90 *AR* 6-1973.

91 DOCOMOMO fiche by D Whitham, 1994 (architect's account); *AJ* 16-9-1970; *JRIBA* 8-1970.

92 *QRIAS* 11-1952.

93 *AJ* 7-4-1965, *AR* 3-1965.

94 *Royal Scottish Society of Arts Bulletin* 23 1967.

95 *American Institute of Architects Journal* 7-1967.

96 Interview with Ron Simpson, 1994.

97 *AJ* 5-12-1962; *AD* 5-1963, 210-1.

98 *Mac Journal* 1 1994: articles by C Mac Callum, M Baines, D Niven; Metzstein, RFACS Minds Meeting seminar 1993; *B* 6-9-1968; MacMillan,

lecture to 20th Century Society, Glasgow, 1994;
D M Watters, *Cardross Seminary*, 1997.

99 J Richards, *EAAYB* 1964, 86ff.

100 W Newman Brown, *EAAYB* 1971, 88ff.

101 *GIA Yearbook*, 1964; *Building Design* 5-1973,
B 27-6-1969.

102 Interview with Sir A Wheeler, 1995.

103 Interview with M Richards, 1995; J Richards,
Mac Journal 1, 1994.

104 Interview with J Richards, 1995.

105 Cd 6852, *Scottish Housing: A Consultative
Document*, 1977, 36-42 and 93. R Boyle, *Urban
Studies* 1993, 309ff.

106 *B* 5-9-1969.

107 Scottish Civic Trust, *The Conservation of
Georgian Edinburgh*, 1972.

108 M Horsey, *Tenements and Towers*, 1990,
Chapter 5.

109 R Marks et al, *The Burrell Collection*, 1983.

110 Begg: *Prospect* Winter 1995. Robinson:
AJ 5-8-1981; *Mac Journal* 1, 1994, article by
Baines.

111 International context, see e.g. P Portoghesi,
Postmodern, 1983.

112 J Jacobs, *The Death and Life of Great American
Cities*, 1961.

113 *Prospect* Winter 1995, 16.

1.75 Pollockshaws Comprehensive Development Area Unit 2, Glasgow: new 'Bison' multi-storey slab blocks (designed by Boswell, Mitchell & Johnston) rear up behind 19th-century tenements under demolition in 1963. (Outram)

PART TWO
PATRONAGE AND BUILDING

INTRODUCTION

This first group of papers, all drawn from the DOCOMOMO Conference, 'Visions Revisited', is dedicated to the general context of building. Its aim is to begin, with the aid of the recollections of key participants from the 1950s and '60s, the reassessment of the 'why', 'who' and 'how' of postwar building as a whole. (Fig. 2.1)

It focuses above all on the 'housing-planning nexus', with two contributors representing the central government viewpoint and one the municipal position. The climax of the Government drive for planned modernisation in the mid 1960s is recalled, especially in the field of housing and planning, by the Scottish Office minister, J Dickson Mabon, who put it into effect, and by one of his key administrators within SDD, Ronnie Cramond. Pat Rogan, on the other hand, recollects the continuing sense of outrage at the persistence of the 'slums', which drove forward the municipal 'crusaders' for housing output. A fourth paper focuses on a different aspect of the 1960s

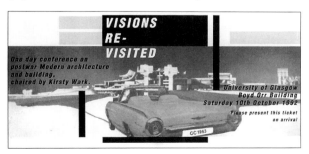

2.1 DOCOMOMO 'Visions Revisited' inaugural conference, 10 October 1992: conference ticket.

rebuilding – the urban roads programme of Glasgow Corporation, which set out to create a full-scale US-style expressway in the densely constrained setting of a European city. Described by the engineer James P McCafferty, the essay deals both with the 'provision' and the 'design' of this vast and, in the event, uncompleted project. But we begin Part 1 of the book with the three short introductory papers which inaugurated the 'Visions Revisited' conference.

VISIONS REVISITED CONFERENCE:
INTRODUCTORY ADDRESSES
CHAIRPERSON'S WELCOME:
KIRSTY WARK

Welcome to 'Visions Revisited'. This is the inaugural conference of the Scottish National Group of DOCOMOMO – the International Working Party for the Documentation and Conservation of Buildings and Sites of the Modern Movement. And it's a mark of the passion that Modern architecture arouses that this conference is well oversubscribed. You've all come here from your own traditions – planners, architects, historians, interested people from the community. And, also, you've come with your own prejudices. This, then, is a chance to hear a great variety of views expressed.

John Ruskin said: 'When we build, let us think that we build for ever'. The trouble is, many people don't see Modernist buildings like that, and they accrue evidence – and it's often not very difficult to accrue evidence – to support their view. Or, sometimes, the problem is just the shock of seeing something different – like the Louvre pyramid in Paris. One interpretation of this is that, no matter how visionary and enlightened people think they are, they always really believe that they are at the end of history. That, to me, suggests that people can't imagine – or don't want to, for fear of their own mortality – they can't imagine what will come after. But if we were to hold this conference in another fifteen, twenty, twenty-five years' time, the chances are that perhaps a lot of your attitudes would also have changed. Take this very building, for instance – the Boyd Orr Building, designed by Ivor G Dorward of Dorward, Matheson, Gleave & Partners, and completed in 1972. Nowadays, people either love it or hate it – and, with its massive, jutting concrete form, it's gone through a variety of adjectives and expletives since it was built. What will they think in the future?

So – this conference is to open the way to this debate. But first of all, two introductory papers. In a moment, we'll hear Dr. David Walker, who's the Chief Inspector of Historic Scotland, the national organisation for protecting our built heritage, and who will address the issue of Modern Architecture as 'Heritage'. First, however, let me welcome to the conference Professor Hubert-Jan Henket, chairman of the international headquarters of DOCOMOMO, who's here to formally inaugurate the Scottish National Group. He, with one other person, founded DOCOMOMO just over three years ago. He's an architect and a Professor at Eindhoven University. Among many commissions, he designed the Boymans van Beuningen Museum in Rotterdam in 1991, and the Missionary Building at Dar-es-Salaam in 1984.

INAUGURAL ADDRESS:
HUBERT-JAN HENKET

I'd like to begin by saying what a great pleasure it is for me to be in Glasgow, the city of Charles Rennie Mackintosh and the birthplace of the late Jim Stirling. As of today, you are the twenty-eighth national working party within the DOCOMOMO family. And I very warmly welcome you into that group.

Now what is this peculiar organisation, with the name DOCOMOMO?

It stands for the International Working Party for the Documentation and Conservation of Buildings and Sites of the Modern Movement. What brings us together is a love of the spirit of the Modern Movement and the buildings which resulted from that. By that 'love' we mean that we try to bring about public awareness of the buildings of the Modern Movement. We act as a watchdog, if buildings of the Modern Movement, particularly the important ones, are not treated in the right way. We act as watchdogs to make sure that the documentation of these buildings is done properly, and kept in the proper way. And we have this large network of – now – 28 countries, all over the world, to exchange ideas and to exchange research results.

At our second international conference, at the Bauhaus in Dessau, less than a month ago, we more clearly defined that the period we're interested in is a very broad one: from the end of the nineteenth century until today. We also tried to define what the Modern Movement is. You can go through all the literature in the world, and talk to all the people who've thought about that, but it's extremely difficult to define. So we came up with a definition of Modernity which helped us slightly. And that is, we said, Modernity was everything, as far as we're concerned, which historically has proved to be innovative in three aspects – either in the social context, or the technical context, and/or in the aesthetic context. Based on that, we also decided: 'All these countries are so different from each other, their histories are so different, that we have to leave it up to the specific countries what to do'. I'll give you a specific example. The Latvians at the conference said: 'For us, the Modern Movement is very clearly defined, because it finishes – we know it starts somewhere, but that's different – but it finishes on the precise day in 1939 when the USSR invaded our country'. Whereas other countries such as, for example, the Brazilians, say, 'Well, we only experienced the Modern Movement from the 'fifties onwards'.

So we've said, 'Well, we'll leave it to every country to concentrate on the specific aspects most appropriate to their own situation.' We've set up quite a few international specialist committees to sort out a few things: for instance, to make an international register of Modern Movement buildings, and to go deeper into the technology of the Modern Movement and the conservation of the Modern Movement. And I sincerely hope that quite a few of you will participate on those committees, and that we shall see you at the next international conference, which will be in Barcelona in September 1994. Our host there will be the Mies van der Rohe Foundation.

Now, as to the conference of today – 'Visions Revisited' – most of the DOCOMOMO countries have concentrated on the prewar period, because, for most countries, that was the 'heroic' period, and that was where all or most of their interesting things were. But the people in Brazil, in Quebec, and a few people in England – I mention James Dunnett, with his attention to Ernö Goldfinger's work – have begun to concentrate, already, on the postwar period. But this conference – your conference – is the first one which takes it as its main item. And I think that's very important. Jean-Paul Sartre, in one of the diaries he wrote in 1939, said

2.2 'Visions Revisited' conference: Professor Hubert-Jan Henket, Chairman of DOCOMOMO-International, seen at Cumbernauld Town Centre on the conference bus tour.

something very interesting. He said, '"I am" only gets meaning when I understand who I was'. Therefore this conference to me is important, because we have to look back to the recent past to understand how we're going forward.

Particularly since the War, quite a few huge-scale developments have taken place; you can see that in Glasgow as well. Scotland has witnessed quite a few disappointments as far as experience is concerned, and as far as idealism is concerned. Indeed, right now, we can see the smoking ruins around us, in political terms! I think we should learn from both the negative and the positive things, and I hope we, together, in this conference, can have a debate which is objective about the subject – because that is what we need. We should look at the negative sides of the Modern Movement, as well as the positive sides. I thank you very much for organising this conference, and wish you, as I said before, a very open and objective debate. (Fig. 2.2)

MODERN ARCHITECTURE AND HERITAGE:
DAVID M. WALKER

Architecture is certainly the most prominent, if not always the most enduring expression of a particular culture. We do not need to look at paintings or – most of the time at least – listen to music if we do not want to, but we all have to live with architecture, day in, day out. Every building we put up should therefore, ideally, be one which adds to the heritage of our country and enriches the life of those who pass by.

We are holding this conference at a time when architects are seeing their buildings demolished in their own lifetime as never in the past. I find it a rather astonishing experience that buildings, whose construction I opposed, not all that long ago, are now being listed as being of architectural interest, or are now under threat. I'm even more surprised to find that, just occasionally, I view their impending disappearance with regret, as the architect had made a serious attempt to match, or indeed better – and said that he believed he was bettering – the quality of what was being replaced. There are, I think, no surer tests of quality than that.

Whatever, personally, we think of the period which is under discussion today, we can be sure it will be the subject of the close scrutiny of historians from every point of view. And, on that reappraisal, perhaps just one personal cautionary thought. Pioneering buildings are, historically, always very important, and their significance in that regard should always be recognised. But I would suggest that we should not become too hung up on whether or not buildings were up-to-the-minute at the time. To take a historical perspective: as time passes, the question of whether or not a building, or a painting for that matter, is 20 years or more behind the times, matters less and less, and eventually becomes only an interesting academic point, within about 30 or 40 years. Apart from the obvious question of whether or not the building can be adapted to changed living and working conditions, we become solely concerned with its artistic quality, and with the pleasure we have in it. It is, I think, quite important to remember that Alexander Thomson himself began by picking up an idiom which, in most other European countries, had been discarded at least a decade earlier.

This is most important; and we should try to evaluate everything on its own terms. At the end of the day, how well or how badly the building was designed will be the most lasting consideration. As in the nineteenth century, which, in this part of the world, produced such giants as David Bryce, Alexander Thomson, Frederick Pilkington, Rowand Anderson, J. J. Burnet, John A. Campbell, Robert Lorimer and Charles Rennie Mackintosh, the postwar period will one day, I'm sure, be found to have its masters: some of these are clearly established already. And a few of these will achieve reputations on the international scale, as did the architects whose unique national tradition they inherited. Some of us may not like their buildings at the moment. But, forty-four years ago, Ian Lindsay, who founded the whole business of listing in our country, made an important point in his instructions to investigators: that, while his generation did not like Victorian Baronial, future generations might. And, indeed, they did! Now it is for us to look at the work of the Modern masters in the same spirit. (Fig. 2.3)

Who these Modern masters will eventually be identified as, is of course a matter for this conference to investigate. And while I'm speaking personally today – especially since Historic Scotland has certainly no extra cash on offer for Modern architecture just now! – let me say that their works are as worthy of proper repair and maintenance as any other. I say this particularly because there was a mistaken belief, in the 1950s and 1960s, that Modern buildings, unlike traditional ones, would not need repair! I can recall it as a constant selling point for demolition and replacement. We are, sadly, paying the price of that misconception now. Inadequate maintenance, compounded by building methods which had not been subject to the test of time, have brought some of the very best buildings of the period to a very poor state indeed. Some application of the mind may at times be required to solve these problems, and preserve the original concept. It's always sad, it's often tragic to see the intentions of the original designer whittled away by ill-considered modifications. It's a bit of a failing in this country that people always imagine they can improve on the work of great masters.

It will not be enough for this conference just to identify. We must persuade building owners and planning authorities that the buildings, the best buildings of the period, deserve respect and care. I am, therefore, delighted to open the conference, and wish DOCOMOMO's Scottish National Group the very best of luck.

REBUILDING SCOTLAND: THE ROLE OF GOVERNMENT
J. DICKSON MABON

Politics, as you all know, is the art of the possible. And those of us who enter politics enjoy the debates, the street meetings, the party conferences – a form of masochism ordinary people don't indulge in! – we enjoy all these things. And we enjoy Parliament, of course.

But what many of us don't achieve is ministerial

(opposite) 2.3 External view of Peter Womersley's Nuffield Transplantation Surgery Unit, Edinburgh (designed 1963, built 1965-8), in 1968.

office. And if we do manage to achieve ministerial office, we then have to work out what the devil to do! That is the great tragedy of people being in Opposition for too long, as, indeed, many in the Labour Party are now. Vigorous young men and women, with a wonderful potential and an ability to do quite a bit – but there they are. It's difficult as a shadow to know what you do. It's very good that we have this system of shadows, and very good that they switch them around, but, really, it's quite difficult for many of them – as they will find when they're re-elected in the next Parliament, if the Government, happily, changes. These youngsters, then, will suddenly be confronted with the choice: 'Do you wish to be a minister, yes or no?'

In my case, this happened after nine years in Parliament. My great hero was Gaitskell, of course, and to some extent Mr. Bevan as an orator; but as a creator I thought Gaitskell would be better. Gaitskell died, and after him we had Harold Wilson, about whom I had no worries or concerns, no 'antis', no 'pros'. And when Harold sent for me – by myself, by the way, I was very impressed by that – to the Cabinet Room, he said, 'Well, Dick, you realise you are going to the Scottish Office?' I'd already realised that that was likely, because of the way the Ministry had been formed over that vital weekend. We'd had results on Thursday night, Prime Minister on Friday, telephone ringing Saturday, leaks to the newspapers Sunday: by Monday, you knew what you weren't going to get, and you knew what you might get!

Willie Ross was safely ensconced in the Scottish Office – he'd been thirteen years in opposition, and he deserved to be in office – and he was to be a very good Secretary of State. From my point of view, he was a wonderful Secretary of State, in that he never troubled me one bit! Willie was quite a character. But he left me alone in the Departments for which I was responsible, and whenever I was in any trouble, I used to go to him: I would get his unquestioning support, if it was an argument further up the line.

I had previously been trained in Parliament to shadow, above all, health, since I was a physician and was, indeed, in practice. And I'd also been involved in shadowing various other things, such as industry, shipbuilding in particular. So I was astounded when Harold said to me, 'Well, you'll go to the Scottish Office, and you'll do the Scottish Development Department!' I'd thought I would be Health, obviously. Oh, I'd be a brilliant administrator in Health – no doubt about that! I knew all there was to know about it! I was frightened I might get Agriculture, because the opposite was true: I'd have been a disaster! And there were other various portfolios that I could have got – I might have stuck Education, for instance. But no – it was to be Development! I said to him, aghast, 'But, Harold, that's all about housing, and local government!' And he replied, 'Yes, yes, I know.' I said, 'I know absolutely nothing about them.' 'Oh, well, that isn't exactly true,' he says, 'but, anyway, you're going there to learn, and to do something!'

I said, 'But if we're building houses, how long have we got? You're sending me to the Scottish Office, in October 1964, to build houses, about which I know very little. How long have we got?' We'd a majority of four. We'd had experience of a majority of twelve, a majority of six and so on, and I realised they didn't last long. So I said: 'A majority of four – well, how long have we got?' Harold said to me – and this is absolutely true – he said, 'Eighteen months!' 'Then,' he said, 'we come out and win!'

I worked it out myself, that by the time one gets organised, that you're only just beginning to declare your 'numbers' – that's what it was at that time, 'the numbers game' – you're only just getting to that at the end of eighteen months. My political instinct was that this task – to build houses, to build them rapidly, to get better numbers than my opponents, and to do it in eighteen months – that this was ridiculous! But the art of the possible obliges you to attempt the ridiculous!

I found the Department geared up to wanting a housing programme, but nothing like that. Public expenditure figures didn't allow it. It happened to be the case that most of us Scots had lived in rented properties all our lives – either in the council, in which you were on the whole lucky, or in the private sector, in which you were, on the whole, unlucky. The worst houses were in the private sector – the houses with baths were in the council sector. 'Coals in the bath' was a joke for the middle classes, but it was true, a very great reality, for the working classes. And, indeed, the working classes consisted of everybody except the aristos and the top middle class. They included, for instance, many very respectable Presbyterian church elders with fine families and wonderful traditions – not at all the kind of 'lumpen-proletariat' that was popularly associated with the slums. In fact, many of them didn't have a bath in their house; they didn't have hot water in their house. They considered themselves privileged to have an inside toilet.

That's what the situation was, not all that long ago. People forget that when they denounce the housing programmes of the '50s and '60s as outrageous political chicanery. We lived in a desperate, desperate time as far as housing was concerned. (Fig. 2.4) Many of us were born in houses which would be called slums now, but which were in fact quite respectable residences of their time. But we all wanted – it's not unreasonable – we all wanted an inside toilet. We weren't quite so sure of a bath, but it seemed to be the modern thing to do, to have an inside bath, and not rely on the public baths! And, then, maybe the logic of that was to have hot and cold water too!

When you examine, today, the housing deficit – and it still is a large housing deficit, between what is needed and what is available in this country – you find all these needs still listed, not in such substantial

2.4 Florence Street, Gorbals, 1947 view of back court.

numbers as before, yet there they are, still there. But now people don't have the same sense of urgency about housing. Maybe it's because most of us have good houses, so the tiny minority, who don't, tend to get lost in the general argument about politics and political needs. That's a disgrace – we should be anxious to finally polish off the fundamentals of the housing programme: namely, to give everybody, everybody a decent house in which to bring up their children. We have not yet achieved that. It's one of the terrible things of the '80s and '90s that we have not done that.

But let me return now to the colossal social need of the '60s. And even the Conservatives – lovely people! – even the Conservatives, at their conference, had been overwhelmed by the mass of people on the floor, demanding that there should be a target figure. I don't know where Mrs. Thatcher was then – she must have been a young chemist, who had no interest in politics at all – but she couldn't have been at that conference, where Lord Wilton said, 'I agree – I will adopt 300,000 as the programme'. That was a resolution from the floor. 300,000 for the whole UK. Houses a year.

And, of course, that figure alerted the other parties, and the competition, the numbers competition – a very good competition, for those who wanted to be housed – began. And our pledge was 500,000 – half a million new houses a year. This at the time, by the way, when we had the heresy of Enoch Powell, who told us, when he was a minister in 1957, that there was no housing shortage! That, if you counted the number of houses in the country, and the number of people in the country, it matched exactly – so there was no housing shortage! Totally ignoring quality, population movement, and so forth! At any rate, by the mid-1960s we, the Labour Party, were pledging 500,000 a year. The figure actually being built was nowhere near that. In Scotland, if you looked at this target, it meant 50,000 – one-tenth of the total. 50,000 – and how were you going to do it? And when we turned to look at the position in Scotland, we found, first of all, that the private sector was absolutely hopeless. Not their fault – but absolutely hopeless. They'd built very good houses before the first war, and good houses even in Victorian times. Trouble was, since 1914 – lack of customers! And so now they were down to less than 5,000 a year. They complained about land banks, banks that were either held by large developers, and which kept them out, or land banks held, in effect, by the municipalities. And they complained about the prejudice of planners, who said, 'No, no, no – houses shouldn't be there, that must be a green space...' or whatever. The private sector found it very difficult to find sites.

And then we looked at the Scottish Special Housing Association, or SSHA – one of the Government's interwar social-services innovations. The SSHA built in places where even the local municipalities hadn't the money to build houses, but where there were terrible housing problems. It built directly from St. Andrew's House. Or, more exactly, it was a kind of agency, but it was controlled centrally, and, at least in its main principles, managed centrally. And then we had the New Towns, a postwar creation, a twinkle in somebody's eye long before the war ended, and which at length became reality. There was East Kilbride, first of all – a New Town of the conventional kind. Then there was Cumbernauld, which was quite revolutionary. Cumbernauld in my time got a prize for the best designed New Town in the world – I never was

absolutely sure why! I used to visit all these places very regularly. Also, there was Glenrothes, and then Livingston, and Erskine, which technically wasn't a New Town but nevertheless perhaps ought to have been. And finally there was Irvine, which was only just getting underway as a New Town in my time. (Figs. 2.5, 2.6)

However, I wasn't to reason why. I was only the Minister. My job was to get the numbers, and the quality too, but as for the styles – I didn't interfere, that wasn't for me to say. I never fought the planners, in the sense of 'they were wrong and I was right'. I always tried to listen to them, and to make a fair judgement, as to what was necessary for their purposes, and what was necessary for mine. But for the numbers, I had to turn not to the SSHA or the private sector, or the New Towns, but to the cities.

Now we have already heard a little about Davie Gibson, Glasgow's Housing Committee Convener in the early '60s. (Fig. 2.7) He was one of the great heroes of the cities' housing drives – hitherto unrecognised heroes, by the way. He was such a contentious, controversial, difficult man that he was hardly regarded as a hero – indeed, he was branded a rebel – during most

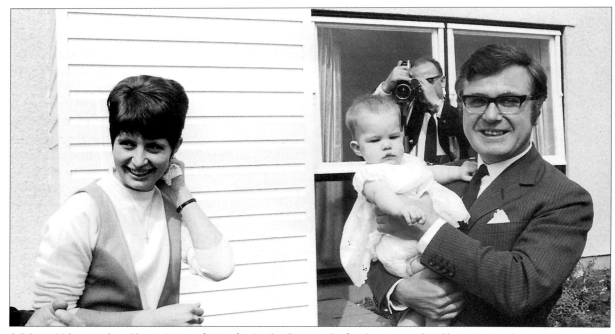

2.5 Dr. J. Dickson Mabon (then Minister of State for Scotland) opens the first house completed by Irvine Development Corporation (18 Ardmillan Square, Pennyburn) on 15 August 1969.

of his political life. But he, undoubtedly, when he got to Heaven, was admitted straight away, and solely on his record as the Convener of Housing in Glasgow. Because he really was absolutely wonderful. He defied everybody, and he built as fast as he could. Why? Because his job was to get houses for his people. And I see nothing wrong with that. I thought that was marvellous. But of course, this meant he contravened many of the 'rules', and he sometimes made life difficult for the rest of us.

And remember, too, that Gibson was asked by the planners, like every other Glasgow councillor, to concede that they had a million people in an area the same size as Edinburgh (which had half the population), that they were clearly too densely packed together, and that therefore there had to be 'overspill'. Now Gibson was someone who – even although he'd been a member of the Independent Labour Party and believed in international Socialism – someone who had been taught from his schooldays that this was the second city of the Empire, that this was a great city, and its size meant something. There was this prejudice: 'We are not going to allow our city to run down to three-quarters of a million!' And, although they half-heartedly agreed to overspill arrangements,

the Glasgow councillors really didn't have it in their hearts to carry them out.

We had these arrangements that we'd send so many Glaswegians out to Kirkintilloch, so many to Haddington, and so many here and there, that there'd be houses specially built in the smaller burghs around the City that would take the overspill, and that gradually we'd get the City's population down to three-quarters of a million. But the Glasgow councillors, such as Gibson, had this prejudice against the plan. Gibson's prejudice was: 'I'm damned if I'm going to wait for overspill, which I don't like anyway! I'm going to build houses in Glasgow, wherever there's a site!' (Fig. 2.8) And you must remember that at that

2.7 David Gibson, seen in 1948.

2.6 Inspection of model of the SSHA's Wyndford redevelopment (Glasgow) at an exhibition at Edinburgh College of Art, 1961. On right, the SSHA's top architect, Chief Technical Officer Harold Buteux; at centre, Edinburgh's Lord Provost Sir John Greig Dunbar.

2.8 1987 view of the Sighthill scheme, one of the most massive undertaken by Glasgow Corporation under Gibson: ten 20-storey slab towers and lower blocks, all designed and built as a 'package deal' by Crudens in 1963-9 on the site of the former Tennants 'soda waste'.

time the four Counties of Cities were very powerful, in as much as they exercised most of the functions of local government – and that Central Government was not as dogmatic and not as overweening, not as overbearing as it was to become in the '80s. Central Government likes to think it can do a lot, but in those days, in the '60s, it didn't have as many powers. You had to persuade rather than order, as appears to be the case now.

So I had, therefore, the cities, including Glasgow, and the three others, Edinburgh, Aberdeen, and Dundee, to rely on. (Fig. 2.9) And we'd got good people as councillors there – Pat Rogan is here today. And then we had the large burghs – people forget that – we had twenty large burghs, of which Motherwell was one, and Greenock, and all these other large communities. And then we had no less than one hundred and seventy-five small burghs, all with the right to build or not to build. Some of them had never built; some of them had built very well, but very little: they varied.

You can imagine what the personnel of these small burghs were like, in contrast to, say, the big cities. And then you had, finally, thirty-three counties. Now I must say that, although I am a Scot, born in Scotland, I never properly knew my country until I became the Under-Secretary of State for Scotland, and obliged myself to visit five cities – I respectfully also include Perth – twenty large burghs, a hundred and seventy-five small burghs, and thirty-three counties! What I eventually found, when I began these visits, was that the problems were always the same, although the numbers varied.

By trying to get everybody involved in housing in this way, we got a huge number built in eighteen months – Ronnie Cramond will tell you all about it. We got enough submissions to the Department, plus about 5,000 from SSHA and 5,000 from the New Towns, and not quite 5,000 from the private sector, to get us reasonably close to our great target. At the end of September 1965, the total number of houses under

2.9 Menzieshill housing scheme, Dundee, under construction in 1964: view from roof of Gowrie Court (a Crudens-built tower block). Hillside Court, another high block in Menzieshill 9th Development, is visible on right. To left of centre is Charleston Drive.

construction in Scotland, by all agencies, had at last edged above 50,000! And that level was more or less, I believe, sustained for several years. Then, of course, inevitably, people came and people went, and, under other ministers and other governments, the priority went out of the programme. If we had had that sustained burst of activity for, say, ten years, instead of three or four, I think we would have solved the bulk of Scotland's housing problem in that time. It became almost a crusade. It became an arithmetical crusade, if you like. That we could definitely do it over a certain time. And that we'd then be able to turn to other problems of housing, which we couldn't address at that stage. That was what somebody said to me right at the beginning, when I got to the Scottish Office. On that first day, when I was trying to work out how on earth I was going to put together my housing programme, I asked if the Civil Service would be kind enough to provide me with all the Labour Party policies on housing. It was a pile about two feet high! And then I asked them if they would kindly read them – and we would discuss them!

In the Department, I had a very fine body of men, from Alan Hume right down. An interesting lot, although it was like addressing a sergeants' mess – nobody spoke unless the sergeant spoke. But nevertheless they were excellent, individually – as I found when I took them out on all these visits – that was how I cracked them! In the Department they'd talk quite freely – all that argument going on – and then they'd face the Minister with one answer. But taking them out, visiting the various local authorities – then I could get them one by one! For instance, you'd say, 'I'm going to Kirkintilloch, Ronnie, can you come?' He might say, 'I can't go.' Then I'd say, 'Oh, all right, I'll take your junior'. And with five cities, twenty large burghs, a hundred and seventy-five small burghs and thirty-three counties, you could break up the Department quite rapidly!

One thing we did decide very quickly was, that there was no question of diverting significant resources to rehabilitate old houses. I always remember what Walter Elliot had to say on that question: he was a former Secretary of State who had greatly promoted social housing in the late '30s, and who latterly, as

Lord Rector of Glasgow University, discussed all kinds of political things quite freely with a young colleague such as myself. I remember him saying to me, 'There is nothing you can do, Mabon, with these castles of misery!' We were walking through Kelvingrove Park, and he was referring to 19th-century tenements. (Fig. 2.10) 'Castles of misery!' And if I'd tried to put forward alternative suggestions – such as that I'd heard from an architect that if we converted the middle flats to contain all the facilities, lavatories and bathroom facilities for the others, we could make these houses reasonably fit – he'd say, 'Oh no, no, no, no, the walls are too thick . . . you can't do this, and you can't do that . . . No, no, tear them down!' In any case, at that stage, we didn't have any room to have a rehabilitation programme. Whereas now a rehabilitation programme has come, and it has come very successfully for many fine old tenements, products of the last century, which are very worthwhile living in. I live in one myself, in Largs, which is a fine building, a hundred years old now, rehabilitated, and I commend

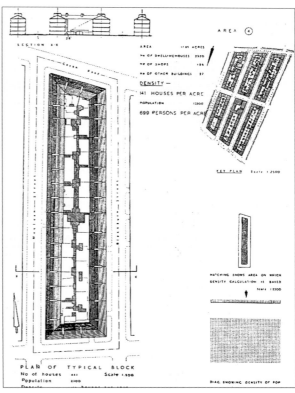

2.10 Diagrams designed to demonstrate high density of typical Glasgow tenement street-layout: from a 1952 article by Robert Grieve.

it. And one of the casualties of the great One Mile Square, that fabulous idea of the late '50s and early '60s, the square of motorway traffic around the City of Glasgow – that was a very early concept, partly the Department's and partly Glasgow Corporation's – the price of that was the destruction of far too many fine old tenements, which could have lived another day in a very comfortable existence. But the climate of opinion was not in favour of that, and so many fine tenements were swept away in our desire to build a Modern city.

Now I was very lucky in having, in the SDD, a marvellous Department. I had planning, I had housing, I had local government, I had roads, I had electricity, in all its forms, I had tourism, I had sewage – people used to snigger at that, but that is really quite a fundamental part! – and I had water. By the way, I discovered that while half the water on this island fell on the top third – namely ourselves – we used to have regular shortages of water, because we relied on antiquated Victorian pipes, laid down in the last century – mainly in small towns and villages – which just couldn't cope. I brought an industry to one town, that couldn't take it, because the industry wanted so much water, and there weren't the pipes, or the supply! And so we had to virtually municipalise water in Scotland, reducing it from a hundred and ninety-nine authorities to eleven. A hundred and ninety-nine, to administer five million people, that really was bureaucracy – and we reduced it to eleven! I don't know why they want to privatise the system now, it seems to me to be doing a good job. But, anyway, water was essential for all we wanted to do.

In housing, therefore, the effort was to really get the numbers up, and to get everybody involved in it. Many counties didn't realise, for instance, that they actually had rural slums. You had to take the good-natured lairds who usually ran the County Councils, to actually see their slums, before they recognised that they had some. It was the argument of *de minimis*. That if *de minimis* exists, it doesn't count, there are no votes, there is no shout, so therefore we can ignore it! And so – because I was selfish, I wanted numbers, I wanted ten, twenty, a hundred from anywhere, to add to my numbers – I therefore went round all the

counties. And many of these good people suddenly realised, 'My God, we've never done anything about this! We have always assumed there was no such thing as slums in the country!' But there were some dreadful slums in the country, as we found.

In this way, we got all these places working within our programme. And we also had the benefit – if you like – of industrialised building. One of the attractions of industrialised building was to get authorities to co-operate. Instead of taking ages to negotiate with a contractor, and all that that involved, six or seven of them could negotiate with one contractor. We were no longer the neutral referee; we were the participating referee. And we would get them together. I always remember a meeting in Galashiels, where we had the six Border burghs all together to discuss a consortium contract, and we finally got them to agree, that if we thought it was a good deal, and it seemed to them to be a good deal, that they should sign it. And the contractor would save on costs, too: he would be able to build here and there in quick succession. That was agreed, everything was fine, absolutely dandy. But as I was going out of the room, one man said to me, one Provost – all the Provosts were there – he pulled my jacket and said, 'Dr. Mabon, one last question. We all benefit from this?' I said, 'We all benefit from this.' He said, 'You benefit?' I said, 'We benefit.' 'Galashiels, here, it benefits?' 'Yes, yes, yes.' 'Kelso, it benefits?' 'Kelso, yes, Kelso.' 'You mean to tell me,' he said, 'that HAWICK benefits?!' I said, 'That's my weak point – Hawick benefits, too!'

But despite these rivalries, you still get the picture, that the enthusiasm was to build. Everybody was anxious to build. And this wasn't a Government off its head, building rubbish and just racing ahead for the next election. It had become a really intense feeling, that we should all get together, and that, even in small areas where the urgency didn't, at first glance, seem relevant, we should still join in. And you got this tremendous fervour, and the desire to have the same as the guy next door. This happened once in a small burgh of my acquaintance, a burgh I almost feel I was brought up with. They were merciless in exploiting their good favour with me, and they came along one day, three elderly Provosts in their seventies, with a young, sparkling Burgh Engineer, newly qualified and anxious to show his spurs to the Department. What they were demanding was that they, Saltcoats, should have a multi-storey block. Now fortunately the predecessors of these men had bought enormous amounts of ground to build houses on. So there was no shortage of ground. And, by the way, they bought it at such prices that they rarely went into deficit in their housing account, and at that particular time there was no problem. They had everything going for them. But here they wanted a multi-storey. Why? Because the people next door had one. And they were building them in Glasgow. And, they had them in Edinburgh. It was now part of the general climate of enthusiasm, to build in style, to build high. That's why today's wiseacres, those 20-20 hindsighters who tell us that multi-storeys should never have been built in the first place, are speaking for their time, but not for our time, when the climate was entirely different!

So, at my meeting with Saltcoats, I said, 'No, you can't have a multi-storey. First of all, you've plenty of land. Secondly, you won't have enough room at the bottom of your multi-storey for parking spaces, or for space for . . . children to play, or for general confluence of the air . . .' (I think I'm getting desperate here!) 'or for washing facilities, you see!' And one of the ex-Provosts says to me, 'We don't need parking spaces. We don't have motor cars.' I said to him, 'My dear Bob, under Socialism, everybody will have a motor car! It's obligatory!' And this was the way it went on. Eventually, we broke up and had an adjournment for coffee. After that I was intending to finally say no – no multi-storeys – because I was in my anti-multi-storey phase at that time (I'll come to that presently). But Bob came up to me with a piece of paper, and he said, 'Umm – look at this.' I said, 'What is it?' He replied, 'It's the mock-up of our election address, which is to be printed in a week's time.' I said, 'So what?' He said, 'Look – I've promised a multi-storey!' So I said, 'Let me see it – Oh, God!' Then he says, 'We haven't the money to reprint!' 'I see, I see,' I said, '. . . all right, I'll give you it – but only a wee one!' He got his 'wee multi-storey', and you can still see it, or, rather, them: the scheme eventually approved was actually for two blocks. It's very nice – with marvellous views of the Island of Arran. He got it! (Fig. 2.11)

But the reverse was true in Glasgow, because David had been building everywhere. He'd been packing them in, he'd built or contracted more houses within Glasgow, in a short period, than the planners had envisaged being exported as overspill – which was really quite a phenomenal achievement! And he was getting ready to build the huge Red Road project, and all these kind of massive constructions. By the way, people had never known multi-storey life previously – they thought multi-storey life would simply be like tenemental life, and those of you who live in tenements know that tenements are friendly places. Whereas social problems like the isolation of many families in great multi-storeys – these were foreseen by relatively few of us at that time.

I tried my very best to make sure that the Glasgow people were allowed to go on building, but not with so many multi-storeys. And the same was true in some other cities – except Aberdeen. Aberdeen, if anything, built slightly fewer than they could have done – although they did have, on the whole, a very good

2.11 Glebelands housing development, Saltcoats, built in 1966-7 as a 'package deal' by J. Miller (Bison): the 'wee multis' referred to in Dr Mabon's paper.

housing programme. Dundee was, I think, very well in balance. Edinburgh was too, in certain parts – such as the famous scheme, at Arthur Street, about which there was at first some controversy. Pat Rogan initially proposed some very high point blocks; there were planning objections, but we eventually settled on quite a good medium-rise compromise.

Now, to return to Glasgow. On one of our visits to the Corporation, the planners – who were fed up with David Gibson, because he was always winning, and they were losing, and good planning really wasn't being treated properly – they produced a wonderful argument, in the form of a block of timber, a topography of the city, made out of matchsticks. Black matchsticks for multi-storeys that had been built, or were so far ahead that they were going to be built, and white matchsticks for the ones that were to come. It looked so horrific, that we prevailed upon Glasgow to start thinking seriously, after their wonderful effort in building up their city, about turning their attention, at last, to the overspill arrangements. Out of that came Erskine, which I wanted as a New Town, but which, at Treasury instigation, we decided would have to be a county council-sponsored development rather than a full-blown New Town; later on, it was Irvine which would eventually become the fifth New Town. New Towns, in my opinion, were the best method of overspill, rather than extensions of existing towns, which tended – at least sometimes – to become almost a foreign part of the host community. The real answer was in New Towns – and I think our New Towns are a matter of great credit to us. (Fig. 2.12)

But the important aim for me was, whatever my negotiations were about, to get the counties to work together with the burghs, for instance, concerning land-use. There were great, great arguments about land – and we got them to agree a strategy, each county in turn, on land use. This would involve allocating some land for our private sector. The private builders couldn't believe it – that the Labour Party was actually going out of its way to find land on which they could build! In this, we were motivated by the fact that people, as they got tenancies in municipal houses, were, more and more, beginning to say, 'This is not the end – we're not going to stay here for ever – we're

going to buy our own house'. The sale of council houses, which never happened in our time, was a logical step from that. But the thing about the sale of council houses is, that you should have been selling council houses AND building council houses at the same time! Because if you don't, and you just sell them, the problem is not solved – you leave all these other people behind.

That is why I feel that the whole question of the scope of public housing provision isn't just an argument about the Public Sector Borrowing Requirement, or anything like that. It's a most solemn matter: that the local authorities, having done so well – oh, terrible mistakes, I know, but having done so well, on balance – should have been allowed to go on and provide for the rest of the people. To provide for the real 'lumpen-proletariat' that had been left behind in the wake of all the various efforts and initiatives up to then. In this matter of broadening the scope of public housing, I tried, largely unsuccessfully, to persuade my Labour colleagues to accept the idea of a co-operative system of management – not a house factor at George Square, but a house factor on your doorstep, in the form of the secretary, the committee, of your own tenement or series of tenements. That was one of my hopes that was never realised.

So I'll conclude on that. From a politician's point of view, you see yourself in various different roles. Going to the conferences, running elections. In

2.12 Kildrum 1 area, Cumbernauld New Town (Gillespie, Kidd & Coia, built 1957-62), seen in early 1960s.

Parliament, arguing, criticising, listening to the Government of the day and getting so frustrated at the fact that they seem to have no answers to our problems. But then, at last, if you become a minister, you're made to find the answers yourself. And if you eventually do succeed in finding some answers, this is the finest thing you can achieve in politics. To really be part of a big social movement that faced up to the realities and got something done – that is what politics, to me, is all about!

THE NATIONAL HOUSING DRIVE
RONNIE CRAMOND

At conferences I usually get the 'cemetery slot' after lunch, when people are asleep. I'm honoured today to get the slot after coffee, when there's a sporting chance you may be awake! So I'd better watch what I say. I'm a historian by training – mind you, it was easier to get a degree in history in those days, because there was a great deal less of it to study! So I'll begin with a historical perspective, because I think it is absolutely essential to put any judgments on what was being done in the housing drive in the '50s and '60s into its context – the social and political imperatives of the time.

It would be quite wrong to assume that the attitudes, assumptions and values of the '90s held good forty years ago. Just think, for a moment, how public tastes and attitudes have changed since the 1950s, in so many ways. Take the Green movement: if you'd talked about being in the Green Party, in the 1950s, people would have wondered what you were – some kind of artist? And dancing nowadays – when, I understand, young men and women dance three feet away from one another. In my day, you grabbed the girl and you engaged in what I call 'joined-up dancing'. When I gave an exhibition of that with one of my geriatric girl-friends at a wedding recently, I heard the mutters from around the floor: 'It's like watching a documentary!' The modern consumer society didn't exist then. Even the words have changed. 'Housing', rather than 'Homes', was the title used in 1890, 1909, 1919 – the Housing of the Working Classes Acts – where now we have 'Scottish Homes'. That indicated that the houses built under those earlier Acts were for the poor and underprivileged. And it implied (a) a need or demand which cannot be satisfied by the ordinary operation of the market; and (b) a recognition of a moral responsibility to the people in need. Those implications seem to me to have been accepted, alike, by the Unionist and the Labour administrations which I served at the time. Indeed, as has just been pointed out, it was a Tory Government which first set the target of 300,000 houses a year, and so started the 'numbers game' that was so politically important then. Who knows, or seems to care, how many houses are built each year now?

Another important difference is household size. Between the wars, and in the decades after the Second World War, the assumption was that what was needed was the family house of three bedrooms: parents, boys and girls in separate bedrooms. To a large extent, this was justified by the postwar baby boom, as returning ex-servicemen started families. But now many households are single people or single-parent families. Many unmarried sons and daughters have separate bases. It was uncommon then. I, and many of my generation, stayed with my parents while at University – and even survived that! More households are elderly – four times as many as there were in 1901. And those demographic and social changes have, in themselves, changed the type and size of houses now in demand.

Idealism inspired us. It's a difficult concept to put across to a modern audience, without inviting condescending sneers. But Glasgow had some of the worst slums in Europe – and it was public health considerations that led to council housing as we know it, after the Housing and Town Planning Acts in 1919. Think about a family, sleeping head to tail, in one room, with only a cold water tap. (Fig. 2.13) No bathroom, and a shared lavvy on the stairheid. But there were also fears of Bolshevism in this country, would you believe! And that was a reason for providing 'homes fit for heroes'. These homes had to be provided for the heroes, if the heroes were not to become revolutionaries. Because, of course, the 1917 Bolshevik Revolution had been only two years before. Shades of 'Reds under the beds' and McCarthyism more recently!

But it was not until after World War II that we got local authority housing on a far larger scale. Up to 1946, most local authority houses, were, in fact, cottage-type dwellings. But in the 1950s flats began to increase in numbers – at first in low blocks, but increasingly in high blocks. Why? In response to the need for numbers and speed. There was some bomb damage – for instance in Clydebank. There had been very little maintenance during the war years – because all the joiners and other tradesmen had been called up. There were also new households, from postwar marriages, and a rising birthrate. Prefabs were one of the responses. Do you remember prefabs? The aircraft plants that had been manufacturing Spitfires were turned into factories for making aluminium bungalows. (Fig. 2.14) Then the Conservative Government came in in 1951, and 300,000 houses were built in 1953 – the numbers game! Remember, it was the slums, above all, that people like Dick Mabon, and Hutchie Sneddon, and Pat Rogan, and Bailie Gibson, were trying to get rid of. As was someone else, who hasn't been mentioned yet: Lewis Cross, Glasgow Corporation's 'Housing Progress Officer', in charge of the production of dwellings. Cross actually organised the city's building drive: an absolute pain to some – but he got things done! (Fig. 2.15)

There was obviously a risk of putting quantity before quality. But high flats were also seen as a sign of progress, and an expression of a new technological age. Le Corbusier in the 1920s, in exhibitions and books, had argued for high flats as the essential building form of the Modern city, as did Walter Gropius and the Bauhaus. And building firms like Wimpey, nearer home, advertised themselves as the means of solving the housing problem. Wimpey advertised pictures of 25-storey-high blocks in Glasgow with the caption, 'Wimpey answers the housing problem'. And high blocks became prestige symbols for both architects and councils – Dick Mabon touched on that too. Some attractive blocks were being built – for instance, in London – at Roehampton – and in Scandinavia. I got a postgraduate fellowship after the war, and went to see some of these. For instance, Bellahøj, in Denmark, was one of the key projects I photographed on my trip to Denmark in 1961. Now there you see point blocks, set in landscape. (Fig. 2.16) Robert Matthew, Architect to the London County Council after the war, advocated high blocks. There were arguments of better ventilation, better light. And we in Scotland had the tenement tradition already – it's warmer if you pile houses on top of each other. There's nothing wrong with living in a flat, high or low. It's not satisfactory for young children. But now the household size has dropped, and perhaps the case for flats can again be made – I certainly live in one! Sociological research into housing had hardly started then. It was also a

2.13 Mrs Irene Daniels in the kitchen of her single-end flat, 1041 Dumbarton Road, Whiteinch, Glasgow (1955).

2.14 Toryglen housing scheme: 'AIROH' aluminium bungalows, supplied by Blackburn Ltd and erected in 1949. A 'permanent' version of one of the standard 'prefab' types. Photograph 1990: most of this group were demolished in 1993.

pragmatic solution to the problems of shortage of land – especially when you put the Green Belt around cities – and an incredibly urgent demand. Speed meant system building.

People went from all over the world to admire Roehampton, on the edge of Richmond Park. There was room for landscape and play, influenced by Scandinavian design. The second phase of Roehampton, with slab blocks and balcony access, was much less popular. And a major fault, with hindsight, was the lack of parking. But who had cars then? Who foresaw the enormous explosion in the number of cars? Dick Mabon did; but, then, he was in the Labour Party! Another argument for high blocks was that it saved on drainage, services and roads. So we encouraged system building, with non-traditional and prefabricated techniques. And Central Government provided subsidies for high building, because of the higher cost per square foot.

But it was bad for children. Nowhere to play. In the words of Adam MacNaughtan's 'Skyscraper Wean': 'Oh, ye canny fling pieces oot a twenty storey flat, seven hundred hungry weans will testify tae that!' And bad for mothers, who felt lonely and cut off. There's also noise, vandalism and frequent lift failures – of course, we had our lift failure here today too! But in 1968 there was the Ronan Point gas explosion in England. It brought increasing dissatisfaction with high blocks to a head. (You remember what

happened? A load-bearing wall blew out, and there was progressive collapse). We have a legacy of houses that were expensive to build, and sometimes, but not always, technically deficient – for instance, with condensation and defective cladding – and unsuitable for families. So, in the 1970s, the Government went anti-high, and enforced cost controls which eliminated high rise and high density blocks.

Apart from the architecture, there were major social and planning defects. In Glasgow, Castlemilk and, especially, Easterhouse, were effectively New Towns – but built without New Town facilities; without schools, without shops, without cinemas, that a town would have had. Easterhouse, with a population of something like 40,000, had one supermarket, one cafe, no pub, no cinema, no jobs. It was a dormitory suburb.

Under Dick Mabon, some of these planning failures were put right. But my argument is that better management, and better maintenance, can solve many of the problems of mass housing, provided you put any design faults right – such as poor insulation, whether thermal or sound. But you must work with tenants: community co-ops as in Easterhouse – the Calvay Street Co-op, for example. Some blocks can be turned into sheltered houses for the elderly, with wardens. And wardens and caretakers are crucial. You must have defensible space, you must have security, if high flats are to work. We didn't realise that then. So some bad housing can be attributed to

2.15 Lewis Cross (on left) in the mid 1970s, when working in the Scottish Special Housing Association.

2.16 Bellahøj housing project, near Copenhagen, Denmark; built 1950-4; 1,297 apartments in 8-12 storey blocks. Architects M. Irming, T Nielsen and others. 1982 view.

mistaken design: for instance to deck-access, the streets in the sky, which is now seen as a mistake, because of the opportunities for vandalism. And to inadequate management. We need community involvement. To quote Prince Charles – I'm surprised nobody at this conference has quoted him so far! – 'If people play a part in creating something, they treat it as their own possession, and look after it!' And whatever we may think of Prince Charles's views on architecture, perhaps he's got a point in that!

However, what Easterhouse and its like offered was fresh air, and better facilities within the house. No more sharing a toilet between three families. And they had baths, and hot water from a tap – the answer to most families' prayers. But these advantages inside were not followed up outside the house. Whereas Scandinavian housing, for instance, was well integrated with landscaping and with local facilities, in our schemes there was generally a lack of effective landscaping round about. There was no place for children to play, and they ended up in the street – which, even with the low volume of traffic in those days, was dangerous. There was no thought of the visual impact of the mess left after you built the houses and moved on to the next scheme. And there were, at first, no shops – but thirty years ago, people didn't demand as much as they do now. That deficiency, in the planning and landscaping, the layout, and the provision of facilities in the neigh-

bourhood, was exactly the same deficiency identified before the war, in the Highton Report's comparison of Scottish and Continental housing. It was one thing to put those blocks down among rocks and birch trees and green areas, and another thing to put them down in nothing. And the Scandinavian blocks had just as high a standard of internal finish! (Fig. 2.17, 2.18)

The lesson I take from all these years is that there cannot be only one answer. There is no single 'housing problem'. There is just a series of quite different housing problems and housing needs. There must be different forms of tenancy, different forms of management, and different forms of construction. On tenancy, I wrote an essay once, called *Housing without Profit* – about the Scandinavian experience of non-profit housing associations. Hence the title – *Housing without Profit*. Because, in those days, you remember, there was nothing between council housing on the one hand, and owner-occupation on the other. I was arguing for something in between: non-profit-making housing associations, the 'third force' in housing. One result was that the Housing Corporation was set up in 1965 to provide funds for housing associations.

I'm on the management committee, now, of a voluntary housing association, providing sheltered housing for old people. But here, again, we are hampered by a lack of a comprehensive approach, an

2.17 Menzieshill housing scheme, Dundee: new bus stop at 351 Charleston Drive, 1965. Construction of dwellings on peripheral schemes often preceded that of shops or schools, necessitating lengthy bus trips.

2.18 Wester Hailes Contract 5 (built from 1969): Crudens slab block photographed in 1990, prior to demolition.

all-round vision of a problem. I won't go into the details, but basically, as people get older – and they do live to greater age in properly defined sheltered housing – they get more frail. So they need to move from sheltered, to extra sheltered – where they get meals – and then to nursing homes, where you can get occasional nursing attention. But Scottish Homes can't give assistance to a housing association for a nursing home: that's a matter for the Health Board! So let's look at it comprehensively, because what matters is a customer-centred approach: what do people need and want? And then let's supply it. And whether the funds come from Scottish Homes or the Health Board doesn't matter. It's all taxpayers' money. And it'll cost the taxpayer less in the long run, because sheltered housing is much cheaper than geriatric beds in hospitals, even with occasional nursing cover.

So let's not get bogged down in one type of tenure. Owner-occupation is not the universal answer. And on management – the lesson of the co-operatives, such as Calvay Street, is that there is a future in even *giving* problem groups of council houses to tenants, and making them responsible for maintenance and repair, either individually, or, better, through community housing associations. Because the individual who hasn't been accustomed to being an owner-occupier can be terrified by the sudden arrival of a major bill for a roof repair. That risk can be spread, if you've got an association with a sinking fund for repairs.

'There have always been arguments about the extent of public aid to housing. But it's not easy to point to any generally accepted statement of aims for public housing policy, or the principle underlying the distribution, and incidence, of financial help.' I'm taking the liberty, there, of quoting from myself! From another thing I wrote, as long ago as 1964: *Housing Policy in Scotland*. That's nearly thirty years ago, but I think it's still true. *Housing without Profit* argued that there was a big role for housing associations, and that this could be not just in new building, but in taking over the management of existing houses, to upgrade them and improve their management through harnessing the interests of the occupiers. I find it odd that it's taken a quarter of a century for that idea to come to fruition, in the co-operatives now being set up in some major cities.

Now, on the subject of idealism, there's one final topic I'd like to touch on briefly. There sometimes was, in those days, a suspicion of corruption among councillors or officials. System building, allocation of big contracts – scope for backhanders, that sort of thing. But my experience was of virtually 100% integrity. Some stuff disappeared off building sites – but in general, there was a very high level of integrity among councillors. There were one or two highly publicised court cases – but that was a tiny minority. I come back to my general point. There was a lot of idealism about, a lot of social consciousness, and a desire to be of service to the public. Bailie Gibson, Pat Rogan, Hutchie Sneddon of Motherwell – people like these, their overriding concern was a driving, moral aim: to get their constituents decently housed.

Now these notions of idealism are no doubt naff, to those who are too young to remember the prewar queues at the Buroo, and the days when there was no Health Service. And the days when only the insured person, and not his wife and children, got medical benefit. They're too young to remember the impact of the Beveridge Plan – God! what an era that was for us, the excitement of the Beveridge Plan, to those to whom it came new! – or the creation of the NHS. They're too young to remember the shared lavvies on the stairheids, and the cold water. Decades of materialist indoctrination have taught people to sneer condescendingly at idealism.

We still have integrity and honesty in the civil and local government service. For how long, though? The relentless denigration of public servants – whether they're civil servants, teachers or councillors – will inevitably have its effect on the standards of recruitment and election. I and many others joined the Civil Service not for high material reward – I knew I wouldn't get that – but because it was open to competitive examination, and not to nepotism; and because of its high public standing as a worthy profession, the envy of other countries plagued by corrupt officials. But if the constant denigration of public officials continues, we will eventually get the public officials, and the teachers, and the councillors, that we deserve. And then it will be too late to wring our hands, and look back in anguish to the days when you took the honesty and fairmindedness of public officials for granted – and were outraged at the very occasional exceptions that came to light. So forget 'corruption'. It was exceptional, and certainly not a reason for rushing out these housebuilding contracts.

To conclude: do remember the context in which we were operating. Please remember that context, whatever your views are on the architecture, or layouts. We have different housing problems now – of homelessness, particularly of young people; of families not being able to afford housing. You could afford housing then, because the rents were so low! Too low, arguably – but that's another matter. These were not the problems then. The problems then were that there were not enough houses. That there were too many appalling slums. Shared lavvies, no hot water, no baths, incredible overcrowding in the Gorbals and elsewhere. Political pressures on central and local government alike. Ministers and councillors were bombarded by their constituents. 'When's my hoose – my slum – comin down? When am I gauny get my new hoose?' We had to react. Insanitary, unhealthy dwellings; TB was still rife. And Bailie Gibson, Pat Rogan, Dick Mabon, Harold Macmillan – they were all responding alike to that political clamour.

To those who argue that we should have gone more slowly, taken time to plan better, build better, preserve tenements instead of pulling them down – I would answer: Yes! With the 20-20 vision of hindsight – it's a marvellous thing, hindsight! Perhaps, from the '90s, you're right. But, in the context of the '50s and '60s – not possible! Not politically possible. For any Government Minister or councillor to have advocated caution or delay then would have been political suicide – and rightly so!

Finally – it was a pleasure to work with Dick Mabon. He would listen to you, and then make up his mind. It would either be, 'OK! We'll do it that way!' or, 'No! we'll do it my way!' And he would then stick by his decision and defend it robustly. That's all one can ask of a Minister. And on one occasion, when I argued black was white with him, it turned out that he was right and I was wrong. And, as a civil servant, I learned a tremendous lesson from that about political judgement.

For the future, let's try to analyse what are the real needs of our 'customers' now. And how, in the overall public interest, they can best be met. Let's have no dogmatic solutions. Let's start from the various groups of users – what they want, what they need, what they can afford – and devise solutions from there. Shelter is a basic human need, and a decent home is essential to human dignity. What are the most cost-effective and socially acceptable ways of meeting the different needs of different people? And how can we involve them – the consumers -in the supply, and – perhaps even more important – in the maintenance of the bricks and mortar?

REHOUSING THE CAPITAL: THE CRUSADE AGAINST EDINBURGH'S SLUMS
PAT ROGAN

In the year 1954, much against my wish, or desire, I was elected a councillor to Edinburgh Corporation. At that time, one third of the Council retired by rotation, which meant that 23 seats had to be filled. At that election, following the usual trend, eight candidates were returned unopposed – or, as we used to say at the time, returned unexposed! In the ward where I was elected, the sitting councillor had resigned, and the Ward Party was unable to find anyone to replace him. Without a candidate, the seat, normally safe Labour, would have been presented to the Progressives. To avoid such a calamity, I was persuaded to enter the ring, but I did so on the strict understanding that I would hold the seat for one year only, which would give the Ward Party ample time to find my successor. Twenty years later, with good behaviour, I was let out!

I had no ambition to hold public office, and I was quite content within the Labour Party to be a backroom worker, and help others become MPs and councillors. In 1950, I was the election agent for Andrew Gilzean, the Member of Parliament for Edinburgh Central; and when he died I was offered the vacancy, which I declined. The man who was selected for the seat, Tom Oswald, held it for the next 21 years until he retired.

So I was not overjoyed at becoming a councillor. But, realising the responsibility that had been thrust upon me, I attempted to find out what the job entailed. I sought advice among my more experienced colleagues, but I learned little from them, mainly because they suffered from what I can only describe as 'committee preoccupation': that is, they knew a great deal about their own committees, but not a great deal about committees that didn't arouse their interest. There was an element of snobbery about committee selection, so I, being a newcomer and a building trade worker – such was the profound knowledge of my leaders – was placed on the Housing Committee, and a couple of others that were considered of little importance.

The composition of Edinburgh Corporation at that time was interesting. The Progressive Party had a high proportion of retired people, businessmen and housewives who could afford the time. The Labour Party had a few small businessmen, some trade union officials, some housewives, but just a handful of artisans. The Progressives had a majority of 2:1. The year before my arrival, councillors, for the first time, became able to claim loss of earnings, which provided a maximum of £1 for a full day, and 10s. for four hours. As these amounts represented about half of what a tradesman could earn, I, and a few others, found ourselves subsidising Edinburgh Town Council. On the credit side, one was provided with a bus pass, and a lunch, if attending committees.

My lack of experience, my ignorance, and my innocence were fully exposed a few weeks after becoming a councillor. One very wet and windy night, a deputation, consisting of half a dozen folk from a tenement in the Canongate, arrived at my door. Their roof was leaking badly, their houses were almost flooded, and what was I going to do about it? I didn't know what to do, but I accompanied them back to their homes so that I could see the extent of the damage. I found their complaints were not exaggerated. People were huddled in corners trying to avoid the worst of the downpour, while efforts had been made to protect their belongings, especially their bedding. Among these unfortunates was a young mother who that very day had returned from hospital with her new-born babe.

In an effort to help them, I called in at the local police station, and unfolded my sorry tale to a sympathetic

and understanding sergeant. No, he was unaware of emergency services for leaking roofs. If the building was dangerous, he knew what to do. But complaints about leaking roofs arrived with every rain storm, and he, unfortunately, couldn't help. At that time, I was managing a small jobbing builders' business, so I opened up the yard, found two tarpaulins, and, with the help of a couple of men from the tenement, spread them over the worst of the rotten slates. And that, for the moment, was as much as I could do.

At the first opportunity, I set about finding out why such conditions were tolerated. The first thing I discovered was that the owners had abandoned the property, because they were unable to meet the maintenance costs. No rents were being collected, and the house agents had no funds to carry out repairs. I also discovered that, throughout Edinburgh, scores of tenements had been deserted, and, in some instances, whole streets of properties had been abandoned by their owners. Meantime, City officials were trying, in a half-hearted way, to trace the owners, and serve notices regarding their duty to keep their houses wind- and water-tight. As many of the owners had left the country, the task of finding them was almost impossible, and, as the Corporation was most unlikely to be compensated for repairs, the unfortunate occupiers of the rundown houses were left marooned. The number of new houses available was insufficient to have them rehoused immediately, so their only remaining hope was through the Council's house letting system – providing, of course, they were eligible.

And here was another problem. House letting was not controlled by the Housing Committee, but by the Finance Committee. Over a long period of years, the house letting officials had devised a scheme, subsequently altered and amended as they saw fit, and approved, I suspect, without argument, from the Finance Committee. The end result was a method whereby points were awarded under various headings – health, homelessness, size of family, waiting time – but not the condition of your present abode. Under health, the only points to be gained were if any member of the household suffered from pulmonary T.B. Heart conditions earned nothing, and the same

applied to the limbless, or people confined to their homes for whatever reason. Fortunately, a cure was found for T.B., and then heart conditions became a priority for rehousing (and, incidentally, it's rather sad that the scourge of T.B. has arrived again in our midst). Sizes of families presented problems, because ages of children determined pointage, and a child only qualified for a full point after its tenth birthday. Waiting time carried little benefit, and was of value only when added to other points acquired. Many people had been waiting since before the war to secure a home.

But there was one loophole in the regulations, and it was exploited deliberately, but legally. At that time, if one was foolish enough to find a room and kitchen, or a single room, no matter how cramped and uncomfortable, and without proper facilities, one was then considered to be housed, in the view of the Council, and then had to wait until the house collapsed or was chosen as being unfit for human habitation. On the other hand, if one was clever, and instead of house-hunting, took refuge with one's parents, or found furnished accommodation, then one was regarded as 'homeless', and shot to the top of the queue, although the living conditions were much superior to those enjoyed by the slum dwellers. This anomaly I placed repeatedly before the Finance Committee, but it took a long time before they appreciated the unfairness of the letting system, and amended the regulations, to give those living in unfit houses a better share of the new homes being built.

Private house-building was restricted because vital materials were earmarked for municipal work, the only exceptions being the conversion of large houses into flats, but here too I suspected valuable materials were diverted from local authority schemes.

But the whole situation was aggravated by a slow-moving house-building programme. The method of tendering for new housing didn't help matters. At that time, tenders were accepted on an individual trades basis, with each contractor, or sub-contractor

responsible for his own work, the overall control or supervision being left to the officers of the Town Council. This involved the Town in arithmetical checking of all these separate tenders before contracts could be awarded. But, worse, at the monthly progress review, we were told repeatedly that delays were caused by certain contractors, who, impeding the whole works, would blame lack of labour, shortage of materials, or lack of cooperation from other trades. I was instrumental in having this changed, so that one main contractor was appointed. He was held responsible for all sub-contract work, and would be answerable for delays or bad workmanship. This move proved worthwhile, but meant the removal of contractors who were not big enough to assume control. A list of subcontractors had to be submitted and approved, before the main contractor could employ them.

At that time, the housing section of our Health Department was controlled by a man named James Robertson, who for many years had worked in that department, and had a tremendous knowledge of Edinburgh's slums. Pre-war, he had supervised many slum-clearance schemes, but his efforts were now blunted until such time as the removal of unfit houses could be renewed. But he proved himself useful in other directions, especially when measuring houses where valuable points could be gained by the occupants for overcrowding. Where he felt the need was urgent, and a family should be rehoused as soon as possible, his measuring tape would shrink, and the dimensions he submitted would ensure the early removal of a suffering family. I called on his help regularly when severe cases of overcrowding were brought to my attention, and he responded magnificently. When discussing housing with him, he often spoke to me about one of his predecessors, a Mr. Allan Ritchie, who defined a slum as 'Darkness, Dampness and Dilapidation'. I have not heard a better description, unless one adds the word 'Despair'.

The slums of the '50s and '60s, which had been festering from pre-war days, were truly hideous, and,

(opposite) 2.19 1959 view of Pat Rogan and Mrs Barclay of 35 Carnegie Street, in the Holyrood redevelopment area, Edinburgh. Rogan wrote on the rear of the photograph: 'Services had been cut by vandals and Mrs Barclay had to collect water from a stand pipe in the street. The dog was her protector.'

2.20 Pat Rogan seen in 1960, standing in front of St Margaret's Church – a landmark in the Arthur Street clearance area. The Cockburn Association's opposition to its demolition for a time threatened to delay redevelopment.

speed, and the Dean of Guild Court, of which I was a member, was in constant demand to visit suspect properties, and adjudicate when necessary over disputes regarding their stability.

So, at long last, the removal of the slums was under way. (Figs. 2.20, 2.21, 2.22) At the same time, action was now being taken to close down unfit houses, and grant, where necessary, overcrowding certificates on a most liberal scale. I discovered at this time that approximately 1,200 houses were available every year, through deaths, moonlights or evictions, but that the bulk of these houses remained empty for long periods because of slowness in preparing them for letting. These obstructions were soon removed, and welcome additional houses were now available.

Progress – but now we were faced with a shortage of building land. This had been anticipated, and some years earlier a number of high flats had been built to alleviate the difficulty. But the problem remained, so our thoughts turned to invading the Green Belt. Private builders, also hunting for building land, hoped

2.21 Cleared site at Arthur Street, 1960: Cowans paper works and Lower Dumbiedykes Road tenements are still standing, while the two new 11-storey blocks of the Dumbiedykes development (1958-60) are visible to the left.

that we would give a lead, but the opposition was too powerful and would have caused delays, which we couldn't afford.

At this time – 1962 – I was made Chairman of the Housing Committee: the first Labour member ever to hold that post. The Council was beset by political stalemate; three Liberal and two SNP councillors held the balance, and – no doubt to stop my perpetual complaints! – the Progressives didn't oppose me. The pressing need for land was still with us, and my first task was to tackle this question. In the immediate postwar years, Edinburgh had erected 4,000 prefabs – the largest number of any city in Scotland – and these houses were occupying valuable land, at a very low density. It was estimated that, by removing them, we could build 10,000 houses on the sites made avaliable.

The first hurdle was to get Government permission, because these houses were intended to last at least 20 years, and there were still a few years to go. However, it was discovered that the aluminium floor joists were showing signs of fatigue, so approval was granted. Opposition from the prefab tenants was another matter. They were very happy in their homes, and, if a brick skin could have been built around the exterior, then they could have stayed forever. But I refused to countenance any delay, and set in motion a system

2.22 Pat Rogan (left) with Harold Wilson (Leader of the Opposition) and William Ross (Shadow Scottish Secretary), on a 1964 visit to the Jamaica Street slums in the New Town during Labour's general election campaign. Rogan was by then the Corporation's Housing Chairman. He recalled: 'That visit was partly for election publicity: we took Harold to the worst slumdom we currently had "on offer"!'

whereby we appointed contractors to remove the prefabs, and design and build their replacements. Understandably, this did not please some architects, but the need for houses was great, and the reward was a production of houses never before achieved in Edinburgh.

Dwellings under contract soared from 700 in 1961 to 2,700 by 1962, and two years later, before I demitted office, the number of houses under construction, contracted for, or tendered for, amounted to 3,617. The very worst of the slums had been demolished, and a programme was in place to deal with the remainder. Today, Edinburgh is free from the awful, disgraceful slums that existed forty years ago. (Figs. 2.23, 2.24, 2.25)

Edinburgh being a very old city, and tourism being a main industry, it was vital that many of our old properties be retained, repaired or rebuilt. Although, at times, I found myself in conflict with conservationists over slum clearances, many buildings, especially in the Royal Mile, were saved from demolition. Unfortunately, the salvage operation should have been started many years earlier. But in the Canongate and Leith, we have many families happily settled in rehabilitated buildings that are a great credit to Edinburgh.

In retrospect, many improvements could have been made on the housing crusade of thirty years ago. Unfortunately, wholesale developments were not controlled entirely by the Housing Committee. In preparing a large scheme, land had to be allocated for a school, but, time and time again, and years later, the land was not used. Requests to include libraries, community centres, and recreation facilities were never received from those committees, and provision of shops – the responsibility of the Finance Committee – was usually left to the good sense and judgement of the City Architect. This meant that many new housing estates were deprived, at the beginning, of amenities that would have made life more comfortable. It was my view then, and now, that in these matters a co-ordinator should be employed, so that all aspects of a new development can be considered well beforehand. But, then, are we ever again likely to see the building of large-scale municipal housing projects?

— HOUSING PROGRESS CHART —

Year:-	1959	1960	1961	1962	1963	1964	1965	1966	1967	1968	1969	1970	1971	
Expenditure:-	2256000	1823000	3209000	2894000	3178000	5998000	6105000	7371000	10770000	6552000	5250000	8174000	8900000	
Houses:-	1316	987	1811	960	1515	2363	1721	2232	2514	985	1656	1272	1449	

Labour Force

Houses Completed
– – – –

Contracts Let [Number of Houses]
– – – – – – –

(vertical scale: 2700, 2600, 2500, 2400, 2300, 2200, 2100, 2000, 1900, 1800, 1700, 1600, 1500, 1400, 1300, 1200, 1100, 1000, 900, 800, 700, 600, 500)

2.23 'Progress chart' of Edinburgh Corporation's housing drive in the 1960s: note the sharp peak at the centre, following Rogan's accession to the housing chair in 1962.

2.24 Topping out of Martello Court, Muirhouse Phase II – at 23 storeys, the capital's tallest tower block – on 14 August 1964. Pat Rogan is standing at the centre. Martello Court was designed by Rowand Anderson, Kininmonth & Paul: the project architect was Ian Gordon.

Recently, when compiling the notes for this paper, I went up to the City Chambers in Edinburgh, and had a talk with the Depute Convener of Housing of Edinburgh District Council. I learned that the waiting list is now no less than 25,000, about half of that number being homeless. When I left office as Housing Chairman in 1965, the waiting list had been reduced to 6,000, but that number's back up to 25,000! In discussing multi-storey blocks, it appears that the public are still divided. Some love them, some loathe them. At present, there are 72 multi-storey blocks in Edinburgh. Seventeen are due for demolition, leaving 55, with 4,500 flats. But the most interesting thing that came out of our discussion was this. The District Council plan, for the next five years, has a paragraph headed: 'Acquisition of Land and New Building'. It reads: 'The District Council owns sites which have potential to be developed to meet housing need. At present, however, the Housing Department lacks the capital finance to embark on its new building programme. It also has to consider the 'Right to Buy' implications of any new building scheme, as tenants will be able to purchase their homes at full discount after five years, leaving the Council with a large, long-standing loan debt on the houses sold, and with a reduced revenue base to service the debt.'

So, in effect, Edinburgh District Council is barred from embarking on worthwhile projects. Meantime, vast sums are being spent on maintaining existing housing stocks, and rehabilitating private properties – the point that was touched on in Dick Mabon's paper, and where, I may say, the money's being used to very good advantage.

2.25 Pat Rogan revisits Martello Court (20th floor) in 1991.

But, overall, the future certainly looks bleak, as the private sector is also stagnant, mainly as a result of the recession. And therefore the whole future, for the homeless, and for those hoping to acquire a new home – especially the young ones coming up, who are looking for new homes of their own – doesn't look too bright at all. However, we can but hope that things will improve as they go along – that's always been my sentiment!

THE GLASGOW INNER RING ROAD: PAST, PRESENT AND FUTURE
JAMES P McCAFFERTY

As the only engineer contributing to this conference, among so many architects and others, I feel rather like the one-eyed javelin player, brought into the team not so much to win medals as to keep the crowd on its toes! I'm not a traffic engineer or a transportation planner. I cannot therefore claim any personal credit for the overall planning of the Inner Ring Road, but I was very much involved in its design and its construction. (Figs. 2.26, 2.27)

When I left university and – a product of the white heat of technology – joined Scott Wilson Kirkpatrick, we were still in the Swinging Sixties. Mini-skirts, the Pill, New Towns, the Beatles, flat roofs, tower blocks – and urban motorways! It was a time of great change and excitement. Everyone wanted to be 'where it was at'. And, as far as urban motorways in Scotland were concerned, 'where it was at' was 6 Park Circus, Glasgow, the home of Scott Wilson Kirkpatrick. For the next ten years or so, I mixed with a group of energetic and innovative engineers from many parts of the world, and we also worked closely with Holford Associates, architects and planning consultants – and, of course, with our clients, the Corporation of the City of Glasgow. In the beginning, where no standards existed, we invented them. We felt that we were involved in the greatest project in Scotland. And when it was over, we scattered, like the remnants of the Seven Samurai, to far-off parts, to share our experiences with others.

I propose, first, to give you a potted history, to set this project in its historical context, followed by an evaluation – and a view of the future.

The first proposals for the systematic modernisation of the Glasgow road network date back to the end of World War II. In 1945, Robert Bruce, Master of Works and City Engineer, proposed two ring roads around the centre of Glasgow, and several radial motorways. In 1949, Abercrombie's *Clyde Valley Regional Plan* recommended an extension to the Bruce roads network, including several other ring roads and radial arteries, along with rehousing in New Towns, new industries for old, and a coordinated transportation plan. In 1954, the Glasgow Development Plan proposed two ring roads again, and nine dual carriageway arterial roads, along with road improvements to reduce traffic congestion in the city centre.

But all these plans for the time being remained on paper – and, by 1956, the average journey speed in the city of Glasgow was just 8.2 m.p.h. 'Stopped time' accounted for one-third of journey time. Traffic was focused on the city centre. Many of the roads were overloaded. Use of public transport was falling, and private vehicle ownership was increasing dramatically. Traffic volumes were expected to treble in fifty years. Road safety records were worsening. This is a quotation from the 1960 Review of the Development Plan: 'The future social and economic health of Glasgow will depend basically on a successful attack on the interlocked problems of housing, employment and communications. In this respect, the campaign of the 1960-80 period should be centred on the redevelopment of 29 Comprehensive Development Areas (CDAs), and on the traffic proposals for the central area'. By contrast, the existing road system was characterised by the Review as 'a plethora of radial routes with multitudinous interchanges, and a complete absence of specially designed ring roads which would link the main radials and enable through and cross city traffic to steer clear of the city centre and inner residential areas'.

The 29 CDAs recommended in the 1960 Review – part of the Glasgow planners' strategy of linked redevelop-

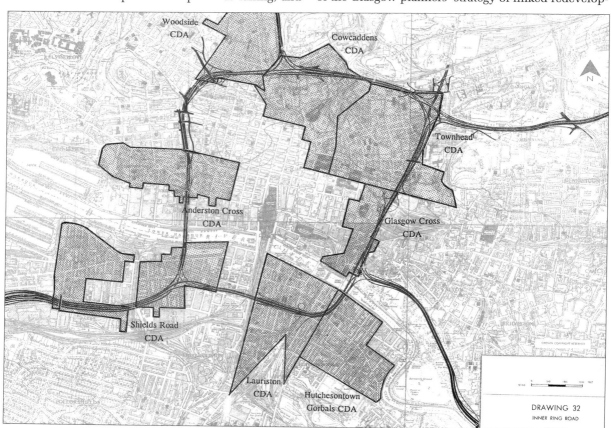

2.26 Glasgow *Highway Plan* (1965): map of Inner Ring Road, with Comprehensive Development Areas superimposed.

ment and overspill – involved 2,700 acres of the city, 2,500 industrial and commercial concerns, and a population of 300,000, and the traffic proposals included an Inner Ring Road. Although this concept had been discussed previously, now the CDA clearance programme provided a readymade framework into which the road could be slotted. By that time, in 1960, significant elements of public and political opinion in the city were ready for this bold step. The *Glasgow Herald*, on 22nd February, proclaimed, 'The timing and the logic of the proposals are both right. Redevelopment of the central areas provides the opportunity for road building on the boldest lines'. A strong element of civic pride was evident: Glasgow was, after all, the nation's largest city and its commercial-industrial hub. And there were also comparisons with the relative inactivity of England in this field. The *Herald* continued: 'The most extraordinary thing, perhaps, about the inner ring road proposals is that they have sprung from local initative. While Mr. Marples, Minister of Transport, is

considering what powers he possesses or can acquire to make a departmental assault on London's traffic problem, Glasgow has produced a blueprint for the first urban motorway in Britain, probably in Europe, and is turning now to consider the prospects for an outer ring route'.

But others were not so keen. In the *Glasgow Herald* three days earlier, Councillor Harry J. Crone had complained that the Planning Committee were 'bulldozing the individual members of the Corporation'. A.S. Warren complained of being 'pulled by the nose'. The person doing the 'bulldozing' and 'nose pulling' was Bailie Bill Taylor, Convener of Planning and future leader of the Labour Group in Glasgow Corporation. He explained, in reply, that 'purely negative restrictions on traffic do not meet the basic functions and needs of the city, and severe restrictions could eventually lessen the importance of the central area as a whole . . . Unless our road system matches the potential challenge, then

2.27 Perspective (1965), by Alexander Duncan Bell, showing the Townhead interchange as envisaged in the *Highway Plan*. The view, from the southwest, shows the Royal Infirmary completely redeveloped at the centre, and, at the left, the originally intended decked layout of Townhead C.D.A. Area 'B'.

the centre of Glasgow is going to die of slow strangulation'. As S. Hamilton, former Town Clerk, subsequently noted, a decisive role was indeed played by the City's Labour administration, who supported this initiative of the Planning and Housing Committees, and forcefully exploited available Government subsidy.

In 1960, therefore, Scott Wilson Kirkpatrick were commissioned to develop an Inner Ring Road proposal. At this stage, the road proposals included the embryonic idea for a ring road round the centre. The Clyde Tunnel was proposed, and there were motorways heading towards Glasgow, but nobody was quite sure what they were going to do when they got there! In 1961, Lord Provost Jean Roberts led a visit to the USA to study redevelopment of urban areas. They visited Washington DC, Baltimore, Philadelphia, New York City, New Haven, Pittsburgh, Detroit and Chicago. They returned convinced that comprehensive redevelopment, mass transportation, and urban motorways would halt Glasgow's decline.

Again in 1961, Scott Wilson Kirkpatrick were asked to undertake a more comprehensive study, and we brought in New York consultants Tippetts-Abbett-McCarthy-Stratton to advise on American experience. The initial proposals for the Inner Ring Road were published in 1962. In 1963 the Highway Plan itself was completed, although it was not published until 1965. At that time, car ownership was predicted to be three times higher by 1990, and the proposals included three ring roads, plus radial motorways and expressways. The ultimate network of roads comprised an Inner Ring Road in the middle, with various arterial roads, and outer ring roads. It indicated the present M74 coming off the Inner Ring Road East Flank at Glasgow Green just north of the Clyde; the Kingston Bridge crossing; and the Renfrew and Monkland Motorways. Going straight out to the north-west was to be the Maryhill Motorway, towards Bearsden, Milngavie and the north of the city.

As already mentioned, the Inner Ring was to make extensive use of the Comprehensive Development Areas, already designated by Glasgow Corporation planners, which covered a vast area of the city. These CDAs, of course, were there not just to cope with roads, but to cope with rehousing and regeneration of the city. They came first, in other words: the road opportunistically made use of their clearance. Although I daresay the tenements in the path of the

2.28 1965 *Highway Plan* perspective of South Flank (unbuilt).

road fell into disrepair even more quickly once its alignment was decided! (Fig. 2.28)

Target 1 of the Highway Plan – the motorway across the city, including the West and North Flanks of the Inner Ring Road – was planned to be completed by 1975, along with pedestrianisation of principal shopping streets and an effective parking policy. By 1965, work on the North Flank at Townhead had commenced, with the Scottish Office providing finance of 50-75% for the contracts which followed. And, in the event, Target 1 was actually completed by 1981, in ten contracts. The cost of all that was about £150m (or £590m in today's prices).

The principles of planning of the Inner Ring Road were similar to those produced in the Buchanan Report, which it pre-dated. Primary roads would be built for main traffic flows; most traffic would be directed away from city streets; large travel and environmental benefits would result. Traffic diverted to well-designed new roads would cause less environmental harm than the same traffic on narrow city streets. The city centre environment would be improved by limiting traffic, and that traffic would be limited by control of parking spaces. Short-term parking was to be encouraged, car commuting discouraged.

The techniques which were used in the 1961 traffic survey were as follows: destination surveys established travel patterns in 1961, and traffic patterns were then predicted for 1990, allowing for traffic growth, and changes of population and employment, New Towns and so on. Future road proposals were then tested for the predicted traffic flows. The results of this 1961 survey, fed into a model of the city streets, demonstrated large flows on either side of Central Station, and crossing the River Clyde: that was why there were already those two bridges there. And there were big flows on Paisley Road West, Great Western Road, and on Parliamentary Road, leading out to Springburn and Kirkintilloch. The 1990 traffic fed on to the same system indicated that there would be massive congestion, were nothing to be done to the road system. Particularly busy would be Paisley Road West and the roads along the south side of the line of

the present Kingston Bridge. All in all, predicted traffic flows were found to be four times higher in 1990 than in 1961. The same 1990 traffic levels, fed on to the Highway Plan's proposed new network, showed a large volume of traffic flowing out across the Kingston Bridge and going up round the West Flank of the Inner Ring Road and out along the North. There was also a massive flow – indeed a bigger flow – predicted for the East and South Flanks. And there were connections to the M74 at the south-east.

The traffic survey models, we believed, provided a rational basis for the design of new roads. Primary routes were located so as to cause least environmental harm, which, it was recognised, could arise from noise, visual intrusion and severance. I mentioned the CDAs a moment ago. But outside those areas, too, the motorways were located along disused canals, adjacent to railways, or adjacent to industrial areas – in other words, trying to snake along lines of existing severance. Construction of the North and West Flanks was staged: the worst areas of congestion, mostly in the early CDAs, were relieved first. It was intended that a sensible, coherent system was to exist at all times. Inevitably, however, this dramatic period from 1965 onwards, when the line of the road became a huge expanse laid bare awaiting construction, was a time of great trauma for the city. Most people travelled by public transport in those days, but there was still a lot of chaos, traffic-jams of buses, and general inconvenience to people who were simply trying to go about their daily business while an urban motorway system was being constructed across their city. (Figs. 2.29, 2.30)

Considerable efforts were made to ensure that the system would be safe, user-friendly and aesthetically pleasing. For instance, the design set out, from the beginning, to provide open-span pedestrian underpasses rather than closed boxes, because it was felt these were much more open and user-friendly, allowing free movement of traffic and people at ground level. A lot of attention was given to the detailing of footways and landscaping. Also carefully considered were the interchange designs, with bridges sweeping down to carry traffic. These are quite interesting structures in their own right – single columns, torsionally stiff prestressed concrete boxes.

Townhead Interchange was the first to be constructed. Its prestressed concrete box girder bridges were quite avant-garde in their day. The red sandstone retaining walls, on the other hand, came in a way from the past: they were built of rubble re-used from demolished tenements.

Models of major structures such as Townhead Interchange were made, to assist in public exhibitions – which were not the same thing, of course, as today's idea of public 'participation'. The Inner Ring Road design work was split between two firms of consulting engineers, Scott Wilson Kirkpatrick (who dealt, basically, with the North Flank) and W.A. Fairhurst and Partners (the West Flank). Another environmental concern was that not just important industry, but also buildings of historical or architectural interest – including their settings – were to be preserved. At Charing Cross, for instance, the motorway was depressed in a cutting, both to reduce noise and to minimise severance of the community and overshadowing of the Mitchell Library; and there was an effort,

through the famous 'Bridge to Nowhere' – which was intended to carry shops across the street – to preserve the 'canyon effect' of the city centre. It would, of course, have been much cheaper and simpler just to continue the line of the raised viaducts on either side, but that would have been unacceptable in such a sensitive location.

So what were the results of all this planning and effort? An evaluation carried out by my firm in 1980 produced the following results. For the motorist, there were of course direct and obvious benefits. Traffic speed had increased from an average of 18 mph in 1961 to 50 mph, largely because of the M8; time savings, largely because of the M8, were about 20%; fuel savings, approximately 9%; and a reduction of street congestion produced similar savings of time and fuel. But other people benefited, too. There was a large reduction in the number of accidents and fatalities on the roads into the city: fatalities were cut from 16.5 per million vehicle-miles to 0.8 in 1977. There were also environmental benefits – a reduction

2.30 Oblique view of the same area in 1974, after completion of the road.

(opposite) 2.29 Vertical aerial view of West and North Flanks under construction, 1969. At the bottom of the picture, the Kingston Bridge is half-built. Above it, on both sides of the Ring Road, stretches the Anderston Cross C.D.A. At the top of the picture is clearance for the Woodside C.D.A.

in noise, fumes, visual intrusion and vibration in the city; and a reduction in the number of heavy vehicles travelling through the city, and elimination of traffic from the main shopping streets – pedestrianisation, even, in places such as Buchanan Street. There were also improved operating conditions for buses. And what of the appearance of the completed road itself? Looking at it today, it is, in my opinion, a green, pleasant, yet at the same time dramatic motorway. Lots of trees, landscaping, footbridges, spiral ramps – the planting has come on well.

But along with, or in the wake of all this, there inevitably also came a 'downfall'. The Greater Glasgow Transportation Study (GGTS) was set up in the mid 1960s to produce a coordinated transportation plan for all modes of traffic. In 1968, they confirmed that the Highway Plan was the highway network they intended to adopt. Several years later, however – in 1973 – the Land Compensation Act gave rights to compensation if property values were to fall due to road construction. That year, the GLC in London immediately abandoned its motorway plans. By 1974, the Greater Glasgow Transportation Study was reporting a 30% drop in predicted 1990 traffic. In the deteriorating economic conditions and changing political climate, the motorway proposals appeared over-ambitious and expensive. Now there was more emphasis on jobs and dealing with urban deprivation. Increasingly, transportation policy encouraged the use of public transport.

The optimism of the 1960s was gone, and attitudes towards urban motorways changed. 'Motorway' became a pejorative word, and the roads themselves were now actually blamed for the clearance of the CDAs! Environmentalists and conservationists led the protests. Confidence among politicians and officials waned. In 1975 Strathclyde Regional Council inherited Glasgow's roads, and by 1981 Stage 1 had been completed. But there were to be no more big urban road schemes.

What, then, of the future? Traffic volumes continue to rise inexorably. There are currently 155,000 vehicles per day crossing the Kingston Bridge, against 120,000 predicted for 1990. Because the Ring Road has not been completed, Charing Cross Section cannot cope with the traffic: under the original plan, half the through traffic on that section would have gone the other way, via the South and East Flanks. So at rush-hour Charing Cross is slow-moving, often blocked. Something needs to be done.

Yet, paradoxically, car ownership in Glasgow is very low, by modern Western European standards. There's a long way to go before we get anywhere near the sort of car ownership levels of Düsseldorf or München! But car-use will inevitably rise fast unless some political move is made to restrict it. We only need to look at what's happened since the most recent predictions, in 1983: a steep rise, above both the 'low' and 'high' predictions of '83! In other words, our predictions have been completely wrong, and, for the past decade, car ownership has been increasing far faster than expected. What is to be done?

Strathclyde Regional Council have proposals to tackle this situation, which they've summed up in a document called 'Travelling in Strathclyde'. This plan proposes a light rail transit system through the city. It will be on roads, with wires overhead: useful, but perhaps not as aesthetically pleasing as some other modes of transport. But what about new roads? The Strathclyde plan shows spreading red lines snaking right round what once might have been called the East Flank and the South Flank, and across the river by the Kingston Bridge. All looking suspiciously like some sort of completion of the Inner Ring Road – but not quite the sort of Ring Road that was planned, originally! (Fig. 2.31)

(opposite) 2.31 Glasgow Inner Ring Road, West Flank: 1988 view of Kingston Bridge.

5 ARCHITECTURAL DESIGN

May 1963 Price 4/-

PART THREE
ARCHITECTS' ARCHITECTURE

INTRODUCTION

Where Part Two focused, in general, on the provision rather than the design of buildings, Part Three examines postwar buildings, especially those of the '60s, in the specific context of Modern Architecture – its theories and its forms. Acknowledging Modernism's combination of highly structured formulas, in some respects, with extreme open-endedness in others, the contributions that follow have been arranged to span as wide as possible a range of applications and interpretations of the Modern Movement in Scotland – in many cases, describing them in the words of the original designers (in papers delivered to the 1992 DOCOMOMO conference and the 1993 RFACS seminar series: for identification, see Table of Contents).

The building programmes tackled vary from massive urban redevelopments and public buildings to small private houses. And the architectural values represented range from, on the one hand, an adherence to Modern Functionalism's insistence on integrating beauty with the practical considerations of solidity and utility, to, on the other hand, a trenchant absorption in the expression of 'form' and 'space'.

Part Two begins at the most elevated and ambitious level of Late Modernist design – the internationally renowned attempt, at Cumbernauld, to radically reshape the concept of the urban central area on multi-level, 'megastructural' principles. Here we reprint, in full, two papers (one written at the time, in 1963, and one more recently, in 1995) in which Cumbernauld Town Centre's architect, Geoffrey Copcutt, described his design, and its governing ideals of futuristic consumerism: the 1963 paper is reproduced in the form of a facsimile from the May 1963 issue of *Architectural Design*. Then, we pass to three papers dealing with other issues of urban reconstruction. Charles Robertson, and the present writer, explore two architectural visions of the rebuilding of Glasgow – the sculptural compositions of Basil Spence, and the more offbeat constructional initiatives of Sam Bunton. By contrast with both these, Sir Anthony Wheeler outlines some of the ideas behind his sensitive small-burgh rebuilding schemes, focusing on his work at Dysart.

Next, Part Three deals with the field of Modernist private house architecture, whose US-influenced open plan tendencies enabled inventive younger architects of the period to use it as a way of working out urban planning solutions in microcosm. The work of Morris & Steedman is explored here from two viewpoints: that of one of the original designers (Robert Steedman) and that of an architect of a more recent generation (David Page).

The remaining contributions are all concerned with the problems of designing large public buildings in the '60s. John Richards explains how the doctrine of a refined Functionalism was expressed in some RMJM projects of those years, especially the Royal

(opposite) 3.1 Cumbernauld Town Centre, model of Phase One original proposal (with two rows of penthouses): aerial view on front cover of May 1963 *Architectural Design*.

Commonwealth Pool. Isi Metzstein and Mark Baines discuss the way in which Gillespie, Kidd & Coia's search for expressive 'form' was combined with social ideals of community in a series of daring sectional designs for educational buildings, culminating (during the Modernist period) in the design of St Peter's College, Cardross. And William Whitfield relates the way in which, at Glasgow University Library, a brief calling both for a symbolic landmark building and a practical 'warehouse for books' was answered by a dramatic, tower-encircled design owing much to the medieval military architecture of Northumbria.

Part Three is brought to an end with a verbatim account of the open discussion which closed the 1992 DOCOMOMO conference, in which many issues concerning the present-day condition and status of Modernist buildings were debated – including the question of whether they should, or can, be preserved. In this discussion, one aspect of our present condition of cultural postmodernity was emphasised: the irreconcilable clashes of opinion concerning issues such as housing, which result from the disappearance of any overarching consensus concerning the 'social'. But, we should remind ourselves, Modern Architecture itself was always a movement of deep-running differences as well as widely shared beliefs.

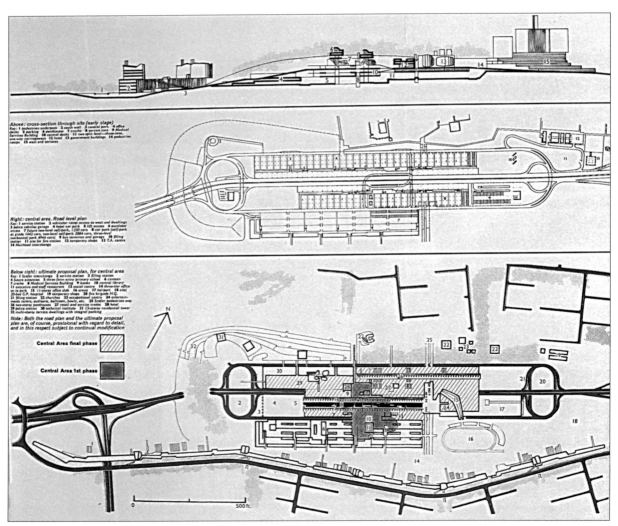

3.2 Cumbernauld Town Centre: layout plans and section of full 1962 proposals, showing the proposed huge linear extensions to Phase One.

Cumbernauld Town Centre – Facsimile from *Architectural Design* (1963)

CUMBERNAULD NEW TOWN CENTRAL AREA

L. Hugh Wilson, D. R. Leaker and Geoffrey Copcutt*

Description by Geoffrey Copcutt

Above: an early sketch of the generating concept for the central area, by Geoffrey Copcutt. This sketch shows the initial formulation of an idea, in which 'penthousing' is cradled on an umbrella structure, inclined towards the south; beneath the cradle are situated multi-level shopping and civic facilities, together with a multiple lane, two-way, servicing carriageway

On the ridge and upper southern slope of the Cumbernauld hill, 200ft. above the reconstructed Glasgow–Stirling trunk road, will rise a single citadel-like structure nearly half a mile long, 200yds. wide and up to eight storeys high. Elevated over a unidirectional vehicular system, this multi-level development, with provision for most of the commercial, civic, religious, cultural and recreational uses for a population of 70,000 will be the largest single employment source, traffic generator and land-space user in the town.

A new town must try to avoid perpetuating the current chaotic urban conditions and attempt to satisfy functional requirements that will in the end have to be solved in existing urban centres. Thus the issue becomes one of giving value for money, and on these terms there is financial advantage in the decision to build a permanent structure with demountable enclosures rather than to provide short-term buildings creating at any one time an indifferent environment or to accept the normal time-cycle of growth and decay with consequent social and economic disruption.

The flexibility reflects accelerating change in the retail and entertainment pattern; there is no reliance, for example, on selecting optimum 'unit' sizes which can be valid in any event only for certain times in certain positions. In the extreme future if particular central area functions decline (a formidable list of facilities that can be piped to the home can already be compiled) the centre could become a gigantic vending machine through which the motorized user drives to return revictualled, or, more remotely, it could be turned over to industrial production.

Provision for the future can be made in four ways: firstly, by rearranging the interior; secondly, by ensuring a considerable space factor of safety within the planned extent of the town centre; thirdly, by allowing the centre to expand 400ft. at each end within its own vehicular apparatus which is arranged within a structural grid; and finally, by reserving sites for completely unknown and unforeseen uses with special buildings sited alone on either the north or south faces of the structure and linked back to the decks.

These considerations were instrumental in channelling research towards improving methods of prediction by relating land use to economic pressures. It was calculated, for example, that the annual turnover in the retail and service trades would be of the order of £10,000,000 in 1959 money terms with, if the efforts of the traders were co-ordinated in an aggressive sales policy, a potential increase in custom from a minimum further 35,000 regional customers. Other aspects of technological, planning and environmental research are running concurrently with the design and continually influencing it.

The site extends to nearly 150 acres lying between two-grade separated interchanges one mile apart, with a crossfall to the south of 25ft. in the centre. The subsoil varies from soft brown clay to stiff boulder clay to a depth of 9ft., from 9ft. to 12ft. soft weathered rock and below 12ft. firm sandstone with no bearing problems. The climate on this exposed hilltop includes annually one month of snow, one month of fog, 200 raindays and seven months from the first to the last screen frosts. It is in addition an area of high humidity and the Beaufort Force diagram accompanying the general plan illustrates the severity of the winds.

These conditions, coupled with topographical considerations and the need for flexibility and pedestrian and vehicular segregation, constitute the major reasons for adopting a single envelope wherein all journeys will be free of hazard and may be, but need not exclusively be, made under cover. Nor will the effect of an infinite cavern or tunnel be presented at the vehicular level. Roads come in and continue through level and all decks are perforated and interpenetrating, resulting in relatively narrow bands of development with continually changing views out of and through the centre.

Within the centre all planes are inhabited both above and below until the final statement of roof is made by long terraces of penthouses. The basic structure of parallel linked frames creating a linear core within the centre are able to accept on this scale, erupting forms, a variety of furnishings and a kaleidoscope of advertising.

While the pedestrian has the broad flank of the centre presented to him and selects out his entry point as he comes uphill, the motorist to whom this is a drive-in town centre, with its section revealed like a map on the approaches, will by virtue of being mechanically propelled, make his selection in the town centre length. After passing through the trumpet interchange he is virtually entering a vast terminal facility, for the component of through traffic in the flows will be something under 10 per cent; demonstrating the effectiveness of the revised town road system in 'draining-off' traffic from the central area. Vehicular approaches to the centre have been given prestige alignment and character involving high standards of design which are intended to promote safe travel at speeds around 40 m.p.h. This extension of the proposed regional semi-motorway system penetrates the structure at the level devoted entirely to vehicle movement and vehicle storage. The general concept of a two-point entry, divided one-way flow and segregation of classes of road user should promote free flow and safety of operation. All carriageway capacities, weaving lengths and cross-links have been checked against anticipated flows.

The proposed parking arrangement of a double layer of cars over the site is an equivalent to the ideal of kerbside parking. Unlike a series of multi-storey parking garages, there are no fierce concentrations of traffic at peak exodus nor dead travel vertically, beyond the thickness of one car. At a stall turnover of 3·3 a day, a comfortable allowance can be given for the predicted car population of the town of 1980 of 1·4 per family plus a regional influx. Covered standing is provided for 300 goods vehicles, 60 buses and a number of service vehicles.

Peak tidal flows are reflected in the signalling system and the dimensions of the arrival and departure platforms which can carry vending machines and parcel pick-up stations and can connect with drive-in facilities for the post office and banks. From these platforms, lifts and escalators will elevate over an average Saturday upwards of 20,000 passengers making return journeys. If the walk-in traffic at the upper levels is added, the amount of pedestrian activity to be handled by the vertical communications system emerges. Horizontal transfers may be achieved eventually by the installation of lateral pedestrian conveyors particularly suitable for a multi-storey centre since it is possible to achieve 100 per cent. use of the band by adopting a one-way service at each level.

Fuelling points, providing a 24-hour service of petrol on one side and diesel the other, are disposed on the exit lanes from the centre, a natural filter barrier segregating the different classes of traffic. At the eastern end inside the U-turns which are 2200ft. apart is the communications node within the central area. Here town and regional bus services link with private cars, taxis and possibly a heliport. As the carriageways divide at the eastern approach a site develops for the fire station having direct access to the radial link and trunk roads. The site makes this an important entry to the centre and the building could take the form of a low shell with air screens closing the ends of the fire fighting deck which would be linked to fire detection and prevention systems within the centre. Adjoining this 'cantonment' is a 2 acre site to the north proposed for a T.A. centre and a similar reservation to the south for the main Medical Services Centre. At the west end the parking lots are terminated by the police vehicles garage which corresponds in position to the police headquarters over; the means of surveillance may include closed television circuits.

Above the vehicular levels is the storage and service deck fed from over one half mile of loading docks. Within this floor either mechanical or manual handling will replenish long-term stores which in turn will serve localized storage islands on the public floors over. Additionally, a main transformer housing, several sub-stations, central fume extraction, refrigeration and vacuum cleaning plant may be installed on this floor and on the level below. Studies are being made for the design of noise control measures for conventional and high velocity ventilation systems, the reduction of noise from lifts and other mechanical plant and the design of structures to control ingress of road and air traffic noise.

continued on page 211

Note*: L. Hugh Wilson was Chief Architect and Planning Officer to the Cumbernauld New Town corporation until 26th October 1962 and is now retained as consultant architect. He has been succeeded by D. R. Leaker. The Group Architect for the whole of the central area is Geoffrey Copcutt.

Cumbernauld Town Centre – Facsimile from *Architectural Design* (1963)

Cumbernauld Central Area

continued from page 210

Above this level the commercial floors terrace down the hillside to form a multi-storey centre, the modern precedent for which exists in the retail market recently opened in Sheffield. Within this area the distribution of economic types is reflected in the storey heights. The shopping arrangement should be particularly conducive to the introduction of non-stop automatic vending by certain distributors as a means of meeting increasing competition, rising costs of distribution and diminishing hours of work. Ultimately groups of sales outlets could be controlled electronically from central panels with radio links to maintenance vehicles, to which complaints could be relayed.

The upper tier of accommodation over the double-height shops or two storeys of shops on the south side is the walk-off office area with accommodation for societies and institutions, professional suites and lettable office space. There is a distribution of joint stock and savings banks throughout the centre opening generally off the squares. The transition from the civic to the commercial use is made via the hotel on the north deck, which may take the form of an inverted pyramid with bars and reception on the lower floor, public rooms and dining-rooms activating the upper level and residential quarters over; while on the south deck the head post office acts as a fulcrum at the pedestrian approach to the civic complex.

The basic form of the commercial zone is a great elongated Z shape embracing a civic platform at the west end and at the east an entertainment square. Sharing the civic podium with the town hall, municipal offices, council chamber and courts of law, and riding over the lower square of central government functions is the technical institute.

This institute should be a potent force in the life of the town and may be expected to offer communal facilities complementary to those of the town hall. A second educational establishment, a primary school is being considered for inclusion on the west end of the terrace one flight up from the main north deck, providing an opportunity for a close link with the seat of local government.

The mid-point of this terrace is devoted to the central lending and reference library, part of which is suspended over the southern ramp access, and the community centre with facilities for all ages at different times of the day, each enclosed in identifiable structures grouped within the main piers. At the east end of the centre is the large span entertainment building connected down to the bus terminus and capable of being subdivided in a variety of ways. This structure which is a further extension of the decks will include auditoria, bowling lanes, dance floors, cafés and

gardens. At the heart of the centre is a multi-purpose gallery for lectures, concerts and meetings which can accommodate either cultural exhibitions sponsored from the library and the community centre or commercial exhibitions originating from the shopping floors.

Four central church sites are proposed projected away from the decks but related to the lateral footpaths.

Participating in the development, will be 1500 dwellings whose presence will ensure that in addition to the 5500 people who will actually live in the central area a good deal of pedestrian service traffic will be generated. With the hazard, noise and fumes, designed out of the public places the centre can become the appropriate environment for children and the less nimble. The dwellings themselves take three forms. Three ranges of penthouses 1000ft. long are elevated above this combination of uses to form an element of visual and physical control. A further 500 dwellings occupy the west-end tiers with integral parking linked to the decks. This arrangement will be refined as information emerges from wind-tunnel experiments designed to throw up locations of conditions of discomfort likely to arise throughout the centre due to wind forces; the resultant form is part of the larger town picture of three high density nodes. Car parking for central area dwellings will be provided within the centre, where space will also be available for those families in the vicinity who may find it convenient to park their second car in the centre. This will ensure round-the-clock use of the facility to the extent of about 1000 spaces. A third dwelling group has been given for test purposes the form of a two-storey town wall, bounding the central park.

Excavated material is used in the construction of the 45ft. high mole and for ground moulding within the central area buildings. Surface water is shed naturally to the south flank where it will be picked up at three points and conducted to a main outfall running east. The system has been designed on a once-in-five years storm to ensure the minimum possibility of standing water. The belt of structural planting on the exposed north face will reinforce the existing shelter belts and canalize views to the hills. From the entertainment locus the arena develops logically as an outdoor recreation area that can provide accommodation for travelling fairs or circuses and space for exhibition enclosed on the east by an arrangement of thick hedges surrounding the amphitheatre.

Note: Work has commenced on site servicing the first stage of the development described here, tenders are being prepared for the structure, comprising about one-fifth of the total cube and the design of additional phases is under way.

Above: road approach to central area from west

Below: maps showing the location of Cumbernauld; plotted as the result of research used to determine the probable population shed upon Cumbernauld as a regional shopping centre. The bottom left hand map is the result of a survey conducted in 1956–57, into 'urban spheres of influence in Western Scotland', and shows the towns commonly visited on a Saturday or market day for shopping. The lines show the pull from scattered towns to the main urban centres. 1 Glasgow 2 Kirkintilloch 3 Coatbridge 4 Airdrie 5 Kilsyth 6 Falkirk 7 Stirling 8 high-ground barrier. This reveals Glasgow, Stirling, and Falkirk as the main shopping centres, adjacent to Cumbernauld, Nos. 2, 3 and 5 coming under the pull of Glasgow. The bottom right hand map shows the areas which are most accessible to Cumbernauld by four methods of transport. 1 bus, 2 car, 3 car and train, and 4 bus and train. The remainder of key indicates:— 5 Stirling–Glasgow road link 6 rail route 7 35,000 population area

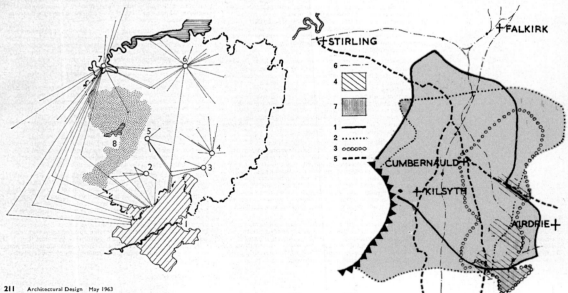

CUMBERNAULD NEW TOWN CENTRE IN RETROSPECT
GEOFFREY COPCUTT (1995 PAPER)

In the Beginning

Arm-wrestling Third World bugs 8000 miles east of those cool Cumbernauld slopes, I keenly recall returning from an early exploration to fold a single sheet of paper into a form which gathered dimensions the Queen would come to baptise, and Prince Philip to blitz as 'bloody concrete'.

We were building a cheap town in severe conditions for a lengthening queue of Clydesiders. I never doubted the logic of a central infrastructure of highways and walkways, layers and ledges promising shelter, warmth and family freedom. (Figs. 3.4, 3.5)

The Future Unfolds

The paper prototype passed from passion to obsession. Hugh Wilson the father kept the faith. Deputy Dudley Leaker kept the peace. In the end, both had to decide to do a caesarian, to get the drawings out of me and up to the excavations.

The paradox of an open citadel was too commanding to risk compromise. So with colleague Alex Kerr, I shamelessly did night classes poaching statistics and traffic planning. By day we engaged rowdy academics on a 100-towns retail-social study, and spent weekends recording the wind regime and sampling test bores. In between, we debated income and spending patterns, projected travel modes, deliveries and solid waste values, juggled structural grids to match parking modules, mitigated venturi effects and correlated tenant, corner shop and sub-centre distribution to match the first phase.

And all the while, like a jeweller fashioning precious metal, I hammered the cross-sections and shaped landscape, to forge an urban morphology.

Friends, Romans, Countrymen

With the succession of roles came a succession of contributions, evidenced in the footprint of Alex Kerr and the fingerprints of Dave Brindle, in the texts of Alan McCulloch and the context of Kilspindie. This fraternal gallery frames professors Hendry (physics, Liverpool), Diamond (economics, Glasgow), and Broady (sociology, ditto). Over the mantelpiece hangs John Faber, son of Oscar the engineer. Without his fun and flair, even the filleted version of the first phase might never have been built. (Fig. 3.6)

Perhaps infected by the interest of Scottish Development Department guru Bob Grieve, our own administrators took 'air rights' in their stride: schooled in municipal halls, they found themselves assembling take-apart models like born-again believers. Every

3.3 Perspective photograph of model of original proposal (from viewpoint corresponding to actual south).

accent, including echoes of the legions of Antoninus, was heard as a band of luminaries from Pier Luigi Nervi, Roma, to Lewis Mumford, Flushing, bought their harps to the studio. They came to witness the evolution of a nine-level package accommodating most of the commercial, civic, cultural, and recreational uses for a population of 70,000, elevated over a vehicular system linked to radials a mile apart. Occupying 150 acres of the ridge and upper south slope between interchanges, its organisation was to be justified by exposure, topography, flexibility of functions, pedestrian separation and the need for vehicle discipline. (Figs. 3.7, 3.8)

Cold Feet

By the time the first phase was committed, my train was departing Glasgow for Belfast, and a second chance to make a city of our time. Meanwhile, back at the Big Hoose, a near top-to-bottom revamp left the Centre under other management. What next? Reyner Banham's *Age of the Masters* gives the answer: '. . . there won't be much next. What has been built so far is a small fraction of Copcutt's original design, but it seems all that is going to be built in this particular mega-mode'.

And, although Banham doesn't say it, this fragment – still big enough to define a future – was shorn not only of its second row of pylons and penthouses, with a host of functional and spatial consequences, but also of the mosaic of sites I had tucked in for flea-markets, the winter-garden front to the tiers of offices, the tube

3.4 Perspective photograph of model of original proposal (from viewpoint corresponding to actual west).

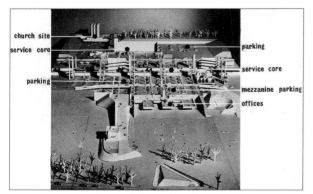

3.5 Cutaway perspective photograph of model of original proposal (from viewpoint corresponding to actual south-east). The six groups of tall columns running across the centre of the photograph support the penthouses at the summit of the Centre: they are completely independent of the main structure of the complex.

3.6 Perspective photograph (c.1963) of model of Phase One as built (from viewpoint corresponding to actual south-west).

3.7 1964 perspective by M. Evans of interior of Phase One.

3.8 1964 perspective by M. Evans of Phase One north wing and motorway running through Centre.

3.9 1965 aerial photograph of Cumbernauld Town Centre Phase One under construction.

roof illuminating the chapel, the glistening 'airplane wing' which was to have tilted open over the library, and even the wall of dwellings with upper promenade designed to curtain the parkland. The curved and stepped terraces of apartments and earthworks arrayed at the 'Glasgow' portal, I always knew would take a lot of shaking and moving to make happen. But countless minor delights clothing the concept were not so much 'simplified' as simply missed. (Figs. 3.9, 3.10)

Cool Head

Still, how lucky I was to have got the brief. Years earlier, reporting on the same day, Derek Lyddon and I cordially agreed (Sir Hugh refereeing) to toss for duties. Derek had the pipe, the coin and the call, I had the beard and the prayer. Out of that spin was to develop a satisfying division of labour, and a life-long respect between us.

Those to whom it may seem that the toss was a poor deal for the Centre can be consoled that the rest of the town was spared my attentions. Those to whom it seems blindingly obvious that there is little alternative in urban hot-spots to a decked development, will as easily observe that the execution of this exemplar was made possible by the awesome powers presented by New Towns legislation.

3.10 Cumbernauld Town Centre, Phase One: 1968 view when newly completed, showing Galbraith store (then the largest supermarket in Scotland).

'A GREAT SHIP IN FULL SAIL': BASIL SPENCE AND HUTCHESONTOWN 'C'

CHARLES ROBERTSON

As the job architect for Basil Spence's Hutchesontown-Gorbals 'C' blocks, I lived through that dynamic time when the country launched into the massive building programmes of the postwar era. (Fig. 3.11) And the Spence office, particularly, grew to its peak then, both in the volume of work that it was doing, and the sheer excitement of being in that atmosphere. I started with Spence in 1956, and left in 1962. It's not only my view, but, I think, that of many of my colleagues, that those years were vintage years for Spence. This certainly seemed so to us, the staff members. I also think that Spence himself probably thought that. He enjoyed, if somewhat coyly, public attention and acclamation – and there was plenty of that in those years. He was president of the RIBA, he got his knighthood, he became a Royal Academician, and he eventually got the Order of Merit.

Most of the senior staff, like myself, had been educated during the war, and, with military service, had graduated as architects around 1952. The prewar years of depression – declining industry, unemployment, poverty and slums, leading on to the six years of war – had left the returning servicemen and women eager to create the new world: a world that had, to that date, cost a great deal in human sacrifice, both in peace and war. Although my generation had not had first-hand experience in the interwar years, or of active military service, we were, nevertheless, imbued with the same spirit of starting afresh. The Victorian and Edwardian eras meant, for most of us, a time that was best forgotten: an opinion held by very many people, incidentally – not just restricted to budding young architects. Although the Victorians had produced great industrial and financial achievements, they had also left a legacy of extremely poor housing for working people. Their successes were also achieved at great human cost, both in this country and in what was, at that time, the British empire. After the war, government and people alike wanted to build a new world.

(opposite) 3.11 Basil Spence's Hutchesontown/Gorbals Area 'C': 1966 view of newly completed blocks.

As architects, we were sure that the new architecture would produce a new and better society. It was a time of high idealism – of visions of the future, where beauty, and happiness, and prosperity would be available to all. One little book, called *Living in Cities*, was written by Ralph Tubbs, who was a well-known architect in the immediate postwar years. It was written, I think, about 1943, and contained, on a page of its own, this little quotation – which epitomises the kind of spirit that we were all experiencing and living with: 'If the cities of the future are to be the places of beauty where everyone can live happily, and where everyone will have a high standard of living, we will require organisation and planning on a very large scale, combined with enthusiasm and determination. In war, the nation unites in a common effort. Everyone plays his part to hasten a common victory. In peace, we must work together on the same scale for our common good. It must not be every man for himself, but every man working to further civilisation. To succeed, we must have the necessary organisation. We must plan now.' Very emotional words, but that was the kind of thinking that was prevalent then.

Coupled with this idealism was, of course, the country's great need: there were enormous housing shortages, decaying hospitals, schools and city centres. In the mid 1960s, Colin Buchanan calculated that we needed to build the equivalent of an entire city every year, to the end of the century, if we were to make up for lost time and satisfy the need that was then obvious. And, of course, after five years of war, there was very little money to deal with those problems. Everything had to be done very economically – which really meant as cheaply as possible – so that what money was available could be spread as far as possible. I think that the fact that we built so much in these postwar years, under such conditions, is not much short of a miracle. The building programmes were impressive in their magnitude – and so were the mistakes! Mistakes they may have been, but if successive governments had not achieved those huge housing programmes, during the '50s and '60s, people would still be living in substantially worse conditions than now.

It is against that background of high idealism, great need, and very difficult economic conditions that we should look at Spence's Gorbals project, and indeed at the whole multi-storey programme in Glasgow. My task is to discuss specifically the Spence blocks, but, just before I get on to that, I would like to just say a word or two about the office and its organisation, and some of its personalities. And then I'd like to try and set the Gorbals blocks in the context of Spence's work in Scotland immediately preceding the Gorbals design, and the work that was contemporary with it.

By the time I joined the practice in 1956, Spence and his family had moved to London from 40 Moray Place in Edinburgh, where he had a flat above the office. (Figs. 3.12, 3.13, 3.14) He, of course, was already well-known. He had established his reputation before the war, with the Empire Exhibition, Broughton Place and other well-known projects. But, of course, by 1956 he had won the Coventry Cathedral competition, and had carried out other exhibition work, notably the Sea and Ships pavilion at the 1951 South Bank exhibition. In Edinburgh, he'd had one or two delightful little jobs, which have now all vanished: the Aperitif Restaurant in Castle Street, Crawford's Tearoom in Queensferry Street, and the Halifax Building Society in George Street. They're all gone now.

There had been lean years after the Cathedral competition: Spence himself has written extensively about that period. I think he spent most of his time then travelling the world, trying to raise money to build the Cathedral! But by 1956, when I got there, the office was extremely busy. He had established an office in Queen Anne Street in London, and another at 1, Canonbury Place, where he, once again, lived with his family above the office. It was at Canonbury Place that I worked, under Spence's personal supervision, on the development of the Gorbals. Hardie Glover and Peter Ferguson were the partners in charge of Edinburgh, and Andrew Renton at Queen Anne Street, all of them previously partners in Edinburgh. And, of course, Basil ruled over the whole organisation from Canonbury. That was the nerve centre, with a nucleus of special, hand-picked staff. Over the year and a half that I worked there, the staff included David Rock, of Rock Townsend, now recently retired; Bob Smart, recently retired Chairman of Building Design Partnership; Jack Bonnington; Gordon Collins; and, perhaps the best-known in recent years, Michael Hopkins. Like all well-known architects' offices at any time, the Spence office was an incubator for the future. Basil originated most of the work of the office, and, not unnaturally, jealously guarded his original ideas. The routine was that a job was started by Basil; after that, there would be an almost daily trot up and down from Queen Anne Street to Canonbury to secure his approval of the latest progress of the job, whatever it might be. Edinburgh staff were not so lucky. Basil

came to Edinburgh, and the grey suits and the cigars were brought out to celebrate the event.

The practice, of course, eventually split up, in the mid/late-1960s. Andrew Renton started what's now known as RHWL at Queen Anne Street, Basil went into partnership with Glover and Ferguson at Edinburgh under that name, and with Bonnington and Collins in London. But he also kept his own practice, in Canonbury, as an individual consultant. Eventually

3.12 Basil Spence, photographed at Moray Place by Lida Moser, 1949. On the table in front of him is a model of Kilsyth Academy (built 1948-53), and hanging on the wall behind is a perspective of the Glasgow University Natural Philosophy extension (1947-51).

Bonnington went off with the Fitzroy Square practice. 40 Moray Place has recently closed, on the retiral of Jimmy Beveridge, who's been running it for several years. The only practice now keeping the Spence name still operates from Canonbury under Tony Blee, Basil's son-in-law.

3.13 Kilsyth Academy, by Basil Spence. The initial, austerely classical design, planned in 1938 as an experimental school for the Scottish Council for Art and Industry, was built after the war with some additions – notably a new south-west block, with sweepingly curved rubble facade.

Now to his buildings themselves. The first thing that really attracted me to Basil Spence was his housing at Lamer Street, Dunbar (1950-3). (Fig. 3.15) Coincidentally, as I was doing my final year thesis in 1951-2, I had chosen a redevelopment of a fishing community in Arbroath as my subject, and Spence's housing at Dunbar was of course very pertinent. At the time, I remember I was impressed by the way in which he had managed to bring what was, for the time, Modern housing into an area of very strong traditional Scottish architectural character in Dunbar. His perspective, which was on the front page of one of the journals – the *Builder* or the *Architect and Building News* – showed the site covered with nets drying, which is something fishermen don't actually do! Interestingly, even today, there are actually creels under the houses, so it's still occupied by fishermen – and still looking very much like Spence had anticipated. There was generous use of the red sandstone of the area, coupled with a kind of deck access, because of the sloping site.

3.14 Spence's Duncanrig Secondary School, East Kilbride (1953-6): partner in charge, P.S. Ferguson. The school comprises a long spine of classroom blocks, with a symmetrical entrance/hall group, around a courtyard, located to its west. This view shows the main entrance hall, with mural by William Crosbie. The spiral stair leads to the assembly hall projection box behind.

My own first job in the office was working on Thurso High School (1958): there were three- and four-storey classroom blocks with precast cladding, and lower buildings with white roughcast walls, timber cladding, and rubble-faced gables; on the south-west side of the group was a sunny, terraced courtyard. (Fig. 3.16) Then I worked on the Physics Building for what is now Newcastle University, but was then King's College, Durham. That's a building of the same character as Edinburgh's Scottish Widows, except that it has a lecture theatre cantilevered from the gable, which became a trademark of Spence's.

I'd just like to briefly touch on some other buildings designed by the office at the same time as the Gorbals – in other words, in the late 1950s and early '60s. St. Andrew's Church, Clermiston, in Edinburgh, was done in 1957-9. In its harled simplicity, it's slightly Scandinavian – it bears a resemblance to Dunbar and the 'style' Basil worked in at the time. There are other examples of this. There's a little private house down at Longniddry, 'The Cottage' (1955), which has the same kind of slated roof, roughcast walls, stone gables and stone chimney. And slightly later (1962) there was the Scottish Widows building in St. Andrew Square, Edinburgh. Then, there was housing in Newhaven (1957), which, again, kept the local idiom of an external stair giving access to the top flats. This time, grey harled walls, and the stonework replaced by the use of ex-Edinburgh granite setts, which gives it a very hard appearance. It's a very successful group of houses; it appears to work very well. Another building that is contemporary with the Gorbals design is the Institute of Virology, Glasgow University, on Dumbarton Road (1961). I saw this recently, and it's in a very badly maintained state – the windows haven't even been re-painted. I think even Basil's windows need to be painted!

3.15 Perspective by Basil Spence of proposed Lamer Street fishermen's housing, Dunbar.

3.16 Thurso High School, built 1956-8. An informally grouped complex of blocks with harling and precast concrete offset with timber and rubble cladding.

Slightly later (1964-7) is Mortonhall Crematorium, Edinburgh. Internally, it still has a very Scandinavian character. (Fig. 3.17) The concept of the building was certainly Basil's. But the internal finish and detailing was much more Hardie Glover's affair. About this time, in the London offices, there was a vigorous programme of work in the universities of Southampton, Nottingham, Exeter, Sussex, Liverpool and many more. When I returned to Edinburgh after

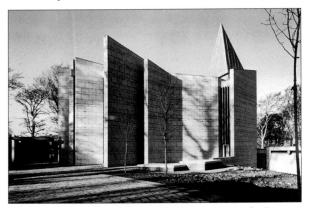

3.17 Elevation drawing of Mortonhall Crematorium (built 1964-7) by Basil Spence Glover & Ferguson.

my sojourn in London, I started work at Abbotsinch Airport Terminal Building (1963-6), and did the preliminary work on that job. It's interesting to compare it with Spence's work at Sussex University, which is at the same time: he uses the same barrel-vaulted form both at Abbotsinch and Sussex. And then, of course, there was Coventry Cathedral, which seemed to go on for ever. When I worked in London, only the crypt was finished, and the Queen had laid the foundation stone.

Well – now the Gorbals. We heard earlier about the problem which faced us in Glasgow's housing at that time: a vast sea of slums. We've seen some of that earlier today. Dick Mabon said earlier that anyone, today, who claims it would have been possible, in 1959, to renovate the tenements, is guilty of hindsight-wisdom. He's quite right – there was no way, politically or socially, that that could have happened. *Everyone* wanted to get rid of them! Now whether that was right or wrong, is for others to judge – but that was the problem actually facing us. The building that eventually rose in the Gorbals was a total contrast: a

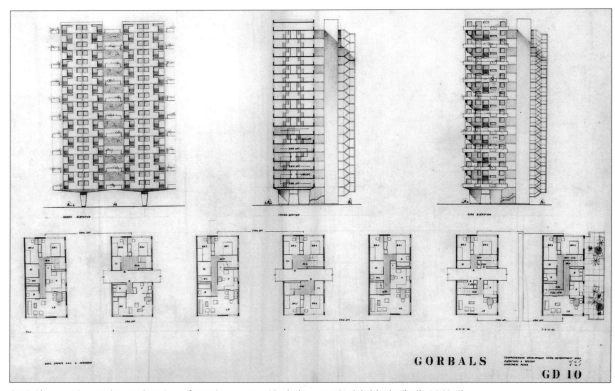

3.18 Plan, section and part-elevation of Hutchesontown/Gorbals Area 'C' slab blocks (built 1960-6).

vision. It was inspired essentially by Le Corbusier's Marseille block – a block which itself, although it went through a very bad time, and was disliked by very many people, has more recently become very popular again. All the flats are now sold, it's had a facelift and the playground at the top's working, so things have gone full cycle, it would appear.

We should also remember that, at the same time, there was another vision in the Gorbals: Hutchesontown Area 'A' – a little group of four-storey blocks done in-house by Glasgow Corporation architects, which, I think, from the day it was built, was a success. The layout of the first three housing areas at Hutchesontown was as follows: Area 'A', in the middle, between Ballater Street and Rutherglen Road; Area 'B' (Matthew), at the north, on an east-west axis; and the Spence blocks, Area 'C', at the south.

Basil's brief was to build three slab blocks on that particular orientation. It wasn't his decision to build them in the form of slab blocks. But he was responsible for the decision to build the scheme in two

3.19 1958 perspective of Spence's proposed Hutchesontown scheme.

blocks, where the brief suggested three. The brief showed three staggered blocks on that site – which, on that orientation, presented some problems, because his blocks were also required to accommodate five different dwelling types. He was required to produce 400 individual dwellings. Lifts, to be 'economic', had to stop at every second floor, which meant the dwellings had to be designed in maisonette form. The decision to build maisonettes – flats on two floors – led to 'crossover' planning, with all the living rooms on one side, on the south, and all the bedrooms on the

north side. The slabs were composed, in effect, of ten individual 'towers' each 40 feet square, linked by communal balconies, or 'garden slabs', entered from the kitchens. (Figs. 3.18, 3.19)

Can I just remind you of a quote from an issue of the *Architects' Journal*, at the time Glasgow Corporation approved the Spence blocks. There was a frontispiece with a photograph of the model, and it was entitled 'The Hanging Gardens of the Gorbals'. It said: 'For far too long the Gorbals district of Glasgow has been synonymous with all that is foul in tenement living. And, until now, Scottish rehousing schemes have not been particularly noted for making any striking contribution towards solving the problems of high-density living. This design for a 20-storey block of maisonettes in the centre of the Gorbals, is an interesting attempt by Basil Spence to develop further Le Corbusier's giant maisonette blocks. The large private balcony has been abandoned in favour of an even larger gallery garden measuring 9 ft. by 22ft . . . arranged in groups of four. Basil Spence sees these platforms as a perpetuation of the green . . .' – and, this is important – '. . . a space for some tubs of flowers, and to hang out the washing, to give the baby an airing, and to provide a garden fence to gossip over. The height between the garden floor and ceiling is 18 ft – the height of the maisonette. Whether this will provide sufficient sun and rain, and exclude sufficient wind, to provide the conditions in which these pursuits will flourish, will depend on the ingenuity and resourcefulness of the architect. We hope he succeeds in his enterprising attempt to civilise the tenement.'

Here's another quote, from a recent book, *Tenements and Towers*. Basil went to the Glasgow Corporation Housing Committee to present the scheme. He said: 'On Tuesdays, when all the washing's out, it'll be like a great ship in full sail!' And the architect who heard this, in committee, commented: 'A patter-merchant, if ever there was one!' I was at that committee too, and Basil did actually say that!

Basil's original idea was to support each of these ten 'towers' on one leg in the centre, and cantilever the tower out from that one leg. This, however – it was pointed out by the engineers – would need a floor slab about six feet thick, so it was dropped in favour of a shaped form. There was one building like that by Moser in Zurich, and other people were doing similar things at the same time. The blocks had an *in-situ* box-frame, with each storey height being one lift of concrete, which was an unusual thing in its day. The finish was board-marked concrete, which was the finish Basil was then trying to achieve. And the infills were precast concrete panels. The panels are each of storey height and full-span width: the windows were fixed at ground level. A lot of time and effort was spent on what we would call the 'technology' of that scheme – for instance, building sample panels to get the board-marking right. It was a pre-industrialised time of building. The actual building was done in rotation, so that we were finishing at the bottom while we were still building at the top.

Now, just a few words on how the scheme was organised, in financial terms. Because the only high blocks completed to that date had been Moss Heights, there was no history of high block costing – and so we had no cost targets as such. We were told that an average two-storey, semi-detached council house was building at about £2,800 or £2,900, and that each flat shouldn't cost much more than that. So it was a case of going up to the Department of Health for Scotland with something and saying, 'Is this all right?' And they'd say, 'No, it's not – it's too dear. Go back and try again.' The fact that there was no target made life very difficult. Because the fact of the matter was that the costs were far too low. We spent hours paring half an inch off the size of a room to try to get the floor area down, so it would conform to a multiplication factor that would give us less than about £3,000 a flat.

The way the scheme was eventually approved was interesting. When the tenders came in, they were of course over £3,000 per flat, and we had several crisis meetings to try and get the cost down. Finally, I remember, a very large meeting was called in the Scottish Office. When it opened, the Glasgow Corporation representative played his trump card right away, and said, 'We've just heard from Buckingham Palace this morning that the Queen's going to lay the foundation stone. To get it ready in time, we need to start the foundations tomorrow. We need approval.' And we got it! There were many ways of skinning a cat! (Fig. 3.20, 3.21)

Since it was completed, what has happened to the building? (Figs. 3.22, 3.23) The concrete has not

3.20 Hutchesontown 'C': laying of foundation stone, 1961. From left to right: Dame Jean Roberts (Lord Provost); Prince Philip; David Gibson (Housing Convener); Alice Cullen, MP; Archibald Jury (City Architect); George Campbell (Direct Labour Manager); George Robertson (Planning Convener); Queen Elizabeth.

3.21 Hutchesontown 'C': concrete pouring, main columns.

weathered at all well, and has deteriorated in many places. The reinforcing is exposed in several places. And I understand that the aggregate in the panels is also showing deterioration. The windows were made by D.F. Bennie in Glasgow: timber windows, single-glazed, very heavy – a sort of prototype of what we now call tilt-and-turn windows. They were made very difficult to open, so that children couldn't open them and fall out – but this meant that they were also very difficult for anyone else to open as well! The open ground area between the legs has been infilled with tenant meeting rooms. The stair towers were painted. And the building also now has a hat on it. It's what Isi Metzstein calls 'Year-Out Architecture'. Only Isi could come up with a phrase like that, but it's pretty true!

The question now remains: what do you do with a building group of this nature? Glasgow District Council have got an answer. They're taking in tenders right now to demolish it, perhaps next year. If, on the other hand, it isn't demolished, what can you do with it? It has not been popular. It has not been

maintained, for twenty years. There have been overflows running for about as many years as that, which have penetrated into the electrical works of the building, causing great problems to the tenants. One of the last few tenants, a very active lady, said to me, only last year, that she liked her house. Because – this could almost have been Basil himself speaking – because, she said, 'It's like a semi-detached house in the air!' She lived about five or six floors up, and she felt that because she'd only a neighbour on one side, and the other side was open, it gave her a feeling of privacy and being on her own, which she liked. What she did not like, however, was the fact that the building was falling apart. Windows were decaying, water was penetrating, electricity was continually failing, and so forth. What we did not realise when we were building things of this nature is that they involve a very high maintenance cost. And that cost was impossible for the local authority to deal with.

And so there we are. Do we keep it as an architectural monument? In which case, you might as well fill it with concrete and leave it as a huge piece of sculpture! Or do we try and upgrade it and use it for something else – or even use it for housing, but another kind of housing? Space standards in the actual rooms are not bad, but the stairs are very tight and very steep. The construction, although it had a lot of technical innovations, like using a lightweight concrete panel as an inner leaf – all the walls are cavities, actually – doesn't have high insulation standards. The wall could be brought up to a reasonable insulation

3.22 Hutchesontown 'C': interior view of kitchen in newly completed block (1966).

3.23 Hutchesontown 'C': 1966 view of newly completed blocks.

standard, but it's got floor slabs running through, which create cold-bridge problems, which would be expensive – not impossible, but expensive – to deal with. And there are other potential problems, other little things that not many people know about the blocks. There's seventeen miles of PVC skirting contained within them, for instance!

Do we keep it simply as a monument to Spence, as an architect? It has good architectural form, but it has not performed very well. But why did it not perform well? We have to ask that too. Was it bad maintenance? Was it bad management? Was it because there's no definable 'defensible space' in the design? Was it because there's no on-site management in the form of a concierge – or was the design and its financial resourcing inappropriate?

POSTSCRIPT
The Hutchesontown 'C' blocks were blown up on 12 September 1993.

SAM BUNTON AND THE CULT OF MASS HOUSING
MILES GLENDINNING

This paper sketches out the career of one of the most colourful figures in early postwar Scottish Modernism, Sam Bunton. Every phase of architecture needs its maverick individuals to provide a certain spice and variety, and Bunton's career shows that Modernism, for all its reputation of grey uniformity, was no exception. However, alongside a vast amount of often inconsequential rhetoric, Bunton was also responsible for several projects of some importance, especially in the 1940s period of innovation in building construction and replanning, but also including Glasgow's tallest 1960s tower blocks, at Red Road.

First, a little about Bunton's early upbringing in Glasgow. He was born in 1905 into a skilled working-class family in Govan: his father was an engineer, and later a senior trade-union official. His brother William recalls that he showed no early inclination to become an architect. Instead, with typical impetuosity, he entered the profession by chance, leaving Bellahouston Academy on the spur of the moment to become a draughtsman. Eventually, he went into practice as an RIBA licentiate. Early work in the 1930s was Art Deco, including a variety of bar-fronts. But before long, Bunton, Like Warnett Kennedy and many other young Glasgow architects in those years, began to be fascinated by Modern architecture, and to be drawn towards the focus of its concerns: mass housing.

All young architects at that time needed a world view on which to build their visions. Bunton was no exception – but, as a largely self-trained architect, the world-view he formed was very much at a tangent to the mainstream intellectual concepts of Modern Functionalism. Looking across the Atlantic, he found his own enduring ideal: not 'Community', but 'Big Business'. This might have seemed out of character for a stalwart of the Labour Party, even the Labour Party right wing. But what Bunton understood by 'Big Business' was very far from today's ideas of unfettered, speculative capitalism. (Fig. 3.24)

It is necessary for us, at this point, to recall the atmosphere of Glasgow in the 1930s. At that time, not only were ordinary citizens fascinated by the cinema-borne imagery of America, but the new Labour municipal regime, led by Patrick Dollan, had begun to look to New Deal corporatism as a guiding philosophy, and to Mayor La Guardia's New York as a model of modern big-city government. This tendency reached its climax with the visit, or rather pilgrimage, to New York in 1939 by Dollan and the City leadership, a visit celebrated in a special Corporation book: *Glasgow and*

3.24 Sam Bunton (centre) seen in the late 1950s with a party of American golfers on an exchange visit (sponsored by him).

New York: A Tale of Two Cities. For the Labour Party at municipal level, the focus of their activity and the bedrock of their power was housing – plentiful, low-rent housing, built if possible by direct municipal labour. Naturally, therefore, Bunton's own breathless conception of 'Big Business' – a Clydeside partnership between interventionist municipal and central Government, organised working class (through the Labour Party and the unions), forward-looking building contractors, and scientifically-minded architects – was focused on municipal housing.

By nature an almost obsessively gregarious person, Bunton began to build up an extensive circle of contacts. In a society increasingly orientating itself around public enterprise, this meant contacts within municipal and central government. Even before the war, these began to bring him an increasing amount of work. He became involved in that major Government housing-reform initative of the late '30s, the founding of the SSHA, and under SSHA auspices began to discover a fascination for experimental concrete building construction. We should remind ourselves of the interwar importance of concrete construction in Scotland. Its use had been advocated by an official committee in 1920, following the sharp rise in stone-building costs: the use of brick as a substitute in the new State housing programme had been discouraged especially by a shortage of bricklayers. Many thousands of concrete dwellings had been built, especially in the North and the islands, and by Glasgow Corporation, where ingenious methods had been developed by the Director of Housing, Peter Fyfe.

3.25 Hoggan Crescent, Dunfermline: late 1930s 2-storey concrete blocks of flats designed by Bunton.

At the end of the 1930s, working at first in the slightly different tradition of in-situ concrete building, Bunton helped the SSHA develop the Dutch-inspired technique of 'no-fines' building (a rather opaque term, meaning coarse aggregate), and 'crosswall' construction, where the loadbearing function is performed only by transverse walls; and he designed major SSHA developments (e.g. at Kilsyth and Kilmarnock) – all still in a rather humdrum Art Deco style, and all still on the prevailing garden-suburb pattern. (Fig. 3.25)

But it was World War II itself that provided Bunton with his vital 'break'. What he relished, above all, was a sudden opportunity which could be exploited with dashing, unconventional initiatives. The war and its immediate aftermath handed him three decisive opportunities in succession. The first literally came out of the skies, on the 13th and 14th of March 1941, when the German air force, in its only major raids on Scotland, rained bombs down on Clydebank. The bombardment left the vicinity in complete chaos. On the first night, Bunton got in touch with Scottish Office contacts and obtained authorisation to go in as a kind of temporary Government representative for clearance and repair work. Working with only a few personal helpers, notably Hal Dykes, he spent the following days and weeks helping the Town Council organise the clear-up operation – arranging trades, transport, demolition work, rehousing of the homeless. As a result of his Clydebank works, not only did he get the direct ear of Government for the future, as someone who could cut through red tape and get things done, but he also secured an appointment from Clydebank Town Council as a consultant architect-planner for reconstruction. As we saw earlier in this book, this provided him with a stable focus for plan-making and experimental schemes.

His second opportunity came in 1944, with the Government's emergency programme for one- and two- storey prefabricated dwellings. In Bunton, already fascinated by experimental building, this sparked off an almost manic period of innovation. Already, in 1939, he and Ove Arup had produced designs for crosswall concrete air-raid shelters suitable for later conversion to housing. Now, the emphasis was shifting to prefabricated techniques suitable for converted munitions factories. So, marshalling his Government, professional and business contacts – above all the contractor John Lawrence, chairman of Rangers F C, and the engineer W. A. Fairhurst of the partnership F.A. Macdonald – he responded with a torrent of constructional projects. For instance, he designed a prefabricated house for Blackburn Ltd, who built 5000 throughout Scotland; he devised, with Lawrence, a way of using gypsum panels as internal walling ('Bellrock' panels); he helped design a thin-leaf concrete blockwork constructional method, the Wilson block, which could be used by major firms such as Lawrence or Stuart in various contexts; and he was the architectural driving force behind the Scottish Housing Group, a committee established in 1946 under Lawrence's chairmanship to coordinate prefabricated systems, train workmen and act as a negotiating body with the Department of Health. DHS recognised Bunton's status – in effect, the heir of Mactaggart and Fyfe as a kind of national impresario

of experimental building – by giving him much help throughout the 1940s and '50s: for instance, in model-making and administrative services. (Fig. 3.26)

During the 1950s, however, Bunton became increasingly marginalised within the world of architecture, as debate moved away from 'mass production' towards more complex ideas. We traced in Part One the growing clash between the planning 'overspill' and the housing-output 'do it all in Glasgow' factions. Increasingly the Clydeside Labourite housing-reformist camp, previously more or less united in support of the Garden Suburb ideal, became polarised between the two recipes. At first, Bunton sided with the planners, and even served on the management board of East Kilbride New Town. Gradually, however, he became drawn away into the opposite camp: perhaps the concept of defending the 'second city of the Empire' was ultimately irresistible to one so strongly linked to the Clydeside Protestant business tradition.

Accordingly, the focus of Bunton's advocacy shifted from cottage-scale buildings to high blocks – to show that it was possible to clear the slums without overspill. In his pragmatic work with various building contractors, he flowed with the current of massed construction of 4-storey tenement blocks in new-build peripheral schemes such as Glasgow's Drumchapel or Clydebank's Faifley, devising ways of achieving these in economical crosswall-construction blockwork. Many were organised by his longstanding associate Kenneth Fraser. Alongside these were fantastic, even bizarre schemes for high-density redevelopment of inner-city slums, which were purely of a propagandising character, arguing with typical hyperbole the case for a 'Glasgow-only' solution. These included a 1949 proposal for redeveloping tenement areas by building multi-storey blocks on top of the tenements, decanting their occupants upwards, then demolishing and infilling below; or a proposal of 1958, put forward along with Lawrence, for squat polygonal and asterisk-plan towers in line with current New York practice, which could accommodate everyone displaced by staged redevelopments.

UNI-SCHOOL CONSTRUCTION

Architects, Engineers, Surveyors and Contractors forming a team, have, by advanced planning and concentration on detail, evolved a simple system of precast and pre-stressed concrete with a high degree of prefabrication in which steel or concrete frames have been completely eliminated and in which the minimum use of reinforcement is an advantage.

The system incorporates concrete cavity block exterior walling to make a welcome alternative to roughcast exteriors, and the fact that the external cavity walling has invariably a double cavity means that a high degree of thermal insulation is produced. The exterior walls are load-bearing, enabling partitions to be freely placed without restriction, while the use of pre-stressed planks with concrete topping provides rapidly formed floors having efficient insulation.

This System Ensures its Six Primary Objectives

(1) To complete a primary school in 12 to 15 months or a secondary school in 18 to 20 months, as against two or more years generally taken to erect traditional school buildings.

(2) To produce a system whose costs are lower than those of traditional building by economies in structural materials, notably the elimination of steel or concrete framing.

(3) To achieve a much higher standard of material, workmanship and finish, both externally and internally, by re-investing the monetary economies accruing from the above.

3.26 Introductory text from 1958 brochure written by Bunton to promote a prefabricated 'system' for school construction, which he had developed in collaboration with the contractor Lawrence.

Although these projects can now of course be viewed, in hindsight, as outrageously maverick gestures –

compared to the mainstream progressivism of Matthew and others – such was the tension over the Glasgow question that they were treated at the time as serious threats by the 'opposition'. The 1958 proposal, for instance, was received with alarm by DHS planners: their Under-Secretary, T.H. Haddow, demanded that his staff and Glasgow Corporation planners get together and 'puncture the Bunton thesis, which is liable to spoil the atmosphere for the whole overspill operation'. A concerted counter-attack was mounted by both groups, using density calculations which asserted the 'diminishing returns' of higher densities. Haddow, on receiving these figures, triumphantly minuted James McGuinness, Planning Assistant Secretary, 'Anti-Buntonia, I think!' – and McGuinness, in his turn, congratulated Grieve: 'The Glasgow planners seem to have made good use of their recent contacts with you!' He pronounced Bunton's scheme 'practically dead'. But many others were to follow it.

From the mid 1950s onwards, we can conclude that Bunton's main impact was as a herald of the massed building of multi-storey flats, driven by local-political rather than architectural pressures. As early as 1949-51, he had drawn up plans to rebuild the bombed area of Clydebank, or part of Glasgow Green, using tall 'point blocks' modelled on Swedish examples; the Clydebank proposal was eventually carried out in the 60s, partly along the lines of his proposal, by the SSHA. (Fig. 3.27) In 1954 he went further: he and Lawrence set up a company, with the brand-name 'Multicon', to build crosswall multi-storey flats using Wilson blockwork. The prototype 'Multicon' scheme, naturally, was built at Clydebank – the first high block in these islands with a load-bearing precast concrete structure. Bunton still involved himself as consultant in other projects – for instance (appropriately for an Ibrox stalwart) in introducing multi-storey flats to Northern Ireland, in 1959, using Wilson blocks. But the main agenda was to apply all this to Glasgow. And it was only with Glasgow Corporation Housing Committee's wholesale switch to high flats in 1960, at the instigation of David Gibson, that this suddenly became possible.

Bunton's first Multicon multi-storey proposal for Glasgow was a scheme for geometrical Y-shaped

blocks, and cruciform four-storey blocks. The prototype contract for these, at Blairdardie South, was built from 1960. This project did not work out at all satisfactorily. There were persistent delays, which stemmed essentially from demarcation disputes with the architects of both Glasgow Corporation and the Government. While Bunton was not 'architectural' enough to be accepted by the architects, he was not 'commercial' enough to build with the ruthless efficiency of the package-deal contractors.

The climax, and undoing, of his career was an audacious attempt to outdo the multi-storey 'package-dealers' at their own game: the Red Road project (built 1962-9). The idea behind Red Road came from Glasgow Corporation's direct labour force, the Housing and Works Department. This department was a powerful element in municipal Labour Party patronage, and, as its name implied, housebuilding was its main activity. It had developed a very forceful tradition of constructional innovation, but also a fatal weakness for abortive and half-baked projects, beginning with its failed precasting factory venture of 1944-6. By 1960, the direct labour manager, George Campbell, was becoming seriously worried by the growing prominence of the multi-storey package-deal blocks of Wimpey and Crudens across the city. He decided to try to organise a Clydeside consortium-based 'counter-package-deal' for standard tower blocks, circumventing the City Architect by using Bunton as designer. The towers would be Lawrence Multicon, using direct labour bricklayers to lay the Wilson precast blocks. A prototype scheme of 20-storey blocks was authorised on a typical gap site – Red Road, Balornock. (Fig. 3.28)

3.27 1951-2 proposal by Bunton for redevelopment of Glasgow Green using point blocks.

Corporation of Glasgow - Housing and Works Department

Report

to

SUB-COMMITTEE ON SITES AND BUILDINGS

16TH SEPTEMBER, 1960

Multi-Storey Flats

Proposed Employment of Consultant Architects

The Manager wishes to inform the Committee that for some time he has been giving consideration to the possibility of his Department constructing multi-storey flats on the same "package" arrangements as those that applied to Messrs. George Wimpey and Company Limited and John Lawrence and Company (Glasgow) Limited.

The Committee will appreciate that the Manager considers that the results shown by Messrs. Wimpey at Royston Road are literally fantastic and in his view deserve the highest commendation. It will be appreciated that Messrs. Wimpey's construction staff, in conjunction with certain architects, produced the designs having in mind a type of construction that would readily lend itself to speedy erection. He, therefore, proposes that these facilities should be made available to his Department; it is, of course, recognised that the City Architect and Planning Officer with his several commitments and lack of staff could not undertake such an assignment.

The Manager, therefore, seeks the authority of the Committee to have Sam Bunton and Partners, Chartered Architects, 7 Somerset Place, Glasgow and Mr. Thomas S. Cordiner, Chartered Architect, 261 West George Street, Glasgow, appointed for the purpose enunciated.

If the Committee agree to this procedure, standard types of multi-storey flats will be on paper at an early date and these designs will be submitted to the Committee for their approval before any further action or heavy costs are incurred.

The approval of the Committee to this suggestion is requested.

SUB-COMMITTEE ON SITES AND BUILDINGS – 1 Report to be submitted with plans

16TH SEPTEMBER, 1960 – 2 CAPO not to be consulted till plans produced

But then matters started developing a lot further, and a lot faster, than anyone originally envisaged. In the heady atmosphere of David Gibson's 'housing crusade', then gathering pace in the City in 1961-2, the Corporation, driven by passionate public demand for maximum housing output, had in effect got into a race with itself. So unimportant was private housebuilding, and so overwhelming was municipal power, that the key tensions and rivalries were internal ones: Housing versus Planning Committee, Architects Department versus Housing and Works department, and so on – all competing with their different recipes of getting things done, of achieving spectacular victories in the 'battle against the slums'. In 1962, the Housing and Works Department decided, largely on the spur of the moment, not to build the 20-storey Multicon blocks at all. What was now to be built at Red Road was a massive cluster of tower and slab blocks of 27-31 storeys – at the time, an unprecedented height for social housing in Europe – and these would not use concrete construction at all, but, rather, steel framing. These seven buildings would contain over 1,300 dwellings. The Housing and Works Department would now act as a kind of management contractor, and also do some of the fitting out, but now there would be huge sub-contracts for steelwork, to be divided between two local firms, Fleming and Redpath Brown. External and internal walling would go to local firms – internal to Lawrence (Bellrock), and external to Weir (asbestos sheeting on timber framing).

So what was the reason for this dramatic intensification of the Red Road project, which converted it from a relatively modest development of an existing system into an leap into the unknown? Various explanations were offered at the time, and subsequently: that part of the site was discovered to be unusable; that the City Architect demanded a higher density development; and that there was pressure from the local steel industry. The best answer may be that, in a time of flux and confusion, but also of high idealism, all of them were probably partly true.

Bunton was now riding on the crest of a wave. DHS chief planner Robert Grieve recalled his increasingly bombastic expansiveness: 'When you went to see him in his office, it was as though you were going to see

Mussolini – seated behind a big desk – the atmosphere was messianic! He'd say, "Bob, it's obvious that fate has marked me out for this! Doors just keep opening in front of me, without my needing to push!" Bunton was intoxicated by the American skyscraper-like connotations of the Red Road project. His son Len recalls: 'I remember my father coming home one evening and announcing over dinner that he'd been appointed to the biggest public-housing contract in Europe. Then, one night, he brought home a drawing board, and sat down with a big broad T-square designing the tower blocks. And he went into the office that Saturday, and threw that design down on someone's desk, and said: "Draw that up!" Then, the same way, came the point blocks and then the slab blocks'. (Fig. 3.29) In 1963 Bunton and Lawrence went further, in an unrealised proposal to develop these plan types up to a height of 45 storeys.

Concerning the severe design that was actually built, Bunton asserted: 'Housing today isn't domestic architecture – it's public building. You mustn't expect airs and graces, and things like different-sized windows and ornamental features'. This explanation recalled, in a somewhat cruder fashion, the prewar preoccupation of the Glasgow Beaux-Arts tradition with the ennobling of the strictly 'practical' and rational. We should also note in passing the similarity, in both height and construc-

3.29 Model of Red Road scheme (1962-9), prepared by Sam Bunton, 1962.

(opposite) 3.28 Minute of 16 September 1960 from George Campbell (Manager of Glasgow Corporation's direct labour department) to the Housing Committee, suggesting the idea of a direct labour multi-storey 'package deal'.

tion (steel-frame with asbestos-clad outer sheeting), between the Red Road blocks and the Tower of Empire at T S Tait's 1938 Exhibition. Tait had defined the aesthetic consequences of such construction in the following terms: 'With asbestos sheets eveything must be kept very simple, relying only on the shape and masses of the building to produce the effect desired'.

Soon, however, things began to unravel at Red Road: delays, overspending and general confusion mounted. One factor in this, without doubt, was the casual grandiloquence of Bunton's conception, throwing together violently experimental constructional methods on such a scale, on a project that was supposed to be not a giant one-off, but a prototype for a standardised series. And so did the fact that (in stark contrast to the Tait/Beaux-Arts tradition) he was not interested in the prosaic detail of design and building, and thus was temperamentally unsuited to the unglamorous task of monitoring a contract of this complexity.

But more important was the role of the Housing and Works Department, which proved to be organisationally incapable of efficient management contracting. The embattled job architect, Bunton's nephew Sam Bunton Junior, summed up the problem: 'The one thing you need on every big building project is a main contractor – and at Red Road, there just didn't seem to be one!' In accordance with standard direct labour practice – endorsed here by David Gibson, to speed up progress – there had been no prior scheduling of trades; the idea was simply to start building, and estimate as you went, but without any checking of actual expenditure by quantity surveyors: in other words, a blank cheque approach. So it was only after seven years, in 1969, that it began to emerge that there had been a 60% excess in spending over the 1962 estimate. There was suspicion in some quarters that this sum was inflated by a policy of using the scheme as a 'scapegoat' to conceal wider inefficiencies: it was claimed that materials were sometimes delivered and registered at Red Road, then driven straight on to other sites.

And if the building of the blocks was controversial, so too was their letting, once completed. Historians of

Modern architecture are only too aware of the danger of blanket hindsight-condemnation of one 'world-view' by its successors – of the multi-storey 'housing crusaders' by the conservationists, for instance. But that does not prevent us from carefully trying to identify individual decisions where, even in the short term, a different balance of outcomes might have been arrived at. One such example seems to have been Gibson's decision, against the advice of DHS housing administrators, that the first two blocks to be built at Red Road, 31-storey blocks with only two lifts, should contain only 4-apartment flats – thus ensuring a very high child population. The apparent result was a reputation for delinquency which stigmatised the scheme even before it was complete, and lasted right through to the '80s. (Fig. 3.30) But this takes us away from the subject of this paper – the provision of buildings – into the vastly complicated area of their later use and experience. However, the considerable popularity of Red Road today, under its present concierge scheme of management, suggests that even seemingly intractable problems of housing use may be soluble through careful management policies.

What is more relevant here is that the troubles of Red Road not only chastened the Housing and Works Department, whose standard package-deal block eventually emerged in the much more modest form of the 8-storey 'Block 84', but also proved the undoing of Bunton himself. He thrived best in a climate of bubbling bonhomie, and the cloud of acrimony which now settled over Red Road – with all the various contractual and professional factions at odds – was deeply demoralising to him. More prosaically, he had great difficulty in getting his fees paid by the Corporation, and his practice went steeply downhill. In the end, he went into semi-retirement in the North-East, where he eventually died in the late 1970s.

The Red Road saga seems to indicate that Bunton's main contribution to Modern architecture – in direct contradiction to his own rhetoric of ruthless business efficiency and machine-like repetition – was through a wilfully individualistic process of constructional experimentation, and through the proselytising of

(opposite) 3.30 View of one of the two Red Road slab blocks in 1989, prior to recent upgrading work, including construction of concierge stations.

those innovations, the useful alongside the ineffective. Bunton was not at home in the world of conceptual socio-architectural debate among first-rank Scottish Modern designers such as Richards, Metzstein and MacMillan. But his quirkish and impetuous ideas added colour to an area of building output often misleadingly portrayed, then and now, as merely banal and repetitive.

THE DYSART REDEVELOPMENT: REBUILDING IN 'CONTEXT'
SIR ANTHONY WHEELER, IN CONVERSATION WITH CHARLES McKEAN

Charles McKean: In this paper, we're going to hear about something very different from the big multi-storey developments of Glasgow. Sir Anthony Wheeler was trained at Glasgow School of Art in the years immediately before World War II, when the Beaux-Arts influence was giving way to Modernism. What he is going to describe to us now, however, is an – up to now – less well-known aspect of the Modern Movement in Scotland: the attempt to reconcile modern redevelopment with a relatively small scale, and strong elements of conservation. This was an ideal which was perhaps inherited ultimately from Geddes, and was certainly influenced by Camillo Sitte's ideas of enclosed space; and it was developed by a number of architectural practices in regeneration schemes in various small burghs. Today, we'll be hearing about one of the most important of these, carried out by Wheeler & Sproson, and in particular by Sir Anthony as senior partner and chief designer: the Dysart redevelopment scheme, implemented over a period of more than a decade, from 1958 onwards.

Sir Anthony Wheeler: You can imagine how daunting a process it is for an architect to go back and recall a

3.31 The Bowery, Leslie: photograph taken by Anthony Wheeler *c.*1956, following completion.

scheme of over thirty years ago! I'll start with a quotation, from the 16th-century Venetian architect, Jacopo Sansovino. He once described a city as 'a place which should be built for the convenience of those who live in it, and for the great surprise of strangers'. In other words, when you go to visit a place, it should be 'different'. This is what I aspired to do at Dysart.

In the 16th and 17th centuries, Dysart was a very lively trading port, exporting coal and textiles. But then things changed, and now there's no industry, it's just residential – and the burgh was absorbed by Kirkcaldy in the 1930s. What we were brought in to do was a scheme of local-authority, social housing, in three or four phases. Phase I was nearest the sea, with Phase 2 – the section we'll be focusing on today, with 92 dwellings of varying sizes – behind it.

After leaving Glenrothes Development Corporation and commencing private practice in 1952, I'd done one or two jobs in Fife, where I'd tried to work out how to deal with dense redevelopment sites in decaying small burghs. The first of these was the Bowery development in Leslie, built in 1953-6, where I did 50 dwellings in cottages and three-storey flats, harled with pantiled roofs and some rubble facing, and also prepared a development plan for the burgh. (Figs. 3.31, 3.32) That scheme won a Saltire award. At Dysart, we at Wheeler & Sproson were given just Phase I to do at first, without an overall plan: that part of the area was ruinous and beyond hope of rehabilitation.

The brief from Kirkcaldy Town Council was to build, on that site, a certain number of two, three and four apartment houses – a pretty loose type of brief, which I resolved with buildings ranging in height from 2 to 5 storeys. The dwellings had to conform to general standards laid down by the Department of Health for

3.32 The Bowery, Leslie: photograph of pedestrian way and pends taken by Wheeler c.1956 to illustrate his Sittesque spatial aim of enclosure and interrupted vistas.

Scotland – although I managed to be extravagant on occasions!

Within the redevelopment area, I identified what I called 'spheres of influence' of historic buildings. For instance, there was a 16th-century house called 'The

3.33 Dysart Redevelopment Phase II: photograph c.1966 of 'The Towers' and adjacent infill. The architects' caption records the aim, in sharp contrast to post-1970 conservationism, of 'grouping together...historic and modern buildings to create a unified new environment'.

Towers' at the north end of the site: I managed to persuade the Town Council not to knock it down. (Fig. 3.33) And – most important of all – there was the Tolbooth. I did try to respect the buildings in these spheres of influence – to preserve the architectural scale – but not to copy them. After all, it was a *Modern* development. But the councillors' attitude tended to be rather different. You'd get councillors who'd spent their youth there, had got sick of it, and would say: 'Let's get rid of all this rubbish, and get on with the Brave New World!' One had to take those kinds of opinions into account, too. I'll come back to the old buildings in a minute.

I'll first deal briefly with Phase I, including the foreshore. That was built in 1958-63. Here we retained the great stone bastion. I decided I wanted a disruptive shape on the skyline. The scheme was designed to give a dramatic sequence, climbing up from the shore into the main group. I used crosswall maisonette blocks, and pantiled roofs: our zigzag blocks – maisonettes with balcony and large sitting room – gave privacy, sun, and a view. We also used them elsewhere: for instance, at Burntisland. (Fig. 3.34)

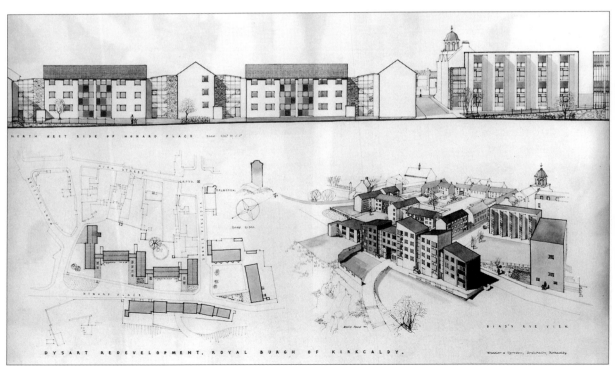

3.34 Dysart Redevelopment (1958-71): perspective of Phase I, c.1958.

At Phase 2 (built 1963-5, by contractors R. Pert & Sons), we moved into the area behind, an inward-looking district of convoluted alleys and broken-down old walls. We opened out this area to obtain sun penetration – one of the major objectives of Modern replanning – while, to get a safe pedestrian setting for children, we cut off a major street, Relief Street. Here we had the idea of building little 4-storey point blocks, each containing two houses, one on top of the other. Around would all be community space, including paving and trees – even today, the place is not yet cluttered with cars. As a foil to these point blocks on the south-west side of the site, a large, strongly-modelled five-storey slab block was built at the north-east. The blocks were built of harled brick with small accents of timber cladding. There were no drying greens – Kirkcaldy had a high standard of housing management, and they provided launderettes, each to be shared by five or ten tenants. The scheme won a Saltire award in 1966. (fig. 3.35) By the time we got to the next phase, Phase 3, we went down to only one of these tower blocks, and we now tried to include more traditional features: deep reds and other colours, roof finials, and pantiled roofs.

Within all these constraints, as I've said, our layout had a particular concern to identify and, where possible, safeguard buildings of architectural interest – and those of historical interest too. For instance, we included a house owned by the first man to walk from one end of Australia to the other! The medieval tower, St Serf's, dominates some views of the site, while the Tolbooth is the focal point on the cross-street. Another building, called The Anchorage, seemed beyond

reasonable recovery. But the National Trust for Scotland, and Hew Lorimer, were very determined to save it. Another significant old building was 'The Towers': although this was a total ruin, we managed to restore it. And adjoining it, we built a two-storey link building, with timber cladding, joining it to one of our 3-storey blocks: I always believe these sorts of links should be uncompromisingly Modern.

Charles McKean: I think there are two things that are perhaps worth pointing out, at this stage in the discussion. First, that the project you've described to us, with characteristic modesty, was in fact not only a distinguished redevelopment design in itself, but also a major link in a chain of important interventions by Wheeler & Sproson in various urban contexts – and by no means all in 'heritage' burghs. For instance, in West Lothian, there was the Old Town scheme in Broxburn, of 1967-70; and in Blackburn, your town centre development of 1968 gave a unifying urban character to a place where it was lacking before. In all of these cases, we see a very confident, cubic Modern style. The second thing is that this Wheeler & Sproson style couldn't be mistaken for those of other architects' burgh redevelopments. What's striking about all the key schemes in old towns, at around this time, is that they're all very different from one another. There's Spence's and Hurd's schemes in the Canongate, Kininmonth's in Linlithgow, and Lindsay's in Inveraray. None of these falls exactly into the same category as yours at Dysart: a contemporary, open Modern layout which is nevertheless sensitive to an ancient setting, and provides for conservation of key old buildings. (Figs. 3.36, 3.37) It's also interesting to

3.35 Dysart Redevelopment Phase II: hessian-covered display board prepared c.1965.

observe the change over time within this scheme: between the cubistic forms of Phase 2, and the chamfered corners and allusions to Scots Renaissance domestic architecture in Phase 3. What were the things which inspired your particular solution here at Dysart?

Sir Anthony Wheeler: One source for our little tower blocks in Phase 2 is the fact that I used to go to San Gimignano quite a bit, and saw how families lived in these slender towers: they command space which could be defended. Instead of having the space chopped up into little gardens, you have these tall towers. But I was also influenced quite a bit by Continental Modernism: people like Oud and Dudok were a great inspiration at the time. Then there was the inspiration of the 17th-century vernacular Scottish architecture itself, in Phase 2 as much as in Phase 3. You can see it, for instance, in the window-spacing: there's a kind of randomness about it, which is characteristic of Scots vernacular architecture – but which also suited Modern architecture, as the openings can be placed to suit the interiors. Or there was the eaves treatment. In the 17th century, they never put a big projection on the eaves, whereas 19th-century Baronial did. If I'd put projecting eaves on these houses at Dysart, it wouldn't have been right – it wouldn't have tied in with the 17th-century buildings. Hugh Wilson was one of the Saltire Society assessors at the time: he greatly approved of 'clipped eaves and gables', as evidenced in Cumbernauld housing. Cumbernauld, like the other New Towns, was, in effect, a great laboratory for housing design and layout design. Many years ago, I can remember an architectural expedition to the Middle East. In a restaurant in Tel Aviv, some architects, including Cyril Mardall, Alex Gordon and myself were discussing housing with some Israeli architects – one of whom could sketch the essence of Cumbernauld layouts on the white tablecloth! I doubt if that could happen today, when every aspect of housing is geared exclusively to profit.

McKean: Phase 2 certainly succeeds in being both small-scale and monumental.

3.36 1965 photograph of 'The Gyles', Pittenweem (1962-4) – one of Wheeler & Sproson's restoration projects for the National Trust for Scotland's 'Little Houses' scheme.

3.37 Backcauseway redevelopment, Culross (1968-70): view when newly complete, showing proximity to Bishop Leighton's Study. A small infill scheme for the SSHA and Culross Town Council in a sensitive site.

Wheeler: In our overall planning, we could have done a more piecemeal scheme, with lots of gaps, but I wanted to concentrate the drama in one large 'hole'. In the details, on the other hand, you depend crucially on your individual decisions as a designer.   For instance, the balconies: that gave a very strong, pure pattern to the elevation. Or the hard landscaping. We felt that it would have to be very simple, that over-use of colours would be very dangerous, and that it would generally be better to stick to grey concrete and texture, setts and so forth. Whereas in Phase 3, which is slightly more romantic and colourful, the whole thing is pretty intricate – for example, the corners are chopped off, like a tower-house. By then, I felt it was right to do that. It was a slightly more romanticised vision. Don't forget, there are cycles of attitude. Today we have an applique architecture, with wee bits and pieces stuck on.   But they don't have to be there! Nowadays, although hard landscaping is treated seriously, it can be over designed; for example, the surface quality of the splendid pedestrian High Street in the city of Perth has suffered from an over-abundance of colours and geometric shapes.

McKean: Could you tell us a little more about the patronage aspects of the project – the influence of local officials, and so forth?

Wheeler: The scheme was a very complex one, and gave us many sleepless nights – dealing with officials who often didn't see things our way! I doubt if the councillors had a real vision of what the new buildings should look like. I had to try and explain to them, that here was something they'd never dreamed they could have.   I went to great lengths, making models and explaining about them, to convince the councillors they were getting something quite unique and new. There were no planning restrictions of the sort we'd get now – because these councillors controlled the planning aspect of the scheme, too! But what they were really concerned with was numbers of dwellings – you had to get the numbers. Whereas the New Towns were different. We did a big scheme at Cumbernauld, and there we got all the support we needed, from the Chairman, Dame Jean Roberts, and from the Development Corporation staff. They were top quality people, and Dame Jean was very enthusi-

astic – she managed to push it through!

McKean: What about Dysart today – how does it seem to you now?

Wheeler: Having revisited it recently, I found that most aspects of the scheme, including the hard landscaping, were more or less still intact. We always believed that the architecture should be strong enough to allow people to do their own thing within it – getting flowerpots, putting on aluminium paint. But if the scheme were totally reconstructed – say, if it were re-roofed – that would kill it dead!

THE CENSORSHIP OF NEGLECT: MORRIS & STEEDMAN'S PRIVATE HOUSES
DAVID PAGE

In our 'revisit' of the past in these papers, we're trying to begin reaching some kind of accommodation with Modern architecture in Scotland. I want to question whether we have to be cynical about such a 'revisit' – whether we must feel obliged to put it into the category of a chore, an unwanted visit to a cantankerous elderly relative. Is the motive for the visit merely that of dry, historical necessity – that somebody's going to have to do it sometime in the future, so we might as well do it first? Or could it be another sort of 'visit', a visit through which we can hope to learn, to establish a new understanding which can actually help shape what we do now? The first purpose of my paper is to pose this question – why we should bother 'revisiting' at all – and I do so because I am a 'real visitor', coming to the period from outside.

I wasn't there, building, in those first three postwar decades – although I did work for some architects who were. I started my education in the 1970s: that was the time when tenemental rehab was being adumbrated. During my very first summer working in an architectural office, a very competent architect said to me, 'There's no hope in architecture! Can I suggest you emulate my son-in-law, who's become a cook, working in France – there's a tremendous future in food preparation!' That was the depressing prospect which faced me. We've had painted for us in previous papers a picture of tremendous idealism in building. But I entered that picture when the idealism had somehow collapsed.

In my first year at architectural school, I have to confess, to my eternal regret, that I missed the first-year bus to Cardross Seminary (I was building a model of the Weissenhof Siedlung at the time). I caught the one to the Bernat Klein Studio and the Pathfoot Building at Stirling University, and I do remember John Richards summarising for us the concept of the Commonwealth Pool. Five years on from then in my studies, there were no more tours to Scottish buildings in our school; five years on, you didn't even consider going to Scottish buildings. Our 'sights' were abroad. Tenemental repair had firmly set in – absolutely rightly so, of course. On reflection, I feel I was educated in the negative equivalent of the Enlightenment: 'The Disenchantment'!

When they stop talking positively, in the architectural schools, about your own national culture, then the rot has truly set in. The sum total of what I know about the first three postwar decades of our architecture is about the equivalent of a Wallace Arnold tour of Scotland. So in some ways you might wonder what I'm doing here today, giving this paper! Perhaps it's because somewhere on that 'Scotland in Three Days' tour – that is, after doing Edinburgh without touching the setts, passing Loch Ness with about five sightings, and then asking what town we were passing through at about 3 o'clock in the morning, only to be told, 'Ssshh! You'll wake everybody! It's Glasgow!' – somewhere, at that stage, curiosity got me off the bus.

Because in my personal history-book, there's a huge hole. From Adam to the First World War becomes ever clearer. McKean's pioneering documentation has illuminated the '20s and '30s. But what follows that? Three decades of stigmatised Black Hole – followed by the Disenchantment of the '70s, and the resulting attempt at repair, renewal, and reconsideration of the city, lasting to the present. So I suppose those three decades, for me, have become a kind of Forbidden City: critically blighted and simplistically censored, in reaction against the stereotypes of the flat roof and the high flat. Our modern architectural history, in short, is censored by neglect.

How can our revisit help remedy this situation? Eliel Saarinen, the great Finnish turn-of-century architect, gives a few clues in the introduction to his book, *Search for Form*. I'm going to quote at some length from it, so I hope you'll bear with me. In it, he says: 'In the search for form, when sincere and honest, the action is twofold: one, to create the form; and, secondly, to diagnose the created form. Accordingly, as the artist proceeds with his creation, there simultaneously develops a rationalising yet unwritten analysis of the work, characteristic of the individual and therefore independent of the thoughts of others. Nevertheless, the nearer the thoughts of the individuals approach indispensable fundamentals, the closer will they engage the thoughts of others engaged in the same search'.

Saarinen's words seem to point to a pressing reason as to why we should 'revisit'. If that unwritten rationalisation of the artist shapes all form, then perhaps an attempt to understand the whole development of form in Scottish architecture, from the pre-Adam period up to now, will enable us, today, to grasp what those indispensable fundamentals are. But then comes the argument which seeks to exempt the three unfashionable decades of Modern architecture from this perspective, just as Lorimer and Anderson exempted the then unfashionable neoclassical and Baronial phases from their definition of the 'national tradition' in architecture. We, today, may all like Adam rooms and Thomson masses, we may be fascinated by Mackintosh space, but – surely not flat roofs and multi-storey blocks?

Saarinen, as a guide, offers further help here. He observed: 'It happened quite often that a piece of art, which I had valued very highly, quickly lost its enchantment. Whereas another piece of art which I had disfavoured, perhaps even denounced, became later on a pet piece of mine. In other words, I had grown further away from the former, while had grown closer to the latter. And, as this was not just an occasional phenomenon, but a regular course in the evolution of my mind, I learned by and by a lesson which is perhaps the hardest lesson for an artist to learn. I learned, open-mindedly, to respect the work of others, even if it be in disagreement with one's own concept, taste or line of development. And if one does not always understand the artist's work, one should at least seek to understand it, rather than to denounce it, and perhaps later on to regret this denunciation. Particularly during a time of transition, such as our time, this kind of openmindedness helps us to keep pace with the progress of things, and with their countless ramifications'.

Saarinen, for me, has hit upon the crux of any good 'guide': namely, to approach the 'visit' – in this case, our 'revisit' – in a spirit of non-judgmental enquiry. And he shows us that analysis of a period which seems at odds with our own can often yield the most fruitful engagement of ideas.

The next issue, of course, is what we 'visit'. What fragment, for me as a 'visitor', could reflect and give a glimpse of the whole? Urban rebuilding plans, as we've seen this morning, can in their complexity describe the functions of a community. Town halls can describe the state of a democracy. But, I suppose, if you search for a less loaded and symbolic, yet still pertinent reflector of the experimental ambition of a society, one key place to look is the one-off house. To that extent, the Morris and Steedman houses of the late '50s and '60s present an interesting case. I want to look, as a present-day 'visitor', at seven of those houses, built between 1955 and the late 1970s. And I'll be doing so from contemporary texts and photographs. My paper acts as a kind of introduction to the following contribution, by Robert Steedman, in which he gives his own recollections about the practice's endeavours to pioneer a Modern domestic Scottish architecture.

Avisfield, in Cramond Road North, Edinburgh (built for Mr B C Tomlinson in 1956-7, and extended in 1964), breaks what I'd call the convention of the 'classic house'. (Fig. 3.38) In defining that latter

3.38 Tomlinson house ('Avisfield'), Cramond (1956-7): view when newly completed.

concept, I want to use Lorimer's Wayside House, built at the turn of the century, as a substantial norm. There the distinction is clear. Here's the house, and there's the garden. In Avisfield, the house holds a fragment of the garden, like a child with a ball. House, like child, becomes recognised through that object. The nature of that new piece – the stone-walled enclosure – does recognise precedents. But in a pre-Modern house, in spite of all those walls that lead you up to the entry, the house in itself is still recognisable as a house above those walls.

In Avisfield, within these walls, the house becomes almost indistinguishable from the walls, stone and plaster, apart from the floating roof-planes. Within the garden, you are in a captured space, looking to the sky. Were they trying to evoke some older plan-form – a traditional kitchen garden, a derelict barn, the

3.39 Wilson house, Lasswade (1958-9).

3.40 Principal's House, Stirling University (1967): landscape view.

enclosures of the farm estates? The wall, in its historical juxtaposition with the framed house, is an emotional relationship – as opposed to, say, Peter Womersley's house, where the framed house is explicit, and the walls arrows, organising the edge. For Womersley, wall is punctuation; for Avisfield, the walled court is its soul.

The Sillitto house, at 32 Charterhall Road, Edinburgh (1960), which followed Avisfield, filled that walled enclosure with bedrooms and service rooms, and surmounted it with a living room. If Avisfield held that garden space, then Sillitto somehow captures air-space in that living room. And an interesting thing happens in the process of doing so. At Wayside, there's house, there's garden, and the walls – big planes and screens of glass – seek to dissolve that relationship between inside and outside. But there's a step between the house and the garden. At Sillitto, the step becomes a storey high, making a distinction between Lorimer's house – a house in garden, inside to out – and Sillitto, inside and down and across.

This idea of the big step, the plinth, also characterises the practice's second house, the Wilson house, at 16 Kevock Road, Lasswade (1957-8). (Fig. 3.39) Here the step, the plinth floats on the edge of a hill. The house does not occupy the plinth completely, making clear the relationship of not just the house on the edge of the hill, but 'house on plinth, on edge of hill'. The house is thus made to float, emphasised by that cantilevering. We'll hear later about Gillespie, Kidd & Coia's

3.41 Principal's House: plan.

Cardross Seminary, which occupies the edge of an existing plinth, made in the landscape – the platform of the original Burnet house. Gillespie, Kidd and Coia sat astride that edge, and, at points, they hurled rooms out, in a heroic celebration of their dramatic setting. Morris and Steedman made a more tentative and careful use of the edge, while using the rear wall to define the approach on the other side. But here, if we look at it on plan, it is no longer sufficient for the building to be straight. Expression is no longer satisfied by a rectilinear geometry, and with the angle of the garage in the wall which leads you to the front entrance, the angle-shape enters Morris and Steedman's vocabulary.

The Principal's House at Stirling University (1966-1967) is the climax of a series of three mid-'60s houses, each seeking different resolutions of the formal issues they had raised in their first projects. (Fig. 3.40, 3.41) Here the edge of the plinth, rather than being can-tilevered, is drawn up as a protective rail around the house. And, to the court side, it is explored in rela-tionship to the line dividing the house and the court: a stepped, faceted wall, stepping across the court. These cranked walls set up a separated shape which finds unusual resolution in the Holden house, East Kilbride (from 1962). Here the stepped planes twist round, not an external space but an internal hall. Perhaps almost, for Morris and Steedman, their first conventional house type, where 'house sits in garden'. But, in formal resolution, there almost seems to be no middle ground in the elevation. There seems just to be

plinth and roof, controlled by that stepping, spiralling shape. (Fig. 3.42)

The Snodgrass house, at Mardwell Farm, Silverburn (1964), refers in some ways back to Avisfield. (Fig. 3.43) This house, if it was bigger, could have totally embraced that captured garden space, as at Avisfield. But it's not quite big enough. It clings to that advantage of being able to have a little bit of garden, to have your own little private piece of land. And, in shape, from the tortured sculpture of the previous, Holden house, a hardly conventional house, the resolution in this case is the universal form of the circle. It's almost as if there's a first bend at the Wilson house – that first crank; then the juddering steps of the Principal's house; and then the twisted profile of East Kilbride. It's almost as if they now said: 'We surrender'. The architects' last recourse is a modern, but almost classical form. For Morris and Steedman, as for – say, an extreme – Ledoux, the extravagance of the Rococo was succeeded by, and found peace in, the geometry of the pure.

The final house I'm looking at today, the Morris house, Woodcote Park, Fala (from 1970), was built fifteen years on from their beginnings at Avisfield. (Fig. 3.44, 3.45) Fifteen years is a long time to gestate, to consider, to contemplate. And, in this house, all the elements of the previous things we've discussed are somehow captured in the conventional form. It is the 'Normal House'. It is, quite simply, 'House and Garden'. From Avisfield, they have come home to the

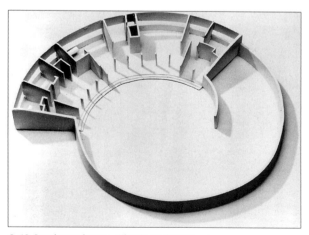

3.42 Holden house, East Kilbride (from 1962).

3.43 Snodgrass house, Silverburn (1964): plan.

conventional. But it's all still there. Shape is there: that tortured theme of the middle years finds resolution in a pirouetting spiral at the heart of the plan, leading up to the captured space of the upper floor plan – which also surmounts a plinth. But, this time, the plinth, the giant step, has become contained within the frame of the house, and now only reads from the double storey swimming pool at the side.

From outside, it is one piece. It is as though Morris and Steedman have come home. No longer house, and court, and garden; no longer house, and plinth, and garden; no longer that bit in between. Quite simply just house, and garden. Lorimer might, almost, be cheering!

What I've just outlined is a necessarily impressionistic, personal view of just part of Morris & Steedman's rich early work. To give this oeuvre a systematic coverage would require, and justify, an entire book. But that would be only one of a whole range of volumes that could be produced on Modern architecture in this country. Quite apart from Coia, Spence or Wheeler (to be dealt with in other papers today), we could just as easily imagine a volume on the collective, institutional endeavours of Robert Matthew and his followers, the individualistic projects of Peter Womersley, or the Lorimerian radicalism of Ian Begg. They, and many others, *would* make a splendid shelf. But our dedicated student, today, finds the shelf to be bare.

Does it matter, in the end, that our Modern bookshelf is empty; that we conclude from this that Scottish Modern architecture is empty and barren as well; and

that we turn to 'British national' or international names and specialist cartels? I believe that it does matter, for one reason above all: that architecture is a reflective and cumulative activity. Whether in sketch or model or written form, it is the duty of a reflective culture to document, record and clarify the origins of our new building, in order to provide a source-book for the next generation and the next after that. Within this framework of continuity, it becomes less important to argue about whether the past was better or worse, about whether – for instance – Modernism was a utopia or a 'dystopia'. What matters is simply that our choices should be properly informed by, should interact with, the past.

I'll conclude with another Finnish quotation – this time, from Alvar Aalto. Concerning the potential inspiration to be derived from the architectural masterpieces of the recent past, Aalto cited Saarinen's work over the previous half-century: 'Saarinen has been helpful in eliminating some of the architectural illiteracy, and some of the inferiority complexes, in a country which, because of its isolation, has been, and still is, removed from the large cultural centres of the

3.44 Morris house, Humbie (completed 1977): exterior.

3.45 Morris house: the hall.

Western world'. And he then went on to relate the comment of a foreign friend: 'In your northerly country, a bridge seems to have been built from that time right into our own. And along that bridge, two important developments have come. First, this bridge seems to connect your architectural heritage with your present form of building. And, second, it seems to have given the architectural form a continuous chance to unify itself with your social pattern'.

MORRIS & STEEDMAN
AND THE 'SMALL SCOTTISH HOUSE'
ROBERT STEEDMAN
(INTRODUCED BY DAVID PAGE)

David Page: In the previous paper, I argued that carefully thought-out small buildings, such as the houses of Morris & Steedman, can act as 'markers' to wider themes of architecture and building – and that they can be of relevance not only to historians of the 1950s and '60s, but also to architects working today. In this session, Robert Steedman will be touching on some of the same buildings: he's going to be describing to us the evolution of the firm's Modern concept of the 'small Scottish house' – beginning with 'Avisfield'.

Robert Steedman: We started work on our first house, the Tomlinson house – that is, Avisfield – in 1955: it was completed in 1957. (Figs. 3.46, 3.47) I was 27, a fifth-year student, when we got that job – it came from my dentist. As students, we'd been exposed to a great many stimuli, and we emerged with a driving idealism to change the world. In particular, we wanted to work out a new way of looking at the house in Scotland – to rethink how to live in this country today. Our aim was

3.47 Tomlinson house: interior view. (*Home* magazine, October 1960).

to build houses which weren't only for the rich: Avisfield cost around £4,000. We wanted to develop a specifically Scottish house, which would fit into the landscape – and Avisfield was an ideal place to begin. There were other houses in different styles nearby, but they were virtually invisible from the site. To get planning permission, we had to prove it would not be seen from the road (Cramond Road North): and here Nicholas Fort, in the Edinburgh Corporation Planning Department, was very helpful.

The governing idea at Avisfield was the combination of house and walled garden. We built the garden wall first, so the client couldn't change his mind; it seemed a way of making the house seem bigger than it was, and provide a sheltered outside area. Flowing, yet interrupted space – always a hidden area, or an 'escape'. The aim was to extend the apparent space, to create a visually limitless, because undefined, space. The principal rooms are inextricably linked to the micro-climate of the walled garden, and visually borrow the tree landscape beyond the site. The stone wall, on the street side, was only a small hurdle to this view – it obliterated cars in the road, but not the trees and the sun. A section of the stone wall was designed as a 'wet wall', dripping, moss-covered – to give close-range interest and movement. Texture was important in the courtyard – grass, pebbles, and water, to give reflection at night. We were trying to create a micro-climate in this garden – and, after 35 years, that's what's happened. On the north side of the house, there's a wonderful view to the Firth of Forth – but it's cold on that side, so it's principally fixed glazing.

The roofs are very clear in outline, emphatically overhanging, protective, powerful, floating, over-lapping planes, with the stone tower, which goes through the roof, as a focus, an anchor; it contained the watertank and chimney. An opening in the middle of the main roof allowed light to come right into the centre of the house, to provide brightness on a dull day and a shaft of sun when available.

We took great trouble with the detail, as with the teak fascias, and the cedar soffit boards. The whole house was intended to weather gracefully, to get better with age – although the white walls would need painting.

The courtyard catches every bit of sun there is, but protects from cold winds. The window to the right slides across to form a wind-break

With a view across the Forth

Fire-place walls rise to encase water-tank and flue

Looking across the courtyard pool towards the house

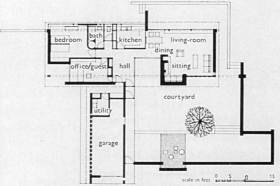

From the road: the house lies hidden behind the trees, garage and courtyard screen walls

The stone walls were very unsophisticated, random-rubble walls, like an old stone dyke.

Inside, the focus of the living area was an all-embracing stone fireplace, a kind of ingleneuk where, on a winter's night, you can draw the curtains, get the fire going. We floated the roof across it, on two big Douglas fir beams. The beams, which ran the length of the house, were supported wherever the plan allowed. The detail of the partition walls was a consciously composed pattern of chipboard panels fitted to the face of the wood framing, shadow gaps painted black, panels white which incorporated the doors, Mondriaan-like but three-dimensional. Ceilings were natural wood boarding, echoing the soffit of the roof overhang. For inspiration, we looked principally towards America – although at that stage I'd never been there, nor had Morris. We looked at the houses of Marcel Breuer, for his planning of space, relationship to site and use of materials, and also those by Neutra, Wright, Kahn. We were also influenced by Zen Buddhist houses and temples in Japan, where all space is flexible, and the play of light a major factor – and we felt that there were exciting possibilities with modern materials in Scotland. In turn, Avisfield, I think, anticipated some aspects of the patio house, which emerged slightly later in schemes such as Leith Fort (Shaw-Stewart, Baikie & Perry) and Inchview, Prestonpans (Edinburgh University Architecture Research Unit). We were all part of the general tendency, in those years, of architects trying to work out new ways of building houses for Scotland.

Our second house was, in a sense, a total opposite to Avisfield: the Wilson house, Kevock Road, Lasswade (1957-8). Here we went to the other extreme, and produced a totally one-sided, extrovert house: a gallery house, a 'promenade' house, which made the most of the orientation, and limited width of the site. (The Wilsons, and Tomlinsons, were just about the only clients who actually said, 'We want a Modern house.') But the actual appearance of the house emanated from the plan. The building was cantilevered out over a bank, from a reinforced concrete slab – it was the only possible way to get a house wide enough on that site. Whereas the Tomlinson house structure relied on those two big beams, this one had a complete 10ft. grid of columns, because of foundation difficulties, within which the plan had to fit. Some of the materials were different too: glass bricks, and the litho stones – Mr Wilson (of Pillans and Wilson) owned a printworks, and had lots of these stones that he could use. Internally, the dressed Craigleith stone hearth was the main element and focus. Looking along inside the house: the whole of its core, with bathrooms and kitchen was wrapped around in wood panelling, and everything else was white painted plaster, with the concrete columns left as such.

Our third house was in Edinburgh once again: the Sillitto house, 32 Charterhall Road, which was done in 1959. (Fig. 3.48) We thought bungalows in Edinburgh were going to have to end somewhere – so why not

3.48 Sillitto house, Charterhall Road, Edinburgh (1960): view from road.

(opposite) 3.46 Tomlinson house: views and plans. (*Home* magazine, 1960).

here? This was a wooden 'living-cube', simply expressed in its overall form – and indeed the planners queried whether it was a suitable design at all for the site. The one opening in the ground-floor wall was where you went in – no problem about finding that. Living/dining/kitchen were upstairs on this platform in space, with a panoramic view of Edinburgh through continuous glazing. There were two bedrooms downstairs. The client was a professor at Edinburgh University, and the brief was contained in three verses of poetry.

Then there was the Berry house, at St Thomas Road, Edinburgh, which was done in 1960. This was built on an unused strip of garden – we seem to be offered sites that other people have given up on. Here we created four courts formed by the house and the existing stone boundary walls, a car court, a forecourt, a central court in the house and finally a garden court where the site widened. There was no view – hence the introspective concept. The client was a kilt-maker and stressed that he didn't like gardening, so as far as possible the outside spaces were finished in slabs, pebbles, trees and shrubs on mounds.

My own first house was built as part of a pair, along with a house for Professor Hunt, in Ravelston Dykes Road (1960). I was looking for a site, and I approached the builder who owned this one, and said: 'If I get permission for two houses, (he had permission for one) will you sell me the site?' He agreed on condition that he built them. The houses were identical in plan but the sloping site allowed for an asymmetrical elevation which acknowledged the fall in ground. Because of the proximity of existing trees, the sitting room, dining, kitchen and utility were all on the first floor, virtually one space which could be divided by full height sliding 'walls'. On the ground floor there were four bedrooms and two bathrooms; a large carport with open balcony above separated the two houses. There is probably something satisfyingly basic about living at tree level, and one is kept well aware of the seasons.

Other houses of the 1960s included the Holden house, East Kilbride (1962), built in an inhospitable, rolling landscape for a potter and her husband. She dictated its form, with studio on the first floor, separated from everything. The result was a spiral house, with some wonderful spaces inside: first a low entrance, then a theatrical, two-storey, 26ft high hall, beams up into the roof, a door into every angle; and a huge country kitchen. That didn't seem the right place for a flat roof: we thought it should have a rough, farming look.

Or there was the Cheyne house, York Road, North Berwick (1961), for a Canadian client: an exploded rectangle. The site was strongly terraced by grassy banks, and it was impossible to resist the temptation to add the line of a long, low roof as a further 'terrace' looking out to sea. Or the Snodgrass house, Silverburn, near Penicuik (1964): the owners had a disabled child, who had to be kept safely inside the walls, so we designed a spiral plan including an area of garden. The site was a wild open hillside – uncompromising, nothing to relate to – and the building was a segment of a circle, leaning towards the sun, with wedge-shaped walls. When I went to the superior to get permission, he said, 'We can't object to this – it looks like a sheep-pen!'

For the Principal's House at Stirling University (completed in 1967), perhaps the main planning constraint, as with Avisfield, was a need for unobtrusiveness. The remains of a steading complex on a rocky promontory was selected as the site, and the existing stone perimeter wall was incorporated into the plan in the south-west corner of the courtyard. This obtuse angle resulted in the private rooms being located along one wing and the guest rooms on the other; the public rooms were at the point of meeting. The roof was raised over the sitting and dining rooms to allow light to enter into the central areas, and give additional height to the principal rooms where the guests were entertained. The blank walls of the house facing the courtyard formed an excellent gallery for the Principal's collection of paintings.

That commission in some ways represented the end of this sequence of early houses, ten years after Avisfield. The diversity of sites with which we were presented resulted in a highly varied series of solutions, and it was that challenge which we enjoyed.

THE ARCHITECTURE OF PRECISION: THE ROYAL COMMONWEALTH POOL

JOHN RICHARDS, IN CONVERSATION WITH ANDY MacMILLAN

John Richards: In this talk, I'm not just going to be dealing with the Commonwealth Pool. Instead, I want to describe the Commonwealth Pool as an episode in the overall development of the Modern Movement in Scotland. And I want to emphasise that our firm's approach represents only one strand of the Modern Movement. What you had in those decades was a great variety of different people working in different ways at the same time.

Now this brings us immediately to a general problem: that of the accreditation of Modern buildings. I'm not really the 'author' of this building: many people worked on the Pool. The architects were Robert Matthew, Johnson-Marshall & Partners: I happened to be the partner in charge – ultimately responsible to the client for the performance of the building. Euan Colam, Andrew Davies and several other key people worked on it too. Often, Andrew or Euan would initiate ideas. And anyway, the building wasn't just designed by architects. For instance, the engineers were Arups, the services were designed by Steensen Varming Mulcahy. Which leads to a more general question: is architecture a fine art process, overseen by one individual, or is it a collective design process in which many individuals participate? Because the collective idea was very prominent in the Modern Movement.

We'll come back to this problem later. But first, I'd like to start with one or two theoretical questions. Nikolaus Pevsner said, in the introduction to his *Outline of European Architecture*, that a bicycle shed was a building, but a cathedral was a piece of architecture. Now, I'm not so sure about that sharp distinction between utilitarian and 'non-utilitarian' buildings. After all, Lethaby said, 'Art is thoughtful workmanship' and 'Beauty is the complexion of good health.' So that question – is architecture a fine art? – must interest thoughtful critics. Personally, I don't see any distinction between utilitarian or non-utilitarian. To me, Pevsner's definition confines 'architecture' to buildings designed for aesthetic appeal – whereas, to

my mind, 'style' is the outcome of addressing all the constraints on a building project. And I don't think I am, or was, alone in this. Because two ideas – that all buildings, for all people, are architecture (or potential architecture), and that all attributes of architecture, commodity and firmness as well as delight, must be completely integrated – were central concepts to my generation of architects.

So first, a little bit of autobiography. I did my training at the Architectural Association in London, where our year, starting in 1949, were the first postwar generation to come straight out of school. The people in the year above had piloted bombers and driven tanks. We shared with these older people an absolute determination to rebuild a better, cleaner, more egalitarian world. We were taught by the new head of school, Robert Furneaux Jordan, who showed us about the social purpose of architecture, and how to look at everyday things. Why, to us in those years, were simple buildings so good, and ornate buildings so overblown? It all seemed to come down to fitness for purpose. Above all, we started with a belief in the idea of progress. Each design must be built on the experiences of previous architects – so architecture had, by definition, to move forward. You couldn't forget that Mondriaan had painted pictures like he had, that Rietveld had built a house like the Schröder House. So there were obsessions, for instance, with cubism and rectangularity – and a preoccupation with the avoidance of sentimentality.

At that time, all the graphs were going up: population, health, the economy. Expectations of a more egalitarian society were high. What we were looking for was a clean, white, healing architecture. The size of the building programme meant that quite a lot of buildings were going to have to be built in factories. Research into modular coordination was going on everywhere. We read Corbusier's *Modulor*. There were international conferences about modular architecture all over the world. We were lectured by Wittkower: mathematical proportions, the lessons of the Renaissance seemed very important, and a new aesthetic seemed possible.

Openings didn't have to be subtractions from a sculptural mass: they could become intervals between panels. The rectilinearity of this kind of Modernism came first from Cubism and second from the practical need to fit panels together. (Fig. 3.49) I became interested in craftsmanship – I admired the Maison de Verre, how everything was so beautifully machined. The Hertfordshire schools were going on at that time; large numbers had had to be built quickly. Some people at the time said that these schools were architecturally flaccid. But, to us, they made their Victorian predecessors look like obsolete hulks.

But by the mid '50s, something else was coming to the fore. We began to hear about new developments in the US. People like Craig Elwood and Pierre Koenig started doing houses in steel and glass, with arc-welded columns. For instance, there was Buck Stahl's house in LA by Koenig: steel-framed, elegant, with overhanging roof, cantilevered out over the hillside. Or there was Neutra's timber house, or the startling and influential house by Charles Eames at 203 Chautququa Canyon, Pacific Palisades. I rapidly developed a love of the West Coast of the US: I'd seen, some years before, a film which featured a West Coast architect – he was tall and handsome, I was small and skinny, and I thought: I'd like to be like that!

So that was my background and training. Now, to move on to the Commonwealth Pool itself – or the Central Swimming Pool, as we called it at planning stage. This project, essentially, happened because Edinburgh Corporation had a visionary Baths and Laundries Department Manager, Jack Black. We had

the view that you couldn't design a beautiful building for an ugly brief. Whereas if the programme was beautiful, all you had to do was reveal it: to open it up like a flower. Now in those days you went to the baths to get clean: they were seen in sanitary terms. But Jack Black had a visionary idea of an alternative, which would shift the emphasis to swimming proficiency: that is, to a mixture of education, leisure and public safety. He wanted to establish a whole system of swimming teaching in Edinburgh, stepping up from the small local pool, to the district pool, and finally to a new Central Pool, which would form the pinnacle of the system. His aim was that every child in Edinburgh should know how to swim. A very simple idea. And the requirement for this happened to coincide with the call for an Olympic-length pool to be ready for the Commonwealth Games in 1970, which meant starting the construction in 1967.

With that client, Jack Black, we went to look at pools abroad. To Germany, for instance – every German city had a central pool and an opera house, and most of these pools worked well. Then we sat round a table, with the structural engineer, the services engineer, and we hammered out the concept of what was to be built here. The first constraint seemed to be that we had to take advantage of the views of Arthur's Seat – so we couldn't just build a big blank box. Then there was the need to avoid condensation, and glare from glass surfaces: so we decided on a big roof overhang, to keep out the glare; we decided to keep the volume down, to keep down the glare; and, to obviate the need for big ducts everywhere, we decided to put all the air supply

3.49 Pathfoot Building, Stirling University, seen newly completed (1968).

3.51 Royal Commonwealth Pool: view from rear, c.1970.

machinery in the roof space, blow the air down, and extract it at lower level.

These functional demands determined the overall form, and led us to begin thinking about the building in terms of overlapping planes. It became clear that the building was going to end up with similar elevations all the way round: the most human scale would be at the entrance (north), while the largest scale would be facing Arthur's Seat to the south. (Figs. 3.50, 3.51) Inside, there would have to be two segregated levels – an access (dry) level, and a pool (wet) level – and we decided, to get lots of transparency, to segregate these by glass as much as possible: double-glazing that you could walk through! In the wet area, there were going to be three pools – an Olympic-length main pool, and diving and learning pools – and changing areas. It began to become clear that we would have to have a two-way-spanning, gridded roof; and that the roof-space would have to be *huge* – in fact, big enough to contain the whole of our Stage I Building at Stirling University (the Pathfoot Building, 1966-7). The roof was even heated, to maintain the 'dry' layer all round the pool. Nobody had ever put all the services in a roof before – or a roof of that scale, anyway! (Figs. 3.52, 3.53, 3.54)

So it was only really at the end that we actually designed the elevations: they were just very plain elevations. To repeat what I said earlier, our view was that if the purpose of the building was good, all you needed to do was reveal it. Indeed, we felt you actually had to strip away the 'architecture' – we called it 'noise'! Economy of expression was our aim. So we used, for the cladding, just anodised aluminium panels bolted on; the lowest level of the facade was white precast concrete. Inside, we designed everything, even down to the door-handles: the diving board supports were simple stainless-steel tubes.

I've continued to be fascinated by buildings you could put up in clean overalls, rather than grubbing about on a muddy building site. That's essentially what we were aiming at in projects like the Pool, or Aberdeen Airport, which we did in 1978. If you prefabricate, you potentially get a very precise type of architecture. With a modern building, with off-site production, many components are designed by subcontractors. You can't 'draw' the building until tenders are

3.52 Royal Commonwealth Pool: general view of interior, c.1970.

3.50 Royal Commonwealth Pool: view of main frontage, 1970.

received. And if that's the case, you've gone a long way from the architect as artist standing by the easel designing.

Now, if I look back at slides of the buildings I was involved in then, things like the Pool, what I'm struck with is their absence of density – a sort of thinness, almost. Our buildings were very simple, very 'thin', but they did have clarity and simplicity. I have to say that I still like that sort of thing: it's still buildings like Neutra's work in the '30s which really turn me on! Whereas, today, we expect broken forms, and, inside, greater density of information. But some architects, at least, do seem to be holding on to the idea of authenticity, with every part supporting every other part. I'm

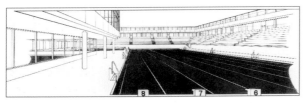

3.54 Royal Commonwealth Pool: interior perpective by RMJM, c.1967.

glad not everybody has gone for the Post-Modern tendency of being overwhelmed by detail!

This, I think, is a lesson for the critics and the historians: when looking back at the history of 20th-century architecture, we must try to allow for the things that seem foreign to us today. There's nothing new about it, after all – it's over 93 years old by now!

Andy MacMillan: You've just given us a very lucid account, but was it also an edited account? I wonder if there are 'skeletons in your cupboard', architecturally speaking, that you haven't revealed – after all, Corb was also building, after the war, buildings in Romantic styles. You subscribed to the programmatic, anonymous, team-spirited – but wasn't that stance also an *aesthetic* stance?

John Richards: Yes – but it was an explicitly non-contextual aesthetic stance.

MacMillan: That's certainly clear! You weren't looking at Corb, but were you looking at Mies – the

3.53 Royal Commonwealth Pool: view of main diving board, c.1970.

hovering planes, the universal space, polarised under the roof, without a context? Isn't there a very definite controlling visual hand? The building's not meant to refer to being in Edinburgh – we'd both agree on that – but surely, far from being a puritan, you were being a poet, but bottling it up!

Richards: I don't think it's as 'universal' as all that. It couldn't be, say, an airport – it looks like a major public building.

MacMillan: Certainly there are grandiose elements: I do like the way the space drops away as you go in. But if we were to build three more of them, would they all still look like important public buildings? At the end of the day, you made your first love clear: the Lovell house.

Richards: I do agree that, for instance, there's not much richness of information inside the building. There's a fine line between economy and emptiness! But that's our perspective today – and it'll be for the historian to evaluate that against our views in the '60s!

POST-COIA COIA: THE POSTWAR WORK OF GILLESPIE, KIDD & COIA.
MARK BAINES

As a one-time student of Andy MacMillan's and Isi Metzstein's, and a one-time employee of Gillespie, Kidd & Coia, I feel privileged to be able to talk about their work – not least because, I believe, this is the first time a public lecture has been given about them, other than by themselves! I've long valued their insights into the fundamental nature of architecture – insights which have made a lasting impression not only on me but on many others. (Fig. 3.55)

Our task today is to begin trying to put Gillespie Kidd and Coia, and their buildings, into some kind of architectural perspective in the postwar period. There was a cartoon in 1974 – at the time of their shortlisting for the competition for Robinson College, in Cambridge – which portrayed their firm in the form of Jack Coia riding a Loch Ness Monster. But in reality, by this time, whatever the media perception, the real driving forces within the practice, alongside many other

talented individuals, were in fact Andy MacMillan and Isi Metzstein – the men behind the mask, the two people inside the monster-suit in that cartoon. There's no space in this paper to set out a full historical account of the postwar work of the firm. So, instead, I'm going to sketch out a general architectural analysis of their key buildings.

I'll begin, although it falls outwith our strict chronological scope today, with a glance at perhaps their largest and most complex commission: Robinson College, Cambridge (competition win 1974, built 1977-80). This, to my mind, is one of the most powerful evocations of their ideas of form, of community in its widest sense, and of space. Essentially, it is an urban form. Here, one influence, naturally, is the local context: the collegiate courts and quadrangles of the English university tradition. But it's also moulded by their experience and perception of urban form generally, and in particular, by the urban context of Glasgow itself. It recognises the value and importance of domain, be it public or private, or those spaces in between. In this building, this recognition is expressed by the parallel walls of varied accommodation, enclosing and preserving the existing meadowland, chapel and library, and providing a variegated and forceful street frontage. The public spaces to the court, to the garden, are surmounted by a stepped section of residences. The whole thing is a little like a concrete megastructure, but draped and clothed in brick. Thus, through the formal manipulation of a very complex and diverse programme, it appeals to one's more humanitarian instincts, as opposed to so many of the megastructures of the '60s, and early '70s. Likewise, their previous college buildings – Notre Dame, Bearsden (1969), and the

3.55 Professors Andrew MacMillan (left) and Isi Metzstein (right) seen with Ian Gow of the National Monuments Record on the occasion of their 1990 Playfair Lectures.

3.56 St Bride's Church, East Kilbride (1963-4): external view, 1964.

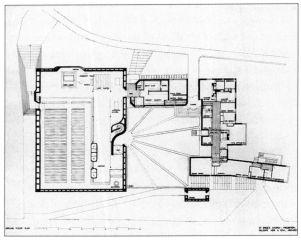

3.57 Plan of St Bride's Church.

3.58 Our Lady of Good Counsel, Dennistoun (1964-5): 1995 photograph.

Halls of Residence at Hull University (1967) – are represented as chiselled walls, which capture the landscape, but also speak of a desire for a collective form, in which individuals feel part of some larger totality, and can relate to the landscape in which they are placed.

A similar quest, for ever more powerful architectural expressions of human association, pervades their church architecture. In the New Towns of Glenrothes and East Kilbride, they built two churches. St. Paul's Church, Glenrothes (1956-7) was the building which launched their trend of highly centralised, worshipper-centred churches, anticipating the liturgical reforms of Vatican II – and which, probably, 'put them on the map' of postwar Modern architecture. And St. Bride's, East Kilbride (1963-4) provides a powerful architectural image for the new, or expanding town. Here, they are concerned to use form as both symbol and a powerful silhouette – an evocation of the religious purpose and meaning of the building. (Figs. 3.56, 3.57)

St. Bride's also makes a very clear, emphatic statement about entry into buildings. Something fairly often neglected in much of modern architecture, it is singularly emphatic here: the folded entrance is the only aperture visible in the solid masonry mass of the external cubic form of the building. Despite its enormous scale, this opening is reduced, towards ground level, to a human scale, by the corbelled and angled adjustment at its base: a receiver and disperser of entry. Internally, light informs the massive brick structure of the church – both from above, filtered through a louvred timber ceiling, and through chiselled apertures, down walls into the very base of this enormous volume. A similar, rectangular internal space, this time with sculpturally chiselled side walls above an arcade, is found at St Patrick's, Kilsyth (1964).

It is, in fact, a general characteristic of their churches that light is used to emphasise the liturgical programme, and especially the altar; in the case of St. Joseph's, Clydebank (1964), the congregation sits under the umbrella of the steel structure above, surrounded by a halo of light, which washes the perimeter brick walls with varying degrees of intensity – a highly evocative and, I think, symbolic gesture. At Our Lady of Good Counsel in Dennistoun (1964), and at the demolished St Benedict's, Drumchapel (from 1965), a similar preoccupation with volume prevails. At Our Lady's, the roof becomes both roof and wall, through the nature of its asymmetrical pitch. Light is employed to help organise the space: the lowest level windows provide a view to a garden; toplighting introduces light to the depths of a fairly deep plan; and finally, above that, in the vertical section of the roof, space within the structure is manipulated to filter a more ethereal kind of light. (Figs. 3.58, 3.59)

In these churches, which were principally single volumes, the architects were able to focus their attention on the surfaces of the floors, the walls, and the roof. The use and experience of light stood them in good stead when it came to far more complex programmes, in which multiple volumes of different size had to be assembled. I think it is a measure of their skill that, when they came to deal with these larger buildings, they were able to give almost equal attention to all parts of them. Even at the small scale of the more recent staff pavilion at the Glasgow School of Art, they were very conscious of the relationship between the external form of the building and its exploitation internally. In this instance, the window is directed – not axially – towards the Art School itself. The gridded structure of the window offers different views and captures different views within its lattice-work frame. Externally, the building is rather diminutive – and, although it tries to achieve some kind of heroic scale, it ends up appearing more like a window in search of its wall.

But let's return to the 1960s. Here, as I say, the firm did some very large and programmatically complex buildings, for various social uses, among which the most prominent are educational buildings.

3.59 St Benedict's, Drumchapel (1965-7): photographed in 1990 prior to demolition.

3.60 Our Lady & St Francis School, Charlotte Street, Glasgow (1958-64).

3.61 Cumbernauld Technical College (1972-5).

3.63 St Peter's College: 1960s view of junction between main block and classroom wing.

Characteristic of the form of these projects is a cross-sectional, somewhat megastructural concept which I call, for my own purposes, the 'Education Section': a preoccupation with a repetitive section, an extruded section, of similar or like volumes. At schools such as Simshill (1956-63) and Our Lady's, Cumbernauld (1963-4), we see classrooms being treated in this way. Within the section of the school, we see carefully expressed differences between the nature of the base, the middle and the top. And equally significantly, we recognise that the spaces within the physical mass of the structure – the occupied spaces – take priority: they recognise that the spaces above and below, in terms of the floor-plates, or from side to side, either side of the walls, or, again, above or below the roof, are of equal, though different value. The consequences of erecting structures in space require a simultaneous consciousness of outside and inside, above and below. The sections also demonstrate one inevitable consequence of assembling multiple volumes, and all the mechanical services they bring to bear in their wake: the depth of the structure, the structural frame, created in part by the use of the cantilever and a central spine corridor, is used to accommodate all such services, and thereby make them discrete, so both services and structure serve the primary, occupied spaces. (Fig. 3.60)

This sectional architecture is developed to a higher degree of elaboration at Cumbernauld Technical College. (Fig. 3.61) In the school we just discussed, the large volumes were substantially placed outwith the linear block. In this building, the cellular volumes are grouped, and stepped, over various volumes, large and small, and are prised apart to allow light-wells to illuminate these large, cavernous spaces below. Another difference becomes progressively more apparent in these sections, this developing typology: the fact that the frame offers a kind of hospitality to a load-bearing structure which is ground-based. The one seems, in a sense, to defy gravity, the other is very much rooted in the ground. They do this in such a way as to become mutually dependent.

And so to St Peter's College, Cardross, conceived in 1959 and completed in 1966: one of the firm's greatest masterpieces. The building was a seminary, a teaching college run by ten priests for 108 students, with a small annexe housing eight nuns. The grouping of the new buildings around the existing nineteenth-century house provides it with a new context, whilst respecting both its presence, and that of the walled garden, which creates a plateau within which the buildings are placed. So the house is placed in a new context, but with some degree of respect. (Figs. 3.62, 3.63)

The new buildings comprise a linear sequence of different spaces, which connect more or less continuously, forming a kind of ring around the garden court. The entry way passes below the full depth of the new main building, housing the chapel and the refectory, and rises up into the garden court, and to the main entrance of the existing house. The complex

programme of this group is articulated into a series of separate buildings, each with its own typology, drawn from the previous experiences of the churches and the educational buildings.

The upper ground level is a linear sequence of spaces, in which each part of the programme determines the form of that specific part of the building. The spaces on this ground level are the communal, shared spaces: the priests' common rooms, the refectory, the chapel, and the students' common room, which sits above the library and below the lecture theatre. And above this, there rises over the main building a ziggurat, again of a kind of extruded section, which gradually narrows as the building rises. The rationale of this arrangement is that its parallel walls, gradually rising to meet each other, are separated by a void and by

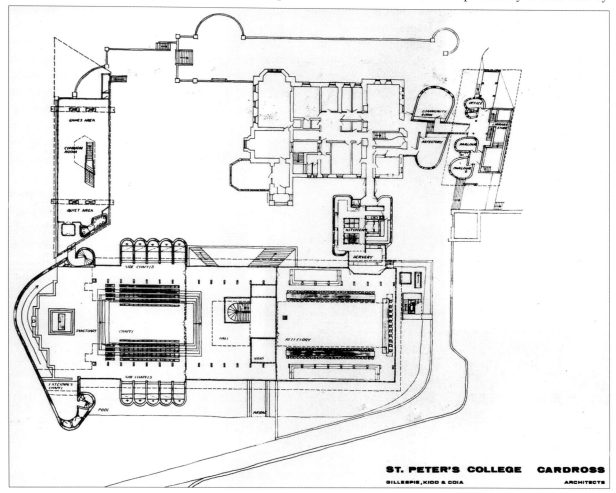

ST. PETER'S COLLEGE   CARDROSS
GILLESPIE, KIDD & COIA   ARCHITECTS

3.62 Plan of St Peter's College, Cardross.

centrally located circulation. This provides an economical position for the circulation pattern, which consists of open galleries to the refectory and closed galleries over the chapel, converging as the building rises – until, at the top, they merge into a single gallery space.

Here, again, the section embodies the basic architectural and psychological concepts which the firm had developed in their other buildings. The primary volumes are a controlled set of spaces, contained within the underbelly of the stepped section. This stepped section, inclining over the primary volumes, has a thickness comprising individual student rooms, whose clasped interdependency, one leaning against the other, provides a very powerful expression of the collective relationship of all the individuals resident at any one time. This simultaneous fashioning of space within and space outside ensures that, externally, the receding planes secure privacy for their occupants, by creating a sense of progressive setting-back from the building edge. The stepped section also serves the more practical functions of fire escape, by allowing access to either end of the building. And it performs two other architectural roles. In its entirety, it creates a continuous entrance canopy: one passes across the moat, below the body of the building, into the garden court. And, within the garden court, the stepped section attempts, in its scale, to acknowledge the presence of the existing house.

In the cross-sections, the 'lack of fit' between the cellular accommodation above and the larger-scale volumes below is exploited in two ways. First, by expanding the accommodation laterally, through a series of side-chapels, in the top left section. And second, in the length of the building, by extending beyond the ziggurat above, exploiting the topography so that the altar is cantilevered out into a space bounded by the loadbearing wall – above which a large rooflight steps up to give light into the interior, and below which a ramp gives access to the practice chapels below.

So this building also engages in a dialogue between the structural frame, the cantilever, and the loadbearing wall. The repetitive structure of the frame section has

to be contained in some way, in order to define the totality of the building. Lengthwise, it is contained by the presence of the end chapel with its upstand rooflight, and, at either end, by the fire escape stair, coiled around the boiler flue. Its lateral extension is contained by maximising the possible limits of the cantilever of the structure above. So the loadbearing structure provides a kind of harbour, a place of repose for the cantilevered stepped section above.

Internally, the stair appears like a kind of timber ladder, dropped down gently on to the ground, from the underbelly of the superstructure above. (Fig. 3.64) The view up into the roof is filtered through the laminated timber beams, through a stepped-section rooflight. And through this, we are allowed to see other parts of the building, from within the building. So the actual view of the interior of the chapel, again, is moulded by the interaction of both light and structure, and its more particular qualities come from its simple and very direct use of materials. Here, as in the firm's churches, one is never really aware of the precise source of light, as it is often indirect, either from a clerestory of what might be described as the 'nave', or through the filter screen of the beams below the roof light. The edges of this space are like aisles beyond the column structure, and one can see the cantilever penetrating what is merely a timber screen between the outside and the inside, again creating a sense of depth to the lateral part of the space. Beyond and below the cantilevered altar are the practice chapels for the students, with access by a curving

3.64 St Peter's College: 1960s view of staircase in main block.

ramp which descends into the undercroft of the building. Again, a play of cantilever versus loadbearing wall.

The admission and regulation of light in these buildings, and, indeed, the views out of them, are very highly controlled, in the sense that the refectory has a glazed window to the end, and low views laterally to either side. The chapel is enclosed, and views into it are restricted, as are the views out, by the presence of these ten priests' chapels to either side. These, provocatively and evocatively, reach out like two hands, five fingers of each hand, as though to help receive the student priests in the stepped building above. At the junction between the library wing – the trapezoidal plan-form on the right – and the body of the building, the one almost nudges the other, in a kind of delicate 'kiss'.

The library building contains the library itself on its lower ground level; this is surmounted by a common room, on top of which are the lecture spaces. Thus,

again, a clear stratification of use, with essentially transparent base and solid top. The cantilever here is used in a slightly different way from that of the other building: it explodes the longitudinal axis of the building, with the lecture theatres overshadowing the common room, and soaring over the walled garden retaining wall, out over the landscape beyond. Internally, there is the same use of light: windows for view, and toplight to light the interior depths of the space. In the lecture spaces on the roof, the trapezoidal subdivision of the spaces creates a latticed timber structure, which again integrates the mechanical, in terms of the light fittings, within the material of the structure, and allows roof-lighting to be filtered through them.

St. Peter's College is, probably, the quintessential embodiment of the architecture of Gillespie, Kidd and Coia, and of Andy Macmillan and Isi Metzstein. It is a kind of microcosm of the fundamental qualities of their work. (Fig. 3.65) So – to sum up – what are those key attributes?

3.65 St Peter's College: original model by Gillespie, Kidd & Coia, c.1959.

Summarised in a single sentence, their architecture is a continual reinvestment of the old into the new. It's an enrichment of and an enlargement upon all previous action: the preoccupation with volume and light, the wall-frame resonating with both past and present. They tried to extend the range of contemporary architecture, without dogma, creating a meaningful complexity in formal and spatial relationships, and producing buildings of sometimes awesome power, which yet somehow sustained both grace and dignity: an architecture in which space, volume and purpose all took priority over preoccupations with structure and servicing. It sought to reaffirm a sense of continuity with the past, to bridge the emerging gap between the past and present.

All this was only achieved, I believe, through the continued pursuit of an architecture based on principles. That they did so with such intellectual rigour, imagination, skill and vision places them among the most significant and innovative architectural practices of the postwar period.

A GIANT MATRIX:
ST PETER'S SEMINARY, CARDROSS
ISI METZSTEIN,
IN CONVERSATION WITH MARK BAINES

Mark Baines: The previous paper described the basic forms and spaces of St Peter's College, in the context of Gillespie, Kidd & Coia's other contemporary work. In this session, I'll be discussing both the architecture and the 'context' – the patronage – with Isi Metzstein, the partner in charge of the Cardross project. Let's deal with the building itself first. Looking at the resulting layout, Isi, would you say that your solution was diagrammatic, and depended on closely relating the new building to the old?

Isi Metzstein: It is definitely diagrammatic, there's no doubt. My principle has always been, to reach the simplest solution to any architectural problem. And this programme lent itself to a very simple solution, because the College came together so coherently as an institution. My idea was a plan in which every part would speak to every other part: an association of many small elements – the cells – within large

volumes. You start with a single cell: it has a degree of autonomy, not just sliced out of a block. Its arched ceiling, stepped window reprises the section of the block as a whole, and emphasises its individuality. I sometimes can't sleep at night, thinking of all those individual rooms, imprisoned for ever within that giant matrix! (Fig. 3.66) From that, the building itself is put together, with the aim of synthesising two potentially conflicting principles: aggregation of small units, and subdivision of large ones.

Now from this concept, of associating large spaces and small spaces within a linear building of repeating cells, there arise one or two architectural problems. The building has to be 'closed'. This we did at one end by a gigantic curved wall, and at the other by a staircase and flue. Built into it is the impossibility of infinite extension. Regarding the relationship to the existing house: that remained the core of the complex, and regulated the relationships of the other blocks. It told you what you couldn't do: you couldn't compete with it. We reinstated it internally, and were careful not to make any external changes to it. We wanted it

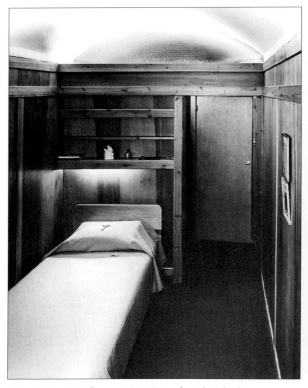

3.66 St Peter's College: 1960s view of student bedroom.

to look like one building, to look like a single 'church' made out of different elements – not like some kind of hotel or youth hostel. A corporate building, where all the occupants make a contribution to the life of the building, and the form of the building reflects this.

The building behind the main house was a convent for eight nuns – a small version of the main building. It has a sweeping curved roof, which wasn't strictly speaking 'necessary' – I never use the word 'functional' – but you have to take account of the psychological effect of the design.

Baines: Let's consider some of the individual elements in more detail. Taking, for instance, the college's relationship with the outside world. Would you say it was quite an introverted complex?

Metzstein: That's the 'entry question'. The rules were simple. Students would live here for four or five years, with no random visiting. You come in under the building along one defined route, to the front door of the old house. That, I agree, is a measure of exclusion. The form, therefore, was collegiate, even 'urban'.

Baines: Could you say a little about your use of materials?

Metzstein: Our aim was to confine the concrete structure to its necessary area, so that exposed concrete would have very little presence: the main frame stops when there's no need for any more of it. Loadbearing walls were a mixture of concrete,

including the walls separating the cells, and brick. We didn't want to disturb any of the stone walls – so we cantilevered the lecture theatre out over them, to protect the walls and hard landscaping. Our attitude was not to mess up the landscape – yet the building isn't pretending to make no impact. We extended the existing terrace and left all the planting as it was, including the vegetation on the walls and the mass of trees collected by the owner in the 19th century.

I wouldn't accept the word 'eclectic' about our use of materials – it was a matter of necessity. We wanted it to look as if it was built by people working on the site, not made in a factory and flown in pieces to the site. So we used render: we certainly didn't want a 'bricky' effect. As a rule, the smaller or less important the part of the building, the wider the choice of material. We could debate about metal versus wooden window frames, but there was no choice about having to use reinforced concrete for the main frame. The precast panels were designed to show some colour, some sympathy to the existing Burnet house – you weren't meant to feel you were inside a concrete building, a concrete box. (Figs. 3.67, 3.68)

Baines: Does the Cardross design demonstrate anything about Gillespie, Kidd & Coia's attitude to history – for instance, about the fact that you admired Romanesque architcture?

Metzstein: I don't think that it's necessary to pin down precise 'precedents' as such. Obviously an architect has to have a well-stocked recall, about relationships

3.67 St Peter's College: c.1965 view of building work. The 19th-century house is on the left.

3.68 St Peter's College: c.1965 view of classroom block under construction.

he or she has seen. I certainly am, for instance, emotionally moved by Romanesque architecture – at Durham, for instance, by the idea of the column at its most elemental level. The cellular form of the building represents the thick wall. We tried to make a rich mix in which history was one link in the chain, between past and future. Our Cumbernauld college arises out of the same obsession as this building, only more so. A terribly confused – or rich! – mixture. All works of art are artefacts, in which people can trace what you've used, and also what you've not used – what's been excluded.

Each building is built on the foundations laid by the previous one. For instance, the chapel at Cardross was an inversion of the Glenrothes church; and the questions Cardross posed about the relationship of large and small volumes, the ideas developed there about stepped sections or manipulation of space and light, were re-addressed at Robinson College, Cambridge – an elaboration, on a different site and in a different culture, of the ideas developed here.

Baines: Can we go on to consider the role of the client, of patronage, in the design?

Metzstein: The influence of the Archdiocese was very powerful, yet enlightened. Archbishop Donald Campbell was an old patron of the firm – at a time when archbishops were very much respected, and made the decisions. His word counted – that was very much part of the history of the college. His office was next to ours – Jack Coia had taken the precaution of moving to 20 Park Circus, right next door to the Archdiocese! – and he was very much committed to architecture. This project was done in close and exclusive collaboration with the Archbishop – not with anyone else, just the Archbishop himself. No committee, no representatives of the future students – none of the proliferation of present-day consultations was brought into play.

We satisfied him as to the form of the building, the plan – we even made a model to convince him! He wanted a building worthy of its purpose. A Modern building, a building of its time, but not a 'modern hotel' dressed up as a seminary – he wanted an old-fashioned seminary transformed by Modernity. For instance, he wanted the building to be isolated: old-fashioned ideas, which we responded to eagerly. And in turn, he responded to our architectural concept, which we were passionately keen on. Now it was a little more complicated because Archbishop Campbell himself died during the course of the project. But there was also the Church as an institution, which had the belief that it had responsibility to make buildings for the future. And so Campbell's successor as Archbishop, James Scanlan, also gave us energetic support. This building was totally dedicated to the spoken and unspoken wishes of the Church, as a client.

Baines: Can we briefly consider the building's more recent problems, and whether it can be rescued from its present derelict state? (Fig. 3.69)

Metzstein: Well, I can certainly say that if they try to pull it down, I'll have the last laugh: the building would be almost as difficult to demolish as it was to build! That's because it was unstable until the top beams were put in position: we had to support it with scaffolding.

More seriously, I can say that, of all the projects I've been involved with, this one is the most important to me personally. It does represent a kind of distillation of my own ideas, and links in with my own wider architectural thinking. Building it was a very painful, but very enjoyable experience: we submitted the proposals in late 1959 and it opened in August 1966: that's three and a half years to develop, and the same amount to build. The building may have its deficiencies in terms of performance – but it's not for lack of effort!

As to possible ways of 'rescuing' it: I don't mind the idea of a conversion – it could be converted, for instance, into a conference centre. I have some ideas myself, about new uses. But it's certainly not a 'flexible box' – and that's not accidental! Or we could go for a completely different solution: in some ways, I would rather enjoy the idea of everything being

(opposite) 3.69 St Peter's College: present-day view of main block.

stripped away except the concrete itself – a purely romantic conception of the building as a beautiful ruin!'

'A WAREHOUSE FOR BOOKS': GLASGOW UNIVERSITY LIBRARY
SIR WILLIAM WHITFIELD, IN CONVERSATION WITH PATRICK NUTTGENS

Patrick Nuttgens: Just before we hear about the University Library, I thought a few background facts might be of interest. William Whitfield comes originally from the north-east of England: he studied architecture at Newcastle University. Since, then, after working abroad for a while, he's designed some major buildings in English cities such as Durham, Newcastle and Sheffield, and more recently, key London projects such as the Institute of Chartered Accountants extension, and Richmond House. But in all this time, his office has never grown bigger than 20 people – and *he* remains the designer. Whereas, for instance, I remember once introducing Robert Matthew to two people working in his office, that he'd never met! Now, on to Glasgow University Library: a big, multi-stage project, built between 1965 and 1981 – and I can remember vividly what a dominant impression it made when it first went up! William, what were the main influences on your design of that building?

Sir William Whitfield: I was first approached at the end of 1959. Joe Gleave was architectural and planning consultant to the University. He had ideas for the whole of the Hillhead area, and had decided that the new Library should be the key building: so he selected the highest point of the extension area as its site. What he wanted, essentially, was visual: an arresting image of what was to go there, years before it was to be built! I felt that first we should find out the practical requirements. So I met the Librarian, Mr McKenna, who told me, 'I want a large area which is freely adaptable, and which I can develop whichever way I want!' From this discussion, I understood his brief to be, more or less, a 'warehouse' for books, and it seemed to me that we might be able to do something to satisfy both him and Joe Gleave. In 1960, I did a drawing to show how the new building might be modelled, so as to form a dominant point in the university extension, while directly addressing McKenna's stipulation of 'a warehouse for books'. (Fig. 3.70)

So the practical requirements, within the framework of Gleave's plan, were my main framework in developing the design. But also present in the background was something very different. It was one of the buildings which has haunted me since my youth – Langley Castle, a tower house in Northumberland. I should point out that I'm a Northumbrian by birth – in other words, barely English! Langley's main accommodation block is a huge rectangle, held in by five towers. That image, of a central space served by peripheral towers, lodged in my mind in my mid teens and stayed there ever since. Thus, when people say that the Library was shaped by the precedent of Kahn's Richards Medical Building,

3.70 Glasgow University Library: perspective prepared *c*.1962 by William Whitfield, showing relationship of proposed Library to existing buildings on the Hillhead site.

Philadelphia, they're wrong – if there was any image in my mind, it was Langley. I was surprised, on my first visit to Copenhagen, to discover there, too, a Renaissance castle surrounded by towers. Then there were the towers of Roskilde Cathedral, and of the west front of Durham. The fascination of *towers* has always been with me. And the fascination with military buildings: for instance, the idea of a glacis is reflected at Glasgow, not as a real one you slither down, but as a bank of granite setts. Lou Kahn once told me that he also had a love of military architecture. Medieval and Renaissance military structures, especially, have always enthralled me: great areas of blank stone, brickwork, glacis, battered walls. (Fig. 3.71)

So I said, 'All right, Mr McKenna can certainly have his "warehouse" – and it must be totally without any service core!' Things like air-conditioning, toilets, everything that wasn't directly to do with reading, should be put out into peripheral towers. Although images such as Langley were somewhere in my thinking, that decision, on practical planning, had to come first.

3.71 The Library's south retaining wall (the 'glacis' referred to by Whitfield).

Nuttgens: So do you, in that sense, subscribe to the Corbusian idea of the plan as generator?

Whitfield: When I start to develop the actual form of a building, I always work from the inside out. I remember, when I was nine years old, my sister reading a book called *The Chimneys*, which led me to what, I think, was the first time I 'designed' anything: trying to plan a house with a secret room between the chimneys! If you think of all the really successful buildings – for instance, St. Sophia, my 'number one' building in the whole world! – they all grow out of the plan.

Most of my designs are planned out in my head long before they go on to paper – I work them out when I'm on a train, or driving, thinking three-dimensionally rather than floor-by-floor or elevation-by-elevation. I proceed in this way. First, I remove certain possibilities. It's like choosing wallpaper. You decide which ones you won't have, so that only one general option remains when you get down to drawing. Then I draw the building out, not absolutely right first time, but as the first outcome on paper of these cerebral exercises. Then the process of refining it begins.

Thus Glasgow began from Gleave's initial plan, and McKenna's raw brief for a 'warehouse'. From that came a central area, with towers at the periphery. Then there emerged, between each tower, double-height spaces, which could be reading spaces. Then, once this plan had grown in my mind, the problem then returned to Gleave's visual image: how to command the hill it sits on, in the same way that Scott's towers do on their site. Most of the towers are exactly the height they needed to be, but the tallest one, a water tower, was heightened a bit for effect.

Nuttgens: Could I bring in a comparative element to our discussion here, by introducing a contrasting case, the Edinburgh University Library, designed by Hardie Glover? I should explain that this was built at roughly the same time (1964-7), but has an almost opposite plan, with services at the centre and big open areas all around, with quite a plain, horizontally banded exterior. Now, at that time, I was on a working party running study courses on academic library planning, and we felt that the Edinburgh University Library turned out exactly as a library needed to be: not a public monument, but a building tailored straightforwardly to its use. We looked at Glasgow, and felt that what Gleave was asking of you – that your library should serve also as a dominant public building – was not what we wanted. What's your feeling about that issue? (Fig. 3.72)

Whitfield: Well, in our case, as I've said, to produce a monumental statement of the new University was a requirement – the first thing I was told to do. In that sense, I was asked to produce just what Edinburgh didn't want. My first reaction was that I couldn't design a building which was just an image! And some further interesting complications followed from Gleave's site. It wouldn't allow a low building of any size – and a big building, in accommodation terms,

3.72 Edinburgh University Library (Basil Spence, Glover & Ferguson): 1967 view.

(opposite) 3.73 South elevation of the Glasgow University Library and Hunterian Museum, taken 1987. In the foreground is the annexe housing the reconstructed Mackintosh house.

was needed. On that site, the basic, cubic shape of a building of that size was going to look exceedingly unpleasant, and it certainly wasn't going to satisfy Gleave's desire to have a sort of architectural explosion commanding the University extension site. So the eventual solution also served as a kind of camouflage, intended to create a different image by careful use of ancillary features. The towers – to return to the military field again – were a sort of 'disruptive camouflage', which set out to completely modify the basic shape: to make it look not like a great cube, but a series of closely assembled vertical elements. (Fig. 3.73) Also, Gleave, perversely in a way, had determined that the new building should be parallel with the Scott building, whereas the existing buildings on the site were several degrees different – so all the existing services became meaningless!

Nuttgens: All universities have a requirement to perpetually expand their book holdings – unless, that is, they throw out old books every time they buy new ones! How does your design cope with this?

Whitfield: The plan was staged, and the second stage would have accommodated extra books. Another possibility was an out-station: McKenna was prepared to accept that, but it didn't happen. When working out the brief, he and I had looked at libraries all over Europe: I remember in one case, the National Library at Bonn, you could get any book from closed stacks to the issue desk in one minute – but the readers had to order the books 24 hours in advance!

Nuttgens: Looking at your work in that period more generally, would it be true to say that you were an exponent of the most utter, rugged Modern architecture? And what are your feelings about the Modern Movement now? I remember when I was a student at Edinburgh College of Art, just after the war, we felt the key to Modern architecture was Socialism: we were concerned above all with housing – quite a contrast with today!

Whitfield: In answer to your first question: yes, I was! My career's been one of exploration. I went through a New Brutalist period: precast concrete didn't really appeal to me, I preferred in-situ. Eventually, at the

Institute of Chartered Accountants in London, I got external concrete out of my system; but I've always felt the need to express the constructional material. My underlying philosophy's stayed the same: a preoccupation with an openly declared articulation of the surface of a building – separating out elements of the building, and bringing them to the outside to make their presence felt. In answer to your second question: I believe Modern architecture's been a great movement, but it's been corrupted badly. The Modern Movement made one terrible mistake, in particular: it dismissed everything which happened before 1917. It became totalitarian, like Communism in Russia. And it crumbled at roughly the same time as Communism. But, unlike Communism, this was just a crumbling of things that obscured its essence: the real Modern Movement is still there. The Weissenhof houses were pure music, wonderful things. The rot began with the Festival of Britain, which trivialised Modern architecture, with gewgaws applied to buildings. However, I think that the Modern Movement, in the broad sense, is now heading for a renaissance. It's not for me personally – but I'm rather excited about it!

VISIONS REVISITED CONFERENCE: CONCLUDING DISCUSSION

Kirsty Wark: To conclude this conference, we've gathered together a discussion panel, drawn from some of our speakers today. (Fig. 3.74) I'd like to begin by re-focusing on what was perhaps the most persistent theme running through these lectures: the drive to build Modern mass housing, and the architectural and building processes which contributed to it. Because that subject seems somehow to encapsulate all the most acute pressures of the time: social, political, aesthetic. And it highlights, in a way that no other building type can, the double chronological tension associated with Modernism: on the one hand, its own ambiguous, generally hostile relationship with the legacy of the 19th century; on the other hand, our own uneasy present-day relationship with the relics of Modernism – monuments of a lost era of utopian dreams.

Let's jump straight into these issues, by picking up the debate that Charles Robertson started. If we take just that one project, Hutchesontown 'C', and ask: how do we, today, go about evaluating its historical and architectural significance? And what do we actually do about the building and its problems, in practical terms? There must be, represented at this conference, a variety of views, ranging from architects, engineers, to planners perhaps; I don't think we have anyone who has ever lived in Hutchesontown 'C', but I may be wrong, and it would be interesting to have their views as well. What do we do with Hutchesontown 'C'? If it needs shoring up and other extraordinary measures to save it – then should it be saved at all? (Fig. 3.75)

Charles Robertson: I think it's structurally sound, and I don't think there's any question of it falling down. In

3.74 'Visions Revisited' conference: discussion panel of speakers. Visible in picture (from left): Charles Robertson, James P McCafferty, David Page, Kirsty Wark.

3.75 Hutchesontown 'C': 1966 view beneath the eastern block.

fact, I think the problem's going to be getting it down! It'll not be so easy or safe to pull down as the tenements it replaced, I can assure you of that – it's a very complicated design, and those concrete legs are absolutely full of steel! No – the main structural problem is that we have external concrete material which is crumbling away, exposing the reinforcement. That can be dealt with. It's simply the panels that are attached to the building which makes this such a difficult problem.

Kirsty Wark: Aesthetically, Ronnie Cramond, do you think it is part of the Scottish architectural tradition – and should it be preserved?

Ronnie Cramond: I'm no architect, and I'm no architectural historian. But I think there's something in the thought that, because it's going to be so incredibly expensive to demolish – and Red Road would be even worse, because its steel frame is encased, for fire reasons, in concrete – because of that, I would have hoped that some conversion could be done, to bring Hutchesontown into another use. As I've said, there's nothing wrong with living in flats themselves, but, in terms of living conditions today, in the 1990s, they have got to be defensible, they have got to have security at the front. They have got to have decent entrance ways and common places. And you have got to have thermal insulation, you've got to have sound insulation. Then flat living is fine.

Kirsty Wark: David Walker, you made a confession at the start, that perhaps you hadn't appreciated the extent of the new 'tradition' – the 'heritage' of Modern architecture – which would arise over these last thirty years. From your point of view, in Historic Scotland, what about buildings like Hutchesontown 'C'?

David Walker: You're asking me if we would list them.

Kirsty Wark: Well, you have listed some Basil Spence works already.

David Walker: In fact, we haven't listed any postwar building of his. But we would have thought very seriously indeed about Hutchesontown, if it hadn't already become so run down – something which

caused me very considerable sadness, as it was a fine thing as first built. Nevertheless, there are, I think, some things in the design that are, perhaps, unfortunate – for instance, that the legs which support the ends of the building do not match the pylons which support it at the middle. But the point is, I think – and it has been the subject of internal debate within our organisation – it is, what listing would actually achieve, if we were to do it. Glasgow District Council have asked us not to list these blocks. And, furthermore, multi-storey blocks do present structural problems which don't arise with other buildings. These problems are by no means confined to Modern architecture, I hasten to add! We have under consideration just now a grant application for one of Glasgow's great turn-of-century master-works: Salmon, Son & Gillespie's office tower of 1905, Lion Chambers. Now there isn't any more pioneering building than that in this country. And the issue has been whether or not we spend a huge proportion of our grant-allocation in supporting something which the engineers say can only be kept going for another twenty years, or even less. And, frankly, decisions as controversial as this, are not decisions that are going to be taken by us professionals alone!

Kirsty Wark: Well, who is going to take them?

David Walker: I think the problem is, that we would have to see what listing would actually achieve, before we do it. One answer as to whether we should list or not, even if we think the building may not last indefinitely, has been that, at the very least, it shows that it should be recorded. But Hutchesontown 'C' is well recorded anyway, and could be recorded further – there isn't any difficulty about that. At the moment, we require to see what listing would actually achieve, before we go ahead and do it.

Hubert-Jan Henket: I'd like to raise the question of whether 'listing' actually means physically keeping a building – David finished on that question. I was fascinated by the discussion this morning, and I learned from the people who spoke this morning that they haven't spoken up, about their ideas, for the past 20 years! Well, here you get a different idea of what 'listing' might be.

Something, an enormous thing, happened in the last 30 years in this country, and I think we should at least keep record of what happened. So the historical accounts, for example, this morning, were to me tremendously important, for they have kept a memory of it, and not just for five years, but for future generations. That might be the path of 'listing', for your postwar Modernist patrimony. Not physically keeping the buildings, but just documenting what is there. It was very much on purpose that we decided to make our name, or construct our name, in the way that we did: DOCOMOMO rather than CODOMOMO. We think, particularly given the vast amount of building which has been done after the war, that it's much better to document a building, and only in very special cases to conserve it, to physically keep it.

Kirsty Wark: I think it's worth saying at this point that the whole proceedings of this conference will ultimately be put into published form. So, in a sense, this conference will be setting the way, by providing a written documentation of some of the testimonies we've heard today.

Mike Galloway: I'm Director of the Crown Street Regeneration Project, which is concerned with the large 40-acre site left by Hutchesontown 'E', right next to Hutchesontown 'C'. We're not involved with those particular blocks, but what we're involved with is bringing back the street pattern, the tenement, the traditional urban form of Scotland, to Glasgow. And that is in conjunction with, and with the cooperation of, the existing community. You may not have anyone here from Hutchesontown 'C' – and that would have been very interesting, because the vast majority of the 24 remaining families in those blocks, who are going to court to contest their eviction, are doing so to make sure that they don't get moved into another high-rise block. In my experience, they want a 'semi' somewhere in the suburbs instead.

I feel that the problem has revolved around an issue of quantity versus quality, and it's fully understandable, for political reasons, that the numbers game happened at the time. But our remit, in this part of the Gorbals, is about quality. And if the numbers suffer a little, so be it. We have to make sure that what we build, this time, lasts 60 or 70 years – stands the test of time. That, I must admit, has often led to a blanket rejection of the Modern Movement in architecture. And that is not, I feel, acceptable. Because there are, obviously, buildings of that period which do deserve proper recognition. I also feel that there is perhaps a feeling, particularly in the Gorbals, that the community's feeling of being hard done by over this last period of years, has really been about Modern planning rather than Modern architecture. There are a lot of Modern buildings, set in a traditional street pattern, that will survive and remain for the future.

Ronnie Cramond: On the matter of quality in Modern housing, I was always impressed in the 1950s and '60s by the high standards of what was done in Scandinavia – the quality of finish and landscaping.

If you build to a high quality, particularly in the common areas, then people respect it. Whereas if you make everything of concrete and iron rails, it looks shabby from the beginning, and it will deteriorate further. But one of the things I didn't mention in my paper, which is of considerable relevance here, is the fact that, in those days, we were subject to the financial constraints of housing indicative costs. These forced standards down – and that led to poor quality finishes, and to skimping on landscaping, because that was an 'extra'. Hence the dereliction around the houses, that I showed in my slides. Now I blame Her Majesty's Treasury for this, and I've spent 40 years of my life trying to persuade Her Majesty's Treasury to allow us to spend a bit more in the short term, in order to save taxpayers' money – much more, ten times more – in the longer term. I have always failed, because the system in this country is of a public expenditure round which never looks further forward than three years – in fact, it really only looks one year ahead, in practice. So the Treasury officials are not interested in anything which shows savings in the longer term. They're only interested in getting down costs in the short term. And that is fatal! Until we get out of this short-term thinking, there is no answer to problems like these. What we have is a public accounting system which goes back to the days of the Stewarts, when you had to stop a king keeping a standing army, and therefore you voted him money on an annual basis!

Kirsty Wark: But what if the tenants, or the tenants-to-be, of the Crown Street Regeneration Project, prove to be opposed to architectural innovation? Why should the people who happen to live in Hutchesontown today, in 1992, be given a veto over the environment to be experienced by future generations of residents, or by people who don't live there, but travel through the area every day? What prescription might that lead to? Is that the way of the future – that we can only have low density, low rise, paltry brick housing with stuck-on twiddly details – even in somewhere like the Gorbals, which is virtually part of the city centre?

David Page: I think, in these debates, we can learn from history, from what's been argued and done before. But to do that, the first and most vital thing is the need to document: we need to know why things were built. Basil Spence obviously aspired to create great housing. He aspired to gardens hanging in the sky, he aspired to a solution of the technical problems of balcony design. When you actually go into these houses, you find that the multi-storey flats don't have internal bathrooms, that these balconies bring light flooding into their bathrooms. They were really trying, within the technical constraints of building high, to bring people humane living conditions, and I think we can learn something from that.

We have to learn from the idea that landscaping was absolutely critical. Spence tried to make hanging gardens in the sky. That wasn't something utilitarian, or second-rate – he was trying to make beautiful things. Look, for instance, at the Olympic Village at the 1972 Munich Games. If you go there now, it's covered in green – multi-storey blocks covered in green! There you have it, achieved – the goal that Spence was seeking. I don't think it's necessary that Hutchesontown 'C' has to be kept, but we have to learn from it. We've got to move forward and say, 'Right! How can we turn tenemental facades round, facades whose living rooms face north?

Can we devise a new architecture capable of turning the building round so it can get the sun – as Modern architects were able to do – while still acknowledg-ing, in today's fashion, the street facade to the front?' We can, I'm convinced, learn from what's happened in the past, and actually achieve a much richer tenemental form of architecture. Our overriding aim must be to avoid being negative and reactive, and, instead, to be as positive as the Modernists were in their own time.

Mike Drury (Edinburgh University): If the Hutchesontown 'C' block is to be kept, it should only be as a monument to absolutist folly. Because one of the basic problems with that sort of building is that it's unresponsive in terms of its local adaptations to the people who actually use it, who live in it. And nobody at that time, politically or architecturally, was taking the long view in terms of maintenance, in terms of use. Nobody cared who the people were that were going into the Hutchesontown block – whether those people had enough money to actually pay for the electricity bills. It was a set of absolutist political and architectural expedients, dressed up in a particular aesthetic form, and imposed on the users.

John Richards: I don't think this corresponds to what actually happened at the time. I was building very shortly afterwards, and I remember there was a great deal of attention paid to the 'users' – in the form of research into user needs and attitudes. Although I wasn't myself building high rise blocks, I was in among many architects who were. And I remember a great deal of published research on tenant attitudes – towards balconies and heating systems in particular! This present-day claim, that there was no thought given to the occupants of different types of housing, is, I think, a myth of hindsight. What would, however, be both interesting and potentially useful would be historical research into this very subject: the evolution of the idea of the 'user', from the Modernist concept of scientifically researched 'user needs' into its apparent opposite, of today's ideal of 'user participation' defending the old from the new. (Fig. 3.76)

Christopher Dean (Co-ordinator, DOCOMOMO English working-party): I was very interested in the unexpected parallel which was drawn earlier, between the situation in the Gorbals before the war, when roofs leaked and the landlords were apparently absent, and the lack of ability of today's local authorities to maintain their stock from the postwar housing programme. Is this just a local parallel, between two generations, or is this a perennial phenomenon?

Hubert-Jan Henket: Our experience in building maintenance may be of relevance here, as it makes a striking comparison with your country. Maintenance has been part of Dutch housing investment, since just after the war. But what, from my perspective, seems to have been missing in all the things I've heard here up to now, is allowance for the inevitability of change. In response to what Mike Galloway said, that you want your new housing to be fit for 60 or 70 years: that, to my Dutch ears, is extraordinary. And I'll tell you why. I think it was Mr. Cramond who said, this morning, that you were trying to build houses in the '50s and '60s, to what was seen then as a very high level; but that these levels wouldn't any longer be good enough for today. In our country, what we've experienced over the past eighty years is that the period of use, the period of the original brief of a building – as houses,

3.76 Springburn C.D.A. Area C (deck blocks built 1971 in the French Camus system): 1989 view, immediately before the scheme's transfer to Scotia House and Wimpey for refurbishment (in a brightly variegated Post-Modern form) and sale.

offices or whatever – has shrunk dramatically, to the point that now, with us, people can come back and renovate their building, with a State subsidy, after 15 years. It used to be 25 years, but now it's 15. And presumably it's going to go even further back, to 10 years. That means that we now have a tremendous problem, which we've never had before: namely, that we're designing housing which might, as a structure, last for 50, 60 or 70 years, but which, we know beforehand, won't endure as a total concept for anything like that time. As Kirsty suggested a few minutes ago, today's idea of design determined by user participation potentially clashes with the different wishes of tomorrow's users. We know that their views will be different, even if we maintain the buildings properly: so it's not just a matter of good maintenance. Thus one of the main problems we have – and this is particularly peculiar for an organisation like DOCOMOMO – is how to save, or record, a throwaway building for eternity! That's basically what you're talking about. And that is a very complex problem!

Mike Galloway: I don't believe that reaction, or rejection, in the future is absolutely inevitable. What we're trying to do at Crown Street is, firstly, to put life back into the community. So they do not think that, 25 years from now, we'll all be back in there, the planners and the architects. So, socially, we put in more investment in terms of the capital cost of the buildings. They've been designed in a way which incorporates all the modern standards we can at the moment, but in a structure which will allow for future adaptation in the same way that – whether you like the architectural style or not – the tenements are now.

Robert Gibson (Glasgow University): It seems to me, as a mediaevalist and a 'Europeanist', that there is a marked contrast between what is happening here and in Europe, and that we here are governed by a very thin, pragmatic culture indeed, determined by short-term considerations. In Northern Italy, or in Prague, the past has been respected, the cities have not been razed. Interventions are generally done with care towards the environment, and new developments – housing in particular – have been developed around, not within cities. Obviously the Green Belt has created some problems here for any such strategy.

Nevertheless their cities don't appear to have the inner-city devastation that has arisen from our situation. And concern for the past means that, in what you're doing now, you start to think of buildings as things that you'd want to have a future. The exhibition upstairs strikes me as particularly plaintive, because it juxtaposes various, frankly, boring buildings which seem to have a perfectly secure present – and, probably, future – with one or two major monuments which seem to be under the greatest threat. For instance, Cardross, or Hutchesontown 'C', which, of the Glasgow high flats, is the most visually distinctive. In most of Europe, there's a sense of monumentality. It's present at all levels of culture, including the relatively popular press. And it means that buildings are generally meant not only to last, but to be significant. The estates that we're preserving are mediocre nonentities, easy to preserve but with no visual identity at all; while our true Modern monuments are threatened, just as were the monuments of each past generation. And they'll remain threatened until they have receded into the past, to become a nostalgic era in which we feel 'safe', in the same way as we, today, look on the eighteenth century – a time when, of course, sanitary conditions were far worse than now.

Kirsty Wark: Can I pick up on your reference to Cardross, and ask Isi Metzstein: are there any general lessons regarding Modernism as 'heritage' to be learnt from the current problems of St Peter's College?

Isi Metzstein: Well, obviously the key issue that Cardross raises, is that of the listing and conservation of relatively new buildings of specialised uses – although Cardross, which was conceived over thirty years ago, is no longer so 'new' as it was! But it is a building which dramatises the issue of Modern buildings of a unique kind, buildings which are difficult to convert to other functions. It raises the question of what those buildings might need in the way of conservation or, should we say, anticipatory conservation. I think this is an issue that hasn't been raised here so far, although it's been hinted at in the idea of documentation. Now I know that Cardross, being listed already, is a special case, and is one of the few postwar buildings in Scotland with statutory

protection. But, more generally, there has to be some kind of mechanism for Modern buildings that are vulnerable – abandoned or distressed. There has to be some method of making a judgement, or of recognising them as having future worth. And the same applies to the buildings of today. In fact, I say to my students that that's just the kind of buildings they must design. I say to them: 'Ideally, leave your designs on paper; but if you have to build them, build them so that they can be "listed" in the near future!'

John Hume (Historic Scotland): Could I add something to the debate on multi-storey blocks – concerning Glasgow particularly, although I think the same is probably true of Edinburgh? That is, that the multi-storey flats represent a transition, not just in architectural terms, but also in social terms. I went to school in the Gorbals, from the late 1940s through to the late 1950s, and I saw the Gorbals at work. There you had a community which had been brought together not much more than a hundred years earlier, of which many of the original members had come from rural surroundings, and which had begun a process of adjusting to modern urban living. That process, in the '40s and '50s, had not fully been completed. The Gorbals was an area, like the Western Highlands or the West of Ireland, where the outside world of the streets was a part of living, where the socialising took place in the streets and pubs, where the house was somewhere you went home to sleep and to eat. The transition from that to what we would now all understand as 'modern living' – living in self-contained, 'privatised' household units – was largely accomplished, in areas such as this, by the construction of the multi-storey flats. And the tenants who are now going to move into the re-re-developed Hutchie 'E', or, rather, the Crown Street Regeneration Project, are people who have very largely become acclimatised to modern urban living, where the home has a defensible space, where the street is an 'extra'. That is a very big transition, and it's taken place within only half of my lifetime. So I think these buildings, regardless of their architectural merits, and regardless of their technically innovative qualities, should also be recognised as historical 'monuments', in view of their crucial role, in making possible that social transition towards self-containment and 'privatised' living.

Kirsty Wark: But was it a valuable role, if what they were doing was acclimatising people to living up on the 23rd storey, to houses which, if the lifts broke, became cells – acclimatising people, in other words, to isolation?

John Hume: But the important thing was that people now had a separate space in which they could live, with separate mod. cons. To extend that separation – previously the preserve of the rich – to working-class people, had been the central aim of housing reformists throughout Europe for the whole of the previous century. To write off that century of effort, on the basis of nothing more than hindsight, is much too easy – especially as we, today, have in no way rejected ideals such as the provision of separate sanitary amenities for each dwelling. You saw the diagrams of a single-end in Ronnie Cramond's lecture. A great many of the houses in the Gorbals in the '40s and '50s were actually 'made down' from middle-class dwellings into single rooms, and enormous numbers of people were jammed into these single-ends, often with a shared kitchen as well as a shared toilet, and with no bathroom or washing facilities. The move from these surroundings into a two, three, four bedroomed house with hot water, a bath, an inside toilet, was a very major change indeed, and one generally seen, at the time, as entirely beneficial. By comparison, the question of where that dwelling was situated, whether it was two storeys up or twenty storeys up, seemed much less prominent. And of course, since those days, the emphasis on the segregated dwelling has, if anything, become even stronger.

Diane Kay (English Heritage): I've got a question about preservation, concerned with where the dividing line should come – between which categories of buildings. Should it fall so as to include buildings which are great works of art, but exclude those of historical interest? Should it be drawn so as to include both, on equal terms? Or is a hierarchical approach the best: to say that something like Red Road should certainly be preserved on grounds of its historical importance, but that something like Cardross College is an irreplaceable work of art, and therefore must have an even higher priority?

Kirsty Wark: Well, David Walker, that's your 'patch'.

David Walker: I think that listing buildings which are difficult to adapt, unless someone finds a way in which, for instance, 'failed' multi-storeys will work again, is extremely difficult. Statutory listing is exactly what it says. It does mean that the statutory process has got to be gone through before the building is demolished or is radically altered. And it's difficult because – here I'm speaking personally – the whole question of postwar listing is governed by the fact that we have a 30-year rule. And within that 30-year rule, I think we will have to take advice before we move on any scale. But we're moving as fast as we can.

Some things we know already. A great deal of university building was very good indeed. There's a lot of very good housing. There's a lot of good church building, not without its problems. Also an enormous amount of extremely good school building, but this has not yet been sufficiently comprehensively analysed. I don't really want to go back to the system English Heritage and its predecessor department had at one stage, of listing only the works of a set of identified major masters.

There are always people like William Kerr of Alloa, of whom no-one had heard until recent years. There are always important people out there, who may not have done very much, but have done good work. Everything should be looked at for what it's worth, in its own terms. This is underlined, for instance, by the contentiousness of the proposals to preserve Hutchesontown 'C'. For Basil Spence was an architect whose name every well-informed household in Scotland, and even relatively uninformed households, have known for a very long time.

That controversy does, I think, indicate the extent of appraisal which is required before we start doing anything too radical. But, that having been said, I do think that we don't have too much time. Far too many buildings haven't been maintained properly. For example, even in a case such as the Provident Institution on the south side of St. Andrew Square in Edinburgh, where there's no shortage of funds to maintain the building, someone, annoyingly, has modified the top of the staircase-tower, and quite spoiled the design – which may be troublesome, in due course, to get put right. So we are dealing with a building stock that isn't perhaps going to be quite as stable as traditional buildings have been. It is important to get on with it before we find that, suddenly, major university buildings have – as indeed has happened – been refenestrated, and have been quite spoilt. I do think we need to start a process of serious evaluation: obviously that's what we are hoping DOCOMOMO will do. And when you have digested it all, we'll look at it again!

David Page: We have to look past what may prove relatively short-term technical problems, to the wider cultural continuities. I feel that a building such as Cardross can easily stand comparison with past monuments like Thomson's St. Vincent Street Church, or the School of Art. Frankly, I've never been to any Modern building in Europe that synthesises quality of plan-form and detailing in that way. Yes, there are technical problems, but this is an astonishing work of art. Even at the Finlandia Hall, for instance, Aalto's classic piece in Helsinki, all the marble panels fell, and are going to have to be replaced. There are always technical failures.

David Walker: As you may have seen in recent press coverage of our recent listing proposals for Gillespie, Kidd & Coia churches, we in Historic Scotland aren't in any way contesting the quality of the work which was carried out by the practice: that's why we moved on listing these churches. But you've only to read last week's newspapers to see what the reaction has been, to what might be thought very obviously 'listable' cases. I've never been in any doubt that Cardross was a great work of art, from the day it was built.

Mike Galloway: Could I just make the point that there's a difference between the design of special buildings in urban areas, and that of background buildings; generally, housing is a background kind of building. And in that case, slightly tongue-in-cheek, I would like our new Gorbals never to win an architectural award, and never to be listed – because that might be the kiss of death!

Ian Stanger (Duncan of Jordanstone College, Dundee): I'm one of the people who could be classed as the 'opposition' today. As a planner, I'd just like to ask any of the panel, any of the people who're into listing these tower blocks, whether they, even after all the modifications in the world, would want to live on the 31st floor of Red Road?

Kirsty Wark: Do we have anyone in the audience that lives or has lived in a high-rise flat, and has liked it, or anyone that would want a flat on the 31st floor? – could you put your hands up? Well, in fact, quite a number of people have their hands up – added to the fact that one of our speakers, Miles Glendinning, has a flat (a second home) on the 20th floor of Martello Court in Edinburgh. This brings our formal proceedings to an end: so I'd like to call on Paul Stirton, Convener of the DOCOMOMO Scottish working-party, to say a few words in conclusion.

Paul Stirton: Our purpose in bringing 133 people together here today to discuss this country's postwar architecture, was to demonstrate that the issues raised by the subject are current ones, and that they are not at all simple. From this point on, our aim, as an organisation, is to promote further events – including publications, such as the proceedings of this conference – to promote the DOCOMOMO strategy of documentation followed by selective preservation. In the latter area, we intend to pursue not a confrontational agenda of oppositional 'campaigning' – which would merely be substituting pro-Modern for anti-Modern utopian rhetoric – but a long-term strategy of persuasion and discussion, to try and ensure that Modern architecture, and postwar architecture in general, is treated seriously, and not dismissed out of hand. I think it's time that we put an end to knee-jerk reactions and blanket rhetoric, and get a mature, considered, sensible approach, which allows for the complex and often, still, problem-ridden situation of Modernist architecture in this country today. And I hope that DOCOMOMO's Scottish national working-party, in particular, will be at the forefront of that process of research and analysis.

PART FOUR
SIXTY KEY MONUMENTS

INTRODUCTION

To begin the task of documenting and conserving postwar Scottish architecture, DOCOMOMO compiled, in 1993/4, a preliminary descriptive register of sixty key monuments from the years 1945-70: the compilers were Claudia Bölling, Miles Glendinning, Ranald MacInnes, and Diane Watters. The subjects in the register were selected with the aim of representing the diversity of building types, and associated values, constructed during this period. In size, they ranged from small individual structures to entire planned areas of towns. In scope, architectural distinction was the most prominent criterion of selection – demonstrating that architecture, as an art, flourished undiminished during those years – but the energy and scale of the wider building drive, and its constructional and technical daring, were not neglected. Architecturally, Modern design naturally predominated, but survivals of older styles, such as Traditionalist classicism, were also included, as were projects anticipating the conservationist and Vernacular tendencies of the 1970s and the Postmodern period.

This preliminary national register, which is reproduced below, formed the basis of an extensive exhibition on postwar architecture mounted in 1993 by the Royal Incorporation of Architects in Scotland. And it will subsequently be put to specific policy use in the field of 'heritage'. For it forms the basis of two key inventories of postwar monuments, which are being prepared for the purposes of heritage documentation and protection. The first of these is a Scottish contribution to a wider international register of monuments currently being drawn up by DOCOMOMO International for the use of ICOMOS; and the second is a report and inventory requested by Historic Scotland – our country's Government heritage agency – to help them in a recently started thematic project for the statutory 'listing' of postwar buildings.

For these purposes, some adjustments to the original selection will be necessary, especially to take account of subsequent developments such as the demolition of Hutchesontown 'C' and the dismantling of the Ravenscraig complex. But this does not diminish the significance of the register itself, as an initial pointer to the acceptance of something which would once have seemed a contradiction in terms: Modern architecture as 'heritage'. Already, DOCOMOMO has been involved in important developments in this field, including the listing, at Category A, of the Lanark County Buildings, Hamilton, and, at Category B, of the Bernat Klein Studio; and the raising of Cardross Seminary to Category A, along with the establishment of a working-party to safeguard its future. In 1994, Historic Scotland also listed a large group of Gillespie, Kidd & Coia churches, including St Bride's, East Kilbride.

What has made this process different from any previous 'rehabilitation' of past architecture as 'heritage' was its intimate link with living testimony – a point emphasised by Dr Dickson Mabon when he opened the RIAS exhibition on August 18th 1993. Noting the exhibition's roots in the 'Visions Revisited'

(opposite) 3.77 Monktonhall colliery (1960-5). View of the No. 1 Shaft Winding Tower.

conference, he explained that 'for Ronnie Cramond, Pat Rogan and myself, and the other "historic" speakers at that conference, it opened up a whole new perspective for us. Especially for politicians, who, with our short-term timescales, don't often get the chance to stand back, and see the good we sometimes do. What that conference, and the selection of sixty key buildings in this exhibition, has reminded us, is that maybe we didn't do such a bad job after all. Oh yes, there were many blunders as well – but on the whole, those years were a joy to live in, a time of high ideals and some solid achievements. And now here is what we built, in all its varied aspects, set out for history to examine and to judge!'

To further this process of reassessment, the preliminary register of sixty key buildings and groups is reproduced in the following pages. They are grouped in geographical order (under pre-April 1996 regions), in each case with an illustration and brief description – summarising the building's historical and architectural importance. Where there has been significant discussion of any building in an earlier passage of this book, a cross-reference is given. To assist in locating the buildings, a six-figure Ordnance Survey grid reference (four-figure, in the case of area items or groups), as well as the number of the relevant O.S. 1/10,000 map, is provided. It should be borne in mind that inclusion of a building on this register does not mean that it is publicly accessible.

BORDERS REGION

1: BERNAT KLEIN HOUSE AND STUDIO, HIGH SUNDERLAND

Peter Womersley, 1956-7 (house), 1969-72 (studio).
OS: (73) NT 473314

These two buildings, commissioned by a Borders textile designer and mill-owner, show that Modern architecture could cope with the planning of highly individualised buildings just as effectively as it addressed the demand for mass social production. The Klein house, one of a series which established Womersley's national and international reputation, was planned in an American-inspired open manner, around features such as chimneystacks and cupboard clusters – a plan described by Womersley as 'subtractive architecture, commencing with one simple volume and breaking it down'. The demureness of the

4.1 Bernat Klein House: 1958 view of living area.

4.2 Bernat Klein Studio: 1972 view.

modular prefabricated-timber structure emphasised the natural grandeur of the high beech trees around it. A decade later, Womersley brought a more monumental sensibility to bear on the design of the Studio – whose refined form combines cantilevered plasticity with floating openness to the landscape. Studio listed by Historic Scotland, 1994. (Figs. 4.1, 4.2)

CENTRAL REGION

2: STATUE OF KING ROBERT THE BRUCE AND ROTUNDA, BANNOCKBURN: ROTUNDA, 1962; STATUE

C. d'O. Pilkington Jackson (sculptor), 1964.
OS: (57) NS 794906

Although protected since 1932 by the National Trust for Scotland, the site of the Battle of Bannockburn was only developed in a representational and monumental manner in the 1960s. In 1962, under NTS auspices, the site was landscaped and the circular, concrete

4.3 Statue of King Robert the Bruce: C. d'O. Pilkington Jackson at work on the clay model, 1963.

Rotunda erected, to focus visitors' attention on Stirling Castle as the English army's objective, and Pilkington Jackson was commissioned by the King Robert the Bruce Memorial Committee to make a massive bronze equestrian statue of the King (unveiled 1964). The information centre was opened in 1967 by William Ross, Secretary of State for Scotland. (Fig. 4.3)

3: WARD UNIT AND OPERATING THEATRE SUITE, FALKIRK AND DISTRICT ROYAL INFIRMARY, FALKIRK

Keppie, Henderson and Partners, with SHHD and Western Regional Hospital Board, 1963-6.
OS: (65) NS 882798

A research and development project built to test out the 'race-track' method of ward design; and an exemplar of the SHHD's innovative approach to hospital 'design-in-use' projects. Advances in medical science, especially in the USA, had rendered obsolete the spaced-out 'pavilion' hospital layout, with its emphasis on ventilation, and interwar architects such as Tait had begun to pioneer much more economical, concentrated plans with smaller wards (allowing greater patient privacy). This three-storey (and basement) prototype Unit, whose two upper floors were planned to simulate floors of a mechanically-ventilated, multi-storey block with services at the centre, and small wards arranged in a 'racetrack' layout around the outside, proved the workability of this system here; it was subsequently incorporated in hospital slab blocks throughout Scotland. The ground floor of the Unit also contained four operating theatres. (Fig 4.4)

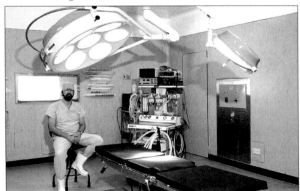

4.4 Falkirk Ward Unit: Operating Theatre 3.

4: STIRLING UNIVERSITY, PHASE 1 (PATHFOOT) BUILDING

Robert Matthew, Johnson-Marshall & Partners, 1966-7. OS: (57) NS 804968

A microcosm of several key Modern values – scientific design, rapid prefabricated construction, and flexibility in use – applied to one of the most characteristic Modern building projects: a new university, the first to be established in Scotland since 1583. The task which faced RMJM when appointed executive architects to Phase I in January 1966 was to design and build, by September 1967, a single permanent structure which would accommodate all the University's non-residential functions during its first three years of existence. The site was the mature parkland of the Airthrey Castle policies. The solution – a single-storey, steel-framed building, with a high degree of prefabrication and almost complete flexibility of internal planning – provided a sophisticated demonstration of the impact of machine-aesthetic design in a landscaped setting. The ground plan was a variant of the traditional hospital plan of central spine and finger-like lateral wings. Actual construction time was 13 months. (Fig. 4.5)

FIFE REGION

5: DYSART REDEVELOPMENT, PHASES I, II AND III

Wheeler & Sproson, 1958-71. OS: (59) NT 304931

This large, multi-phase rebuilding of the decayed centre of a historic burgh represents an amalgam of the

4.5 Stirling University, Phase I: display board, prepared *c.*1967 by RMJM.

informality of smaller-scale infill projects such as Dunbar and Lerwick, and Modern ideals of open, 'comprehensive' redevelopment: Phase II includes a group of small, detached 4-storey 'point blocks', while Phase III, with its heavy forms and small windows, reflects the ideas of 'cluster' planning prevalent at the time. (Fig. 4.6)

6: ST PAUL'S CHURCH, GLENROTHES

Gillespie, Kidd & Coia, 1956-7. OS: (59) NO 281004

A low-cost New Town church for an avant-garde priest, and the first of the practice's innovative centralised, expressionistic designs. The carefully controlled daylighting and the massive, geometrical forms of the larger 1960s churches are presaged in this simple, white-painted structure. Notable metal cross by Benno Schotz as internal centrepiece. Listed by Historic Scotland, 1994. (Fig. 4.7)

4.6 Dysart Redevelopment Phase II: 1965 view.

4.7 St Paul's Church, Glenrothes: late 1950s view.

7: KINCARDINE POWER STATION

Robert Matthew, Johnson-Marshall & Partners,
1958-63. OS: (65) NS 925881

The first of a series of giant coal-burning power stations commissioned by the South of Scotland Electricity Board on its formation in 1955 as part of moves towards an integrated Scottish national energy policy (following the break-up of the British Electricity Authority). Kincardine was brought into service in five stages between 1958 and 1963, with an ultimate generating capacity of 760 kilowatts – at the time, one of the largest in Europe. Adjoined by two 400-ft. chimneys, the main building has a steel-framed structure (by Redpath Brown) with light cladding of aluminium and glass – a decisive break from the interwar 'cathedral of power' tradition. The station was designed to burn low-grade coal from local collieries. The Kincardine area's coal extraction/energy generation complex was further augmented from 1966, when the country's largest conventional power station, the Longannet plant, also designed by RMJM, was built. In comparison with the slender elegance of Kincardine, Longannet's single-chimneyed massiveness purposefully expresses its far greater capacity. (Fig. 4.8)

8: KIRKCALDY TOWN HOUSE

David Carr, 1937-56. OS: (59) NS 277914

The Traditionalist classicism of this building was, by the end of the 30s, *the* internationally accepted idiom for design of public buildings anywhere in Europe. Yet individual instances of this monumentalism – just like the international 'vernacular' of *c*.1900 – were typically justified by rhetoric of a national 'essence'. Here, the text which accompanied Carr's successful competition entry claimed the design was a response to the 'inborn characteristics' of Scots towns. Its construction delayed by the war, the Town House was eventually built in little-altered form. (Fig. 4.9)

9: ANDREW MELVILLE HALL OF RESIDENCE, ST. ANDREWS UNIVERSITY

James Stirling, 1964-7. OS: (59) NO 495167

A 250-room residences 'settlement' contained in two splayed wings stretching downhill towards the sea: originally envisaged as part of a programme of up to six such settlements, but no more were built. Although the building's general form seems to echo the Scots tradition of splay-planned classical buildings (e.g. Minto House), Stirling's design is also significantly influenced by the New Brutalist conception of residential buildings as radiating 'clusters' which, it was hoped, would foster 'community' spirit among the occupiers. Here, 'sociability' was to be encouraged by the wide, glazed-in decks emanating

4.9 Kirkcaldy Town House: original perspective by David Carr, 1937.

4.8 Kincardine Power Station, 1958.

from the central services building at the apex. The crystalline architectural form, and homogeneous colour, resulted from the decision to set the study bedroom windows diagonally, and to use surface-ribbed precast concrete, prefabricated in Edinburgh and transported to the site. (Fig. 4.10)

GRAMPIAN REGION

10: GALLOWGATE REDEVELOPMENT, ABERDEEN

G. McI. Keith (City Architect), 1964-6. OS: (38) NJ 942067

The most immaculate and refined realisations of those quintessentially Modern forms of urban housing – tall blocks set in open, geometrical layouts – are to be found in Aberdeen. In the City's redevelopment areas, dramatic slabs and towers in superbly finished concrete, with gable-end rubble panelling, rear up from the midst of dense landscaping. Provided from the beginning with generous facilities, including ground-floor launderettes, Aberdeen's multi-storey flats, like all its municipal assets, have been maintained with scrupulous care, and have always attracted long waiting lists. (Fig. 4.11)

11: GRAY'S SCHOOL OF ART, ABERDEEN

D. Michael A. Shewan, 1964-8. OS: (38) NJ 910030

An elegant, steel-framed complex set in a well-planted area north of the river Dee: the informality of the land-scaped setting contrasts with the highly formal, sym-metrical 'U' plan layout with raised sculpture court at the centre. The building's steel framing is exposed

externally and enclosed in a glass skin. A disciplined, sophisticated style, somewhat reminiscent of the work of Arne Jacobsen or Mies van der Rohe. (Fig. 4.12)

12: PETERHEAD CENTRAL AREA (ST. PETER'S STREET, 1ST PHASE)

Baxter, Clark & Paul, 1968-71. OS: (30) NJ 131462

The most monumental of a series of small-burgh rede-velopments by these architects, transitional between the jagged agglomerations of Late Modernism and the Vernacular of the 1970s. A staggered five-storey row of 34 maisonettes and flats built by Peterhead Town Council in a prominent harbourside location; con-

4.11 Gallowgate redevelopment, Aberdeen.

4.10 Andrew Melville Hall, St Andrews.

4.12 Gray's School of Art, Aberdeen.

struction comprises brick with coloured rendering and some slate facing, while steep roofs and raised margins on some windows enhance the 'vernacular' feel of the scheme. (Fig. 4.13)

HIGHLAND REGION

13: DOUNREAY EXPERIMENTAL RESEARCH ESTABLISHMENT

R.S. Brocklesby (Chief Architect to the Industrial Group of the UK Atomic Energy Authority), 1955-8; extension 1966. OS: (11) NC 9867

The original UKAEA project, built on a former airfield site, comprises a prototype experimental fast reactor – the familiar white reactor sphere, known as 'DFR' – together with laboratories and fuel element manufacturing and processing plants. The reactor, which was designed to operate in such a way that it generated more plutonium fuel than it consumed, was the first such installation in the world to supply grid electricity; more recently, however, it has been closed down. In 1966-74, the UKAEA complex was enlarged by construction of the Prototype Fast Reactor (PFR), intended, with its full commercial-scaled fuel assemblies, as the forerunner of future nuclear power plants: a 250 MW station, supplying the equivalent of the power requirements of a city the size of Aberdeen. This reactor was scheduled to close in 1994. The complex also includes a separate military establishment, whose task was the development of submarine reactors. (Fig. 4.14)

LOTHIAN REGION

14: FISHERMEN'S HOUSES, DUNBAR

Basil Spence, 1949-52. OS: (67) NT 680792

Twenty houses on four nearby sites in the harbour area. An influential scheme designed to evoke a traditional fishing-port atmosphere. Typical of the many smaller projects of the immediate postwar years in its ambiguous combination of features indicating 'vernacular' character (the pantiled roofs), features indicating Modern character (the metal-framed windows), and elements pointing both ways, such as the concrete forestairs and balconies, or the rubble base walling, with its allusions both to small-burgh heritage and to the avant-garde 1930s 'organic' tendency of architects such as Corbusier. Storage space for tackle and fishing-nets was integrated into the design. (Fig. 4.15)

4.13 St Peter's Street development, Peterhead.

4.14 Dounreay Experimental Reactor Establishment Fast Reactor (DFR): view during construction, 1957.

15: 'AVISFIELD', EDINBURGH

Morris & Steedman, 1956-7; extended 1964.
OS: (66) NT 195764

A pioneering Modern private house – envisaged by its authors as 'a new way of looking at the house in Scotland'. Built in stone and painted brick, with timber beams and windows. With its rubble-walled courtyard garden, overhanging and interpenetrating flat roofs, and open-plan interior focused on a massive rubble fireplace, this prototype of the influential patio-house pattern reconciles postwar American trends in domestic design with associations specific to this country. (Fig. 4.16)

16: CHESSELS COURT
REDEVELOPMENT, EDINBURGH

Robert Hurd, 1958-66 (project architect, Ian Begg).
OS: (66) NT 263738

The culmination of a distinguished series of Royal Mile slum redevelopment/improvement schemes by Hurd. Planned and executed in three stages, the project contains a mixture of preserved tenement blocks and new infill, with a front range to the Canongate and rear wings framing Chessel's Buildings (a tenement block of *c.*1745) at the rear. It is unified by coloured harling and self-consciously Traditionalist features, such as arcading, in a simplified Lorimerian style. This formula, which developed 'conservative surgery' ideas first enunciated by Sydney Mitchell and Patrick Geddes at the turn of the century, was parallelled in the contemporary reconstruction of bombed German historic cities, such as Münster and Nürnberg. (Fig. 4.17)

4.16 Avisfield, Cramond Road North: rear view as originally completed.

4.15 Dunbar, Lamer Street housing: view of c.1953.

4.18 Leith Fort: rear view of one of the point blocks.

17: LEITH FORT DEVELOPMENT, EDINBURGH

Shaw-Stewart, Baikie & Perry, 1960-6.
OS: (66) NT 263767

An unique encapsulation of avant-garde Modern housing design trends of the late '50s. The scheme, which originated in a competition win by three newly graduated students, comprises three different elements, all of striking novelty: single-storey 'patio housing'; a seven-storey 'deck-access' block; and, most prominent, two 20-storey point blocks faced with precast concrete slabs. The north facades of these towers are of an uncompromising grandeur, with their industrial-aesthetic glass-brick windows and boldly jutting stair-towers (inspired, according to Perry, by Kahn's work). (Fig. 4.18)

18: MOREDUN TEMPORARY HOUSING AREA, EDINBURGH

J.A.W. Grant/City Architect/Sam Bunton, 1948-9. OS: (66) NT 292697

This housing scheme on the south-east edge of the capital is the last area in the country where emergency prefabricated dwellings of the immediate postwar years – above all, the aluminium 'prefabs' produced by aircraft factories – remain in any numbers. Following the main programme of temporary 'prefab' bungalows, numbers of strengthened 'permanent' bungalows – a total of 1,500 across Scotland – were supplied by the same firms. At Moredun, 145 of these latter, along with 186 of the composite aluminium/brick 'Blackburn Mk III' house (designed by Sam Bunton in 1948) and 170 of the steel 'BISF' house, were erected. The scheme's layout had originally been designed by J.A.W. Grant with traditionally-built, Lorimerian-style cottages in mind: 251 of these were eventually built here. (Fig. 4.19)

4.17 Chessels Court: 1957 elevations, drawn by Ian Begg.

19: MORTONHALL CREMATORIUM, EDINBURGH

Sir Basil Spence, Glover and Ferguson, 1964-7. OS: (66) NT 269683

A woodland cluster of crystalline shapes, discreetly alluding to the North European expressionistic tradition of church architecture. The group comprises two linked chapels and service block, with detached remembrance chapel to the west. Built of concrete blocks with sparkling flint-aggregate finish on the outside, and austere plaster facing within. Indirect coloured lighting filtering down from chevron windows. (Fig. 4.20)

20: NATIONAL LIBRARY OF SCOTLAND, EDINBURGH

Reginald Fairlie (completed by A.R. Conlon), 1937-55. OS: (66) NT 257735

The last national setpiece of interwar classical monumentalism – completed after the war, its steel frame

4.19 Moredun, permanent aluminium bungalow.

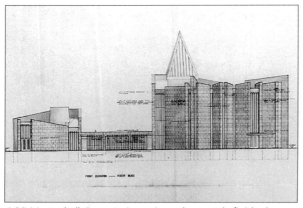

4.20 Mortonhall Crematorium: view when newly finished.

having lain unfinished throughout the conflict. A nine-storey block built on deep piling, with striking sectional arrangement reflecting its dramatically precipitous site and high-level viaduct entrance. The top two floors contain public areas, including a lofty, austere reading room; below are seven stack floors. Architecturally, the public accommodation is expressed by a sheer, pilastered screen wall between broad, flat piers and lower flanking pavilions, echoing both the overseas classicism of the later '30s, and the earlier neo-classical heritage of this country (notably Archibald Simpson's New Market, Aberdeen, 1840-2). The facade was decorated with attenuated sculptures by Hew Lorimer. (Fig. 4.21)

21: NEW CLUB, EDINBURGH

Alan Reiach, in association with Stuart Renton, 1966-9. OS: (66) NT 253739

One of the most sumptuous building projects of the postwar period. A self-rebuilding scheme by one of the country's oldest and most prestigious private clubs. Following the removal of the existing 19th-century building (by Burn), a reinforced-concrete structure of five storeys and basement was erected, with shops at the front, a grand stair-hall at the centre and a four-storey bedroom tower at the rear. The irregularly-windowed front facade, in Rubislaw granite, incorporates a first-floor terrace to conform to the 1967 Princes Street Panel Report formula of bi-level shopping. Internally, a quietly luxurious atmosphere was created through use of hessian wall finishes and

4.21 National Library of Scotland: 1967 view of front facade.

re-used elements of the old building, including both furniture and an entire dining room reconstructed out of Lorimer panelling. (Fig. 4.22)

22: POLLOCK HALLS OF RESIDENCE, EDINBURGH

Rowand Anderson, Kininmonth and Paul, 1952-9. OS: (66) NT 271723

An elegantly formal ensemble of severely classical buildings, ranged around two open courtyards. Most of the group comprises residence blocks, with rendered walls and shallow copper roofs, some with slender lantern towers. The axial focus of the project is a large dining hall, fronted by a slender arched concrete colonnade of a loosely Renaissance character. (Fig. 4.23)

23: PLANT HOUSES, ROYAL BOTANIC GARDEN, EDINBURGH

George Pearce, Superintending Architect, Ministry of Public Building and Works Scotland (in association with L.R. Creasy, structural engineer), 1965-7 (project architects, A Pendreigh, J Johnson, C Mackay). OS: (66) NT 247755

Two glasshouses – a large exhibition plant house (420 ft. in length) and a smaller exhibition orchid house set

at right angles – of a startlingly innovative suspended portal-frame system of construction, allowing, in a somewhat megastructural fashion, a sharp segregation between fixed frame and free-flowing contents. Built on the initiative of the then RBG Curator, Dr E E Kemp, who in 1961 noticed corrosion in the old exhibition house and argued successfully for the building of new, Modern structures. A full scale section of the new buildings was erected and tested to destruction in 1964. All structural support derives from an intricate external structure of high-tensile steel tubes and cables, from which the glazing is suspended. As a result of the absence of internal framework – stipulated by Dr Kemp – serried potted-plants are done away with, and the entire space can be given over to exotic landscape 'environments': African and American desertscapes, East Indian tropics, and Australasian temperate areas are only a few steps apart. (Fig. 4.24)

4.23 Pollock Halls of Residence: mid-1950s interior view of refectory.

4.22 New Club: dining room, including re-used Lorimer panelling from the previous building.

4.24 Plant Houses, Royal Botanic Garden: 1965 view of model.

24: ROYAL COMMONWEALTH POOL, EDINBURGH

Robert Matthew, Johnson-Marshall & Partners, 1967-70. OS: (66) NT 269724

Swimming complex contained in a single, massive rectangular block. Set on a sloping site, which made possible a complete separation between 'dry' accommodation, at the top, and 'wet' accommodation (including the three pools) below, and allowed the pool hall to be framed by spectators' galleries and other accommodation. Through this plan, heat loss and glare were reduced to a minimum, and the external bulk of the building was concentrated on its rear, southern side. Here, John Richards was able to elaborate the clean, 'dry-assembly' aesthetic and emphatic horizontality of Stirling Phase I, in the more grandiose context of a major public building. (Fig. 4.25)

4.25 Royal Commonwealth Pool: main entrance.

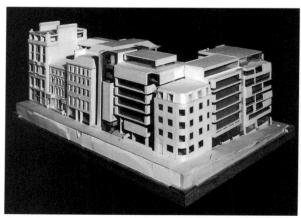

4.26 Scottish Provident Association, Edinburgh: model of redevelopment by Rowand Anderson, Kininmonth and Paul, early 1960s.

25: SCOTTISH PROVIDENT INSTITUTION, EDINBURGH

Rowand Anderson, Kininmonth & Paul, 1961-9. OS: (66) NT 256741

A large, L-shaped office infill, stretching between two streets, and designed by William G Leslie, one of the group of individualistic young Late Modernists who transformed the practice, in the late '50s and '60s, into one of the most innovative in Scotland. Spectacular main facade to St. Andrew Square, with violently juxtaposed patterns of granite-clad solids and sheer glazed voids, horizontals and verticals, crowned by a boldly glazed stair-tower (now altered). An arresting statement of the freedom of Modern composition, executed with exquisite refinement of material and proportion. (Fig. 4.26)

26: SIGHTHILL HEALTH CENTRE, EDINBURGH

Robert Gardner-Medwin (Chief Architect, Department of Health for Scotland), 1951-3. OS: (66) NT 195707

The first health centre to be built in this country: an early focus of state-sponsored, research-driven health architecture. Opened by the Secretary of State, James Stuart, on 15 May 1953. The one- and three-storey group is ranged in an informal square around a garden courtyard, and contained at its opening a comprehensive range of NHS services, including general practi-

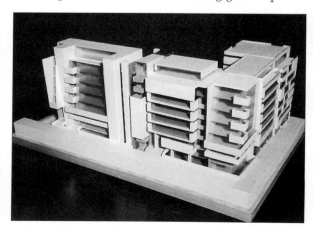

4.27 Scottish Provident Association, Edinburgh: model of proposal for larger-scale redevelopment, mid 1960s. The classical corner block, designed 1954 by J R McKay, and two buildings to the east, would all have been removed.

tioners' and dental surgeries, along with school health, child welfare, district nurses' and midwives' accommodation. It is built of precast-concrete blockwork, with foamslag concrete internal walls. The interior was intended to banish the sombre gravity of prewar institutional interiors, with their 'tertiary' colour schemes. The upper level is reached by a slender concrete spiral staircase, hailed by the *Lancet* as 'strikingly bright and gay'; the same journal noted that the bright internal colours 'range through, and sometimes, it seems, beyond the breadth of the rainbow; but the chocolate hue once revered by hospitals and public-houses is nowhere to be found'. (Fig. 4.28)

27: TURNHOUSE AIRPORT TERMINAL, EDINBURGH

Prof. Robert Matthew, 1954-6.
OS: (66) NT 159739

Returning home after his seven years as Architect to the London County Council, Matthew resumed his

4.28 Sighthill Health Centre: view of staircase.

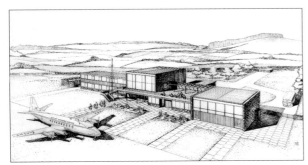

4.29 Turnhouse Airport: 1953 perspective.

work here with this demure terminal building, steel-framed on a rubble base, and clad in the timber weatherboarding typical of Matthew's search for a Modern architecture based on a Scottish 'theme'. Designed, like most of his public buildings, as a sequence of interpenetrating spaces and forms, the building was initially intended to handle 70,000 passengers annually, but to be capable of easy extension. By the early '60s it was handling ten times that number, and was twice enlarged (in 1959 and 1965); eventually a completely new terminal was built in a separate site. Demolished in 1995. (Fig. 4.29)

28: UNIVERSITY OF EDINBURGH REDEVELOPMENT

Robert Matthew Johnson-Marshall: Arts & Social Sciences Faculty Buildings, Phase 1 (David Hume Tower), 1960-3; Phase 2, 1964-7. George Square Theatre, 1967, Basil Spence, Glover & Ferguson: University Arts Library, 1964-7, Reiach, Hall & Partners: First Year Science Building (Appleton Tower), 1963-6. OS: (66) NT 259729

When RMJM began their pioneering greenfield-site university development at Stirling, they (and other designers) were already deeply involved with this, Scotland's most architecturally ambitious university scheme involving redevelopment of existing urban fabric. The individual developments along the south and east sides of George Square included setpieces by Reiach, RMJM and Spence. The stone-clad projects by the latter two firms – especially the cantilevered George Square Theatre – conformed to the 1960s predilection for more massively articulated forms; the eight-storey library was planned with central service core and elevations dominated by the bold horizontals of Portland stone-faced balconies. This redevelopment scheme, which replaced the pleasant but unexciting 18th-century classicism of George Square with a richer and more variegated architectural ensemble, including multi-storey blocks (first proposed in Basil Spence's plan of 1955), was later incorporated in a much more ambitious strategy by Percy Johnson-Marshall for a decked, multi-level redevelopment of the entire University precinct, stretching to the Pleasance. While the horizontality and slightly megastructural character of the RMJM Faculty

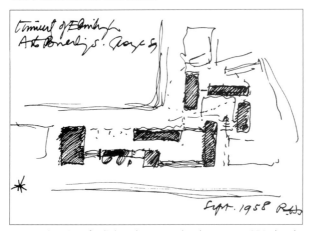

4.30 University of Edinburgh Arts Redevelopment: 1958 sketch by Robert Matthew.

4.31 Proposed George Square redevelopment, montage by RMJM, c.1960.

4.32 1991 aerial photograph of George Square redevelopment, as implemented. Anticlockwise from top left: University (Arts) Library; George Square Theatre; Social Sciences Buildings and Arts Tower; First Year Science Building.

buildings echoed this theme, the wider scheme, like most of Percy Johnson-Marshall's visionary projects, remained unrealised. (Fig. 4.30, 4.31, 4.32, 4.33, 4.34)

29: TRANSPLANTATION SURGERY UNIT, WESTERN GENERAL HOSPITAL, EDINBURGH

Peter Womersley, 1965-8. OS: (66) NT 232751

The world's first experimental building specifically designed for the transplantation of human organs. A spectacular medical innovation expressed in a forceful

architectural form: the culmination of Scotland's tradition of research-driven hospital architecture. The stringent and complex technical demands laid down by Dr. John Bowie, consultant bacteriologist at the Royal Infirmary of Edinburgh – notably, the requirement for a sterile atmosphere, and segregation of patients from one another and from staff – were brilliantly answered by Womersley in a bold, deeply modelled building built of smooth ochre-coloured concrete. Womersley commented: 'This building has been dismissed, I know, as a piece of sculpture, not architecture. I don't see why a building should not be both'. The Unit was the climax of the most monumental phase of Womersley's stylistic evolution; already, he was turning to more 'vernacular' forms (as in his contemporary medical surgery at Kelso), which anticipated more general trends of the 1970s. (Fig. 4.35)

30: FORTH ROAD BRIDGE AND CONTROL BUILDING

Sir Giles Scott, Son & Partners; consulting engineers, Mott Hay Anderson; 1958-64. OS: (65) NT 1278

The long-delayed construction of a large-span, spun-cable suspension bridge was proposed in outline by Mott Hay and Anderson as early as 1935. At its completion, it was the longest suspension bridge outside the USA – and the first to break decisively from the solid, monolithic aesthetic of structures such as Verrazano-Narrows (1963), towards a new, soaring lightness: the depth-to-span ratio was reduced to 1:178. Twin towers of high tensile steel 156m in height, supporting a twin-truss suspended structure. The north

4.33 1967 view of entrance to Edinburgh University Library.

4.34 Edinburgh University First Year Science Building (Appleton Tower): interior view, c.1966.

4.35 Nuffield Transplantation Surgery Unit: entrance hall, showing concrete coffer work.

pier rests on the submerged Mackintosh Rock, and the width of the main span (1,006m) was determined by the distance from there to water sufficiently shallow for the economical construction of the south pier. To the south of the bridge is a squat control building with observation platform, and toll booths. (Fig. 4.36)

31: MONKTONHALL COLLIERY

Egon Riss (Divisional Architect, NCB Scotland), 1960-5. OS: (66) NT 322703

Scotland's most fully realised integrated deep coal-mine complex. Located in the Midlothian Coalfield: a last, great survivor from a period of energetic Coal Board investment during the 1960s. From 1955, two shafts were sunk at Monktonhall, both over 3,000 feet deep, and production commenced in January 1965. The mines built in this programme, such Rothes and Killoch, were characterised by monumental concrete winding-engine towers, and concrete and brick surface buildings, all designed by Riss and his staff. They may be compared with postwar mine-building projects in the Ruhr coalfield, often of similarly

colossal scale and refinement, but usually faced in brick. (Figs. 4.37, 4.38)

SHETLAND ISLANDS

32: HEDDELL'S PARK AND ANNSBRAE HOUSING SCHEME, LERWICK

Richard Moira and B.L.C. Moira, 1956-9. OS: (4) HU 477413

The first stage, on two small sites, of Lerwick's Lanes redevelopment, designed by the burgh's town planning consultant. In contrast to Spence's combination of exaggeratedly rough and frankly Modern elements at the slightly earlier Dunbar scheme, here the effect was more homogeneous, with generally plain rendered walls and timber windows. The meticulously complicated grouping of dwellings into small, pedestrian-planned 'precincts' (Moira's own expression) was designed to reflect the existing character of 'traditional' Lerwick. However, this solution was only arrived at after abandonment, on cost grounds, of an original, more overtly Modern scheme by Moira,

4.36 Forth Bridge: North Main Tower under construction, November 1960.

4.37 Monktonhall Colliery, No.1 Shaft Winding Tower.

which would have been bisected by a wide, diagonal road. The landscape architect was Jane Wood. (Fig. 4.39)

STRATHCLYDE REGION

33: VALE OF LEVEN HOSPITAL, ALEXANDRIA:

Keppie, Henderson & Gleave, 1952-5.
OS: (63) NS 384808

Vale of Leven, the first postwar hospital to be built in these islands, shows that the war-inspired drive for prefabrication of all kinds of buildings had provided a new outlet for Glasgow's Beaux-Arts-derived tradition of architectural rationalism. Designed in the final years of the ascendancy of the pavilion plan, Vale of Leven's layout comprises a permanent brick-built north-south service-spine of 3 storeys, flanked by pre-fabricated 2-storey units of modular-based dimensions, built in a lightweight concrete system (based on a 3 ft. 4 in. mullion spacing) devised by the architects. The project parallels key postwar Continental initiatives in prefabrication of large social complexes, such

as Max Bill's Hochschule für Gestaltung, Ulm (1950-5) (Fig. 4.40)

34: AWE HYDRO-ELECTRIC PROJECT (CRUACHAN SECTION)

North of Scotland Hydro-Electric Board (consultant civil engineer J Williamson/electrical and mechanical engineers Merz and McLellan), planned from 1959, built 1962-5. OS: (50) NN0827

A huge, 400-megawatt pumped storage hydro-electric scheme, including dam, underground machine hall, tunnels, and outfall works: climax of the Hydro Board's development programme. Originated in the late '50s, when the increasing costs of conventional schemes forced the Board to look to the alternative of pumped storage, which pumped water uphill cheaply,

4.39 Heddell's Park, Lerwick: photograph when new, c.1959.

4.38 Monktonhall Colliery, fan house.

4.40 Vale of Leven Hospital, 1955 view.

at night, and allowed it to flow back down, generating electricity, at peak times. While the spectacular Cruachan site, with its steep ascent from Loch Awe, was ideal for pumped-storage (in its high head and short distance between upper and lower reservoirs), it posed corresponding difficulties of construction. The building of the massive buttress structure of Cruachan Dam itself was relatively straightforward. The real challenge lay in the power station and tunnels, which for reasons of space and appearance had to be built deep underground: a gigantic undertaking, involving removal of 330,000 cubic yards of rock in the face of unforeseen geological problems. To increase plant capacity to match the costs of contemporary new thermal plants such as Kincardine, a bold innovation in machine design was also required: the development of the world's first reversible pump/turbine equipment. (Fig. 4.41)

35: ST. PETER'S COLLEGE, CARDROSS

Gillespie, Kidd and Coia, 1959-66.
OS: (63) NS 353782

Rhetorical culmination of the romantic, 'form-giving' tendency in Scottish Modernism, and of the sectional planning formula for educational institutions developed by Gillespie, Kidd & Coia. A seminary for training of a hundred student priests, set on an abrupt wooded bluff, adjacent to an existing Baronial house by John Burnet Senior. On the outside, studiedly rough concrete surfaces, blocky geometry, and

dramatic cantilevering over the trees; inside, spectacularly flowing spaces intended to express the unity of the community's activities, through the enfolding of chapel and refectory by stepped ranges of study bedrooms. Following several years of dereliction and vandalism, the College is now stripped to a tree-enveloped skeleton. In 1993, at the request of DOCOMOMO's Scottish working-party, Historic Scotland raised the college's list status to Category 'A'. (Fig. 4.42)

36: CUMBERNAULD NEW TOWN, ORIGINAL HOUSING AREAS (KILDRUM, PARK, CARBRAIN, RAVENSWOOD, SEAFAR, MUIRHEAD)

Cumbernauld Development Corporation architects and others, 1959-74. OS: (64) NS 7574

In reaction to the segregated 'neighbourhood unit' planning of previous New Towns, Cumbernauld's designers clustered its first housing areas right next to

4.41 Awe Hydro-Electric Project, Cruachan Section: underground machine hall under construction, 1964.

4.42 St Peter's College, Cardross, 1966 view of ramp behind sanctuary.

the Town Centre. But, in contrast with the latter's architectural extravagance, this housing was studiedly unobtrusive. Two-storey pitched-roof rows, designed by the Development Corporation's own architects, predominated, but these were punctuated by other types designed by architects such as Gillespie, Kidd and Coia. The most celebrated of CDC's own schemes was the abruptly contoured and lavishly landscaped Seafar 2 development (1961-3), whose 147 two-storey dwellings featured complex split-level plans. As a visual punctuation for this ridge-top site, groups of sleek Bison point blocks were built in the mid-1960s. Cumbernauld's band of original housing developments, together with the Town Centre at its heart, constitutes Scotland's most significant ensemble of postwar urban architecture and planning. (Fig. 4.43)

4.43 Seafar housing area, Cumbernauld: 1991 aerial view. Seafar 2, with its irregularly aligned terraces, is at the centre; also clearly visible are the Bison point blocks, added to provide 'punctuation'.

37: KILDRUM PRIMARY SCHOOL, CUMBERNAULD

Gillespie, Kidd & Coia, 1960-2.
OS: (64) NS 771752

The postwar reaction against hygiene-determined school planning in long ranges led to more compressed planning, with classrooms clustered around halls and courtyards. Usually, large windows were still retained, in deference to the Modern insistence on daylight penetration, but Gillespie, Kidd & Coia's smaller schools abandoned even this. Their innovative formula is exemplified at Kildrum, whose infant wing, and primary block (containing twelve classrooms), are ranged around deep-set courtyards, and linked by split-level access to hall and offices. Here, 'light and air' are renounced in favour of a massively muscular treatment, with relatively small, variegated openings and chunky concrete and brick detailing –

4.44 Kildrum Primary School, Cumbernauld: 1960s view.

including a strikingly heavy chamfered precast 'railing' around the site. This aesthetic, distinctly reminiscent of the firm's churches, produced internal spaces of a enclosed, muted character. (Fig. 4.44)

38: CUMBERNAULD TOWN CENTRE PHASE 1

Cumbernauld Development Corporation (Chief Architect and Planning Officer: L. Hugh Wilson/ D.R. Leaker, Group Architect Central Area: Geoffrey Copcutt), 1963-7. OS: (64) NS 758744

A massive multi-level, multi-function town-centre building set on an elevated ridge, straddling a dual-carriageway through road. One of the key monuments of postwar European architecture, and the most important postwar work in this country. Significant chiefly as *the* international exemplar of 'megastructural' planning – the conception, central to avant-garde 1950s/60s architecture, of single, agglomerative buildings containing multiple functions juxtaposed in a visually exciting manner with traffic routes. In a postwar context, the Centre is almost completely original as a conception – although possibly influenced, further back, by the multi-level imagery of Italian Futurism, or by Schindler's Lovell Beach House – and it was hailed by international Modern Movement historian Reyner Banham as 'the canonical megastructure'. More prosaically: it was the world's first multi-level covered-in town centre. (Figs. 4.45, 4.46)

4.45 Cumbernauld Town Centre, Phase One: 1964 drawing (view from south) by M Evans. The block supported by a slender stalk, on the right hand side, is a water tank.

4.46 Cumbernauld Town Centre, Phase One: 1965 view (from south-east) during construction.

39: DOLLAN BATHS, EAST KILBRIDE

A. Buchanan Campbell, 1965-8. OS: (64) NS 632542

Theatrically emphatic reinforced-concrete structure, comprising a single giant parabolic arch 324ft. long. A high-point in the postwar reinvigoration of Glasgow's tradition of constructional panache. Externally, at the sides each rib splays out to form two colossal diagonal struts. Campbell originally intended an even more daring design, using huge laminated timber beams, but transportation problems forced a change to concrete. In this new form, he drew inspiration from the buildings of the Tokyo Olympics and from the work of Nervi, whose Palazzetto dello Sport (1957) in Rome he admired. (Fig. 4.47)

4.47 Dollan Baths under construction, c.1966.

4.48 St Bride's Church, East Kilbride: 1964 view of upper balcony.

40: ST. BRIDE'S CHURCH, EAST KILBRIDE:

Gillespie, Kidd and Coia, 1963-4. OS: (64) NS 641543

In its original condition, the finest work of postwar church architecture in the country. One of a series of expressionistic R.C. church designs by the firm, beginning in the mid-50s with St. Paul's, Glenrothes. A single, roof-lit volume enclosed by a massive but subtly modelled loadbearing wall of rough-textured brick, pierced by a slit-like entrance door in a curved embrasure. Owing to structural problems, the sheer, 90ft. high campanile, which consisted of two brick slabs with slatted timber screen infilling, was dismantled in 1987, and has not yet been reinstated. Listed by Historic Scotland, 1994. (Fig. 4.48)

41: ANDERSTON CROSS C.D.A. INDUSTRIAL ZONE, GLASGOW

Jack Holmes & Partners, 1965-9. OS: (64) NS 574654

Megastructural group of decked factories in reinforced concrete and common brick, with banded windows. An attempt to reach a high-density solution to the thorny problem of accommodating 'overspill' industries displaced by nearby slum redevelopment. Contains over 500,000 sq.ft. of flatted-factory floorspace (the top floor being column-free), above three decks of vehicle-accessible warehousing and car parking. The structure is of reinforced concrete flat plate floors, supported by a grid of columns of constant dimensions, with inverted pyramid capitals. The overpowering south frontage provides an emphatic traffic-architecture landmark alongside the Clydeside Expressway. (Fig. 4.49)

4.49 Anderston Cross CDA Industrial Zone: original perspective drawing.

42: CRATHIE DRIVE DEVELOPMENT, GLASGOW

Ronald Bradbury, Director of Housing, Glasgow Corporation, 1949-52. OS: (64) NS 551668

The first multi-storey public housing project to be built in the country: an eight-storey block of 88 one-room dwellings for single women (and caretaker's flat). Here, the modernity of high building was used to distance this new type of small dwelling from the, by then, unsavoury connotations of the old-style 'single-end'. In contrast to the layout of the Corporation's 1944 Castlemilk proposal as parallel 'Zeilenbau' slabs, Crathie Court is an asymmetrical slab-like block, faced in concrete blockwork, with massive projecting balconies. Bradbury was an admirer of American sky-scrapers, and his reliance on what he termed 'the grouping of masses' harks back to the Art Deco monu-mentalism of the 1930s. (Fig. 4.50)

43: GLASGOW INNER RING ROAD, NORTH AND WEST FLANKS

Engineers Scott Wilson Kirkpatrick; consultant architect W. Holford, designed from 1962 and built 1965-71. OS: (64) NS 606660 (Townhead)

The first urban ring-road motorway in these islands, and the initial, component of Target 1 – a ten-year plan to build a 21-km network of primary roads to divert traffic from surface streets. Its daring ambitions were inspired by American precedent, yet it had to fit into the closely confined space of a European city – threaded through a narrow corridor opened up by Glasgow Corporation's slum-clearance – and only half of it was built. Highlights are the grade-separated com-plexity of Townhead Interchange, and the juxtaposi-tion of the sunken artery of Charing Cross Section with soaring Kingston Bridge (now facing a major repair scheme). (Fig. 4.51)

44: GLASGOW UNIVERSITY LIBRARY AND ART GALLERY

William Whitfield, 1965-81. OS: (64) NS 568668

A Kahn-like reversal of the 'service core' principle inspired this densely clustered, castle-like outcrop, which crowns the skyline of the University's Hillhead extension area. Variegated concrete service towers congregate around the outside of the building, leaving internal areas exceptionally uncluttered. The low, massive Art Gallery, incorporating a reconstruction of Mackintosh's demolished house, was added later at the foot of the library wing. (Fig. 4.52)

45: HERON HOUSE, GLASGOW

Derek Stephenson & Partners, 1967-71. OS: (64) NS 583655

Megastructural commercial complex occupying a steeply sloping street-block: dominated by a 200ft.

4.50 Crathie Drive multi-storey development: south (garden) side.

4.51 Painting of Glasgow Inner Ring Road under construction in the late 1960s.

high, 19-storey office tower. Skilfully embraces Alexander Thomson's St. Vincent Street Church at its northwest corner, forming a single, sophisticated composition, with powerful juxtaposition of substructures. The development dramatically envelops St. Vincent Lane in a skylit tunnel. (Fig. 4.53)

46: HUTCHESONTOWN/PART GORBALS C.D.A. AREA 'C', GLASGOW

Sir Basil Spence, Glover & Ferguson, 1960-6.
OS: (64) NS 594638

The centrepiece of the architecturally prestigious redevelopment of the Gorbals: two dramatic 20-storey

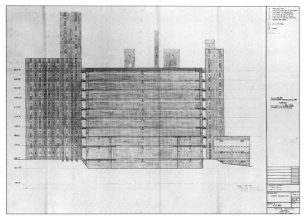

4.52 Glasgow University Library: 1964 Dean of Guild plan of north elevation, showing service towers at sides, and blank area for future extension.

4.53 Heron House: view from northeast, showing the building's grouping with St Vincent Street Church.

slabs, whose inset communal drying areas were intended as a multi-storey re-enactment of the tenement 'community' they replaced. Rugged external modelling combined with intricate split-level internal planning. Following intractable management and structural difficulties, the blocks were dynamited on 12 September 1993. (Fig. 4.54)

47: LOURDES SECONDARY SCHOOL, GLASGOW

Thomas Cordiner, 1951-7.
OS: (64) NS 535637

After the war, Cordiner remained faithful to the brick-built, Art Deco four-squareness of his earlier work. However, a much greater simplicity became evident – expressed most audaciously here at Lourdes School in the sweeping window-bands of the south facade. His largest project – eight 26-storey Corporation slab blocks at Hillpark – was turned down at public inquiry in 1964. (Fig. 4.55)

4.54 Hutchesontown/Gorbals Area 'C': 1966 view of side of one block.

48: MEADOWSIDE GRANARY EXTENSION, GLASGOW

Clyde Navigation Trust (L. G. Mouchel & Partners in conjunction with Archibald Thomson, Engineer to the Trustees), 1956-67. OS: (64) NS 548663

A group of giant granary blocks built to cope with a rapid postwar increase in grain imports. In 1955, the decision was taken to more than double the existing 1914/38 facilities by building a 387-ft. long, 9-storey extension: construction was brick or precast-faced reinforced concrete frame, with storage bins also cast in-situ. The extension was supplied by travelling suction elevators at the quayside and linked by transfer conveyor to the existing building. The contractors were Holst & Co. By 1967, a further extension of similar design and cyclopean scale had been added at the west end. The buildings' monumentality derives not only from their size – which ensures the now disused group a status as one of the city's most prominent landmarks – but also from their unselfconscious, cubic starkness. (Fig. 4.56)

49: NOTRE DAME HIGH SCHOOL, GLASGOW

Thomas Cordiner, 1939-53. OS: (64) NS 563674

Cordiner's prewar work closely paralleled the contemporary architectural tendency of Modernity tempered by Traditionalist classicism, that became widespread

4.55 Lourdes Secondary School, south facade.

4.56 Meadowside Granary Extension, south frontage.

4.57 Notre Dame High School: centre of main facade.

in public buildings of the Netherlands during the late 1930s and '40s. Here – as at the postwar Linn Crematorium – the basic grouping is symmetrical, its brick and concrete simplicity offset by geometrical flourishes. (Fig. 4.57)

50: RED ROAD DEVELOPMENT, GLASGOW

Sam Bunton & Associates, 1962-9.
OS: (64) NS 620674

Five 31-storey towers and two 27-storey slabs – at their completion, the highest housing blocks in Europe. The climax of Glasgow Corporation's drive to 'give the people homes', and the fulfilment of Sam Bunton's quest for an extravagantly tall, skyscraper-like expres-

sion for mass housing. Asbestos-clad, steel-framed structural design highly unusual in a housing context. (Fig. 4.58)

51: ST. TERESA'S CHURCH, GLASGOW

Alexander McAnally & Partners, 1956-60.
OS: (64) NS 591674

Designed in 1955, this Possilpark church by one of the country's leading Roman Catholic ecclesiastical architects, demonstrates the continuing postwar vitality of the deep-rooted tradition of neo-Romanesque architecture. Close parallels to this thick-set brick style are to be found in the postwar Catholic church-building of the Netherlands and West Germany: it is perhaps relevant that the main basilica of St Teresa, at Lisieux, is a massive Romanesque 1920s building. (Fig. 4.59)

52: SMITHYCROFT ROAD SECONDARY SCHOOL, GLASGOW

A. G. Jury, City Architect, 1964-7. OS: (64) NS 634665

A demonstration of the persistence of the tradition of rationalistic, geometrical design within the Glasgow municipal architectural establishment: a secondary school planned with all teaching and assembly accommodation set in a concentric pattern of two circles. The outer circle contains a ring of wedge-shaped class-

4.58 Red Road development in 1967, showing Blocks 1 and 2 (foreground) complete, and the remainder still under construction.

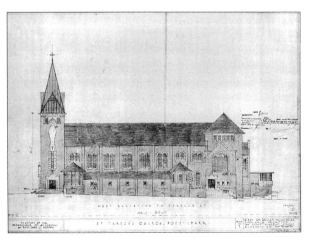

4.59 St Teresa's Church, Possilpark: 1956 Dean of Guild drawing by Alexander McAnally & Partners.

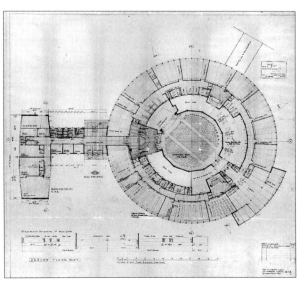

4.60 Smithycroft Road Secondary School: 1964 Dean of Guild plan.

rooms; at the centre, with open areas around, is a 13-sided, 716-seat hall. Typically of the matter-of-fact approach of Glasgow Corporation's architecture department, the elevations are sober reinforced-concrete grids. In a smaller-scale echo of this design, a series of standardised circular primary schools was subsequently built by Lanark County Council across the whole of Lanarkshire in the early 1970s. (Fig. 4.60)

53: STOW COLLEGE OF BUILDING AND PRINTING/STOW COLLEGE OF DISTRIBUTIVE TRADES, GLASGOW

Wylie, Shanks & Underwood, 1960-4.
OS: (64) NS 594657

Designed by Peter Williams, these two adjacent multi-storey college buildings combine a sheer main body, clad in vitriolite/glass curtain walling and Roman travertine, with boldly modelled, Corbusier-like roof-structures. Both employ service-core plans, allowing maximum use of the perimeter walls for teaching. The 13-storey Building and Printing tower, standing on its squat columns, dominates the group; the Distributive Trades College was limited to 100 ft. height (7 storeys) by planning restrictions. (Fig. 4.61)

54: ST LAWRENCE'S CHURCH, GREENOCK

Gillespie, Kidd & Coia, 1951-4. OS: (63) NS 296754

The culmination of the massive, brick-built style of church architecture pursued by Coia from the 1930s to the mid/late 50s: capacious, basilican structures, sometimes overtly classical or Romanesque, but equally often recalling expressionistic German interwar churches, with their soaring parabolic arches or triangular motifs. St. Lawrence's, with its hillside setting and monumental, heaped-up profile, also alludes to the tradition of stepped or terraced architecture represented by Thomson's St. Vincent Street Church or Hamilton's Royal High School. (Fig 4.63)

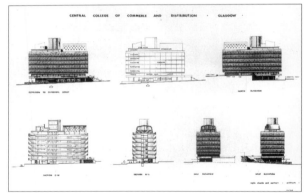

4.62 Stow College of Distributive Trades: elevation drawing.

4.63 St Lawrence's Church, Greenock: interior view.

4.61 Stow College of Building and Printing: view when newly completed, c.1964.

55: LANARK COUNTY BUILDINGS, HAMILTON

D.G. Bannerman (County Architect), 1959-64.
OS: (64) NS 714559

A 17-storey, 200 ft. high administrative slab block, juxtaposed with a circular council chamber and other low buildings. An exemplary realisation of a particularly Modern building type, the monumental, curtain-walled administrative/governmental tower (as pioneered at the UN Headquarters in New York, and at Brasilia), and a noble civic 'acropolis' for urban Lanarkshire. Lavish materials and finish worthy of a great public building, including curtain walling and ceramic mosaic-clad gable walls. Listed (at Category A) by Historic Scotland, in November 1993. (Fig. 4.64)

4.64 Lanark County Buildings, Hamilton.

56: HUNTERSTON 'A' NUCLEAR POWER STATION

General Electric Company Ltd. and Simon-Carves Ltd (design consortium); consulting architects Howard V. Lobb & Partners, 1957-64. OS: (63) NS 1851

The first civilian nuclear power station in this country: a 360 megawatt plant originally designed to supply approximately a quarter of the total electricity demand in the SSEB area. The station comprises two

4.65 Hunterston 'A' nuclear power station: simplified cut-away model of one of the reactors.

4.66 Hunterston 'A' nuclear power station: interior view, 1989.

natural uranium-fuelled, graphite-moderated, gas-cooled 'MAGNOX' reactors, together with associated steam-raising units, situated adjacent to a turbine house and control room. Uniquely, the reactors here were loaded and unloaded from below, and as a result are perched high above ground level, in gigantic but elegant curtain-walled, steel-framed blocks. The station was closed in 1990. (Figs. 4.65, 4.66)

57: RAVENSCRAIG WORKS, MOTHERWELL

Colvilles/British Steel Corporation, 1957-87.
OS: (64) NS 7756

Before its closure in 1992, Ravenscraig was an integrated iron and steelworks situated on a 1,000 acre site, with a liquid steel capacity of up to 2 million tonnes per annum. Built on a greenfield location in 1957, the plant underwent steady development over the following three decades, increasingly orientated towards specialised, high-quality steel-production. Latterly, about 75% of its steel output passed through the strip mill, where it was converted into hot rolled coil for further processing elsewhere. Some of the vast physical remains of the works still survive, awaiting disposal or clearance. (Fig. 4.67)

58: PAISLEY CIVIC CENTRE

Hutchison Locke and Monk, competition 1964, built
1966-71. OS: (64) NS 487640

Complex and sophisticated headquarters grouping, serving two different local authorities (Paisley Burgh,

Renfrew County Council) and a police authority. Despite a 6-storey height restriction, because of the proximity of Paisley Abbey, the design, in the words of the competition assessors, succeeded in reconciling its 'intimate yet respectful relation to the Abbey' with an 'appropriate grandeur of urban space'. The original layout plan envisaged a sinuous line of buildings focused on a complex of council suites serving both authorities, with a 'civic concourse' beneath; but this central group was not fully completed. All buildings are of reinforced-concrete frame with precast cladding, and are designed on a four-foot module. (Fig. 4.68)

TAYSIDE REGION

59: ARTS TOWER AND FACULTY BUILDING, QUEEN'S COLLEGE, DUNDEE

Robert Matthew, Johnson-Marshall & Partners,
1958-61. OS: (54) NO 397298

The most fully developed example of Matthew's rubbly, timber-clad Modernity of the 1950s, before new interpretations of Functionalism began to surface in his office in the early '60s. One of the first built realisations of multi-storey tower blocks in Scotland, this group adds an informal but urbane vertical punctuation to Perth Road. The tower chiefly contains departmental and administrative accommodation, including the nascent University of Dundee's Senate Room; the lower spur contained the university library. (Fig. 4.69)

4.67 Ravenscraig Works, Hot Strip Mill: view of rolling mill line, following closure in 1992.

4.68 Paisley Civic Centre: view of County Buildings, showing council chamber.

WESTERN ISLES

60: EAGLAIS MATHAIR NAN DORAINN, GEARRAIDH NA MONADH, UIBHIST A DEAS

Richard J McCarron, 1964-5. OS: (31) NF 758164

Roman Catholic chapel-of-ease for a congregation of 300, designed by a newly-graduated architect (working with RMJM at the time). Built in fifteen months, in rendered brick, with prefabricated roof beams and RC columns. The building's compact, highly geometrical 'broad front' form, with small, deeply recessed windows and wide, square plan, reflected both liturgical requirements (for intimate contact between celebrant and worshippers) and the extreme maritime climate of the island; the design was influenced by the work of Coia, who was consulted by McCarron at initial proposal stage. The building programme was organised innovatively, with the parish priest, Mgr. McKellaig, acting as contractor. The mosaic over the front entrance was the work of David Harding, later celebrated as Glenrothes Development Corporation's artist-in-residence during the late 1960s and '70s, and (more recently still) an influential teacher at Glasgow School of Art. (Fig. 4.70)

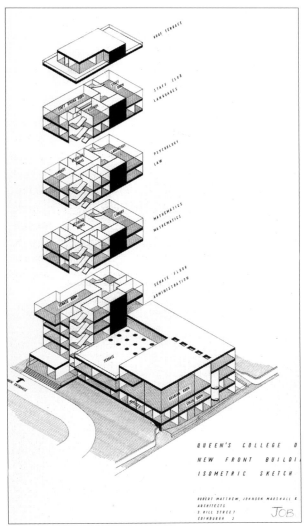

4.69 Queen's College Dundee: isometric sketch of Arts Tower and Faculty Building.

4.70 Eaglais Mathair nan Dorainn: 1960s view.

4.71 Fairydean Stadium, Galashiels (Peter Womersley, 1963-5): view when newly completed.

BIBLIOGRAPHY

To facilitate use, this Bibliography is arranged in roughly the same manner as the book itself. General texts, corresponding to Part One and Part Two, are listed at the beginning. Then follow references corresponding to the papers on architects and architecture in Part Three, and to the Sixty Key Buildings in Part Four.

PARTS ONE AND TWO

GENERAL HISTORIES
J Cunnison, J B S Gilfillan, *Glasgow*, 1958
T Devine and R J Findlay (eds.), *Scotland in the 20th Century*, 1996
A Dickson and J N H Treble (eds.), *People and Society in Scotland*, iii, 1992
T Gallagher, *Glasgow, the Uneasy Peace*, 1987 (chapter 6)
C Harvie, *No Gods and Precious Few Heroes*, 1981
M Lynch, *Scotland, a New History*, 1991 (chapter 25)
M Lynch (ed.), *Scotland 1850-1979*, 1993
London Scots Self-Government Committee, *The New Scotland*, 1942
R Saville (ed.), *The Economic Development of Modern Scotland*, 1985

THE ROLE OF GOVERNMENT
J S Gibson, *The Thistle and the Crown*, 1985
Guardian Society of Scotland, *Scottish Municipal Annual* (various dates)
G Pottinger, *The Secretaries of State for Scotland*, 1979
Scottish Government Yearbook (various dates)

BUILDING (GENERAL)
Concrete Quarterly April/June 1964, 'New Buildings in Scottish Universities'
Edinburgh Pictorial Ltd, *Scottish Building and Civil Engineering Yearbook* (various dates)
E Gordon, *A Handbook on the Principles of Church Building*, 1963
North of Scotland Hydro-Electric Board, *Annual Reports* (various)
P L Payne, *The Hydro*, 1988
P Reed (ed.), *Glasgow: The Forming of a City*, 1993
The Scotsman, 'The New Scotland' (annual building

supplement), e.g. 1959

Scottish Development Department (SDD), *Annual Reports* (from 1963)

Scottish Education Department (SED), *Education Building Notes* (No. 1, 1964, etc.)

HOUSING

T Begg, *Fifty Special Years*, 1987

R Bryant, *The Dampness Monster*, 1989

R Burnett, *Scotsman Weekend*, 31-8-1996 (on Penny Tenement)

Castlemilk People's History Group, *The Big Flit*, 1990

Corporation of Glasgow Housing Department, *Review of Operations*, 1947

R D Cramond, *Allocation of Council Houses*, 1964

Department of Health for Scotland (DHS), *Housing Handbook* (various dates; especially Part I 'Housing Layout', revised 1958, and Part III 'House Design', 1950/1956)

DHS/SDD, *Housing Return for Scotland* (quarterly: various dates

M Glendinning and S Muthesius, *Tower Block, Modern Public Housing in England, Scotland, Wales and Northern Ireland*, 1994

A G Jury, *Glasgow's Housing Centenary*, 1966

Scottish Housing Advisory Committee (SHAC), *Council House Communities*, 1970

SHAC, *Modernising Our Homes*, 1947

SHAC, *Planning Our New Homes*, 1944

Scottish Office Building Directorate, *A Guide to Non-Traditional Housing in Scotland*, 1987

Strathclyde Regional Council Education Department, *20th-Century Housing in Glasgow: Documents 1914 to 1990s* (available in Glasgow Room, Mitchell Library, Glasgow)

R B White, *Prefabrication*, 1965

TOWN AND COUNTRY PLANNING

P Abercrombie and D Plumstead, *A Civic Survey and Plan for Edinburgh*, 1949

P Abercrombie and R Matthew, *The Clyde Valley Regional Plan 1946*, 1949

H Begg (ed.), *100 Years Town Planning in Dundee*, 1992

R Bruce, *First Planning Report*, 1945/*Second Planning Report*, 1946

W Dobson Chapman and C F Riley, *Granite City*, 1952

R Grieve, *Grieve on Geddes*, 1990

M Keating, *The City that Refused to Die*, 1988

M Keating, *The Designation of Cumbernauld New Town*, 1986

J Lindsay, *Elizabeth B Mitchell*, 1993

J Mann (ed.), *Rebuilding Scotland*, 1941

F Mears, *A Regional Survey and Plan for Central and South-East Scotland*, 1949

F J Osborn and A Whittick, *New Towns*, 1977

Scottish Council (Development & Industry), *Inquiry into the Scottish Economy*, 1961 (Toothill Report)

Scottish Development Department, *Central Scotland, A Programme for Development and Growth*, 1963

R Smith, *East Kilbride*, 1979

R Smith, U Wannop (eds.), *Strategic Planning in Action*, 1985.

ARCHITECTURE (GENERAL: INCLUDING CONSERVATION)

ABN, 27-5-1959, 17-6-1959

ABN, 6-5-1964 (N Taylor article)

The Architect's Journal, 6-5-1964 (W Sinclair Gauldie article)

Architectural Design (*AD*), 6-1952, 1-1962 (P Nuttgens article), and 9-1966 (F A Walker article)

R Bailey, *Scottish Architects' Papers*, 1996

Buildings of Scotland series (published volumes: *Lothian, Glasgow, Edinburgh, Highland & Islands, Dumfries & Galloway*)

Edinburgh Architectural Association, *Yearbooks* (various dates)

B Edwards, *Basil Spence*, 1995

Glasgow Institute of Architects, *Yearbooks* (various dates)

Glasgow Institute of Architects, *RIBA Conference*, 1964

M Glendinning, R MacInnes, A MacKechnie, *A History of Scottish Architecture*, 1996

Inland Revenue, *An Introduction to Centre 1*, 1968

M Kelsall and S Harris, *A Future for the Past*, 1961

C MacGregor, 'Gribloch', *Architectural Heritage* 5, 1995

C McKean, *The Scottish Thirties*, 1987

R Matthew, J Reid, M Lindsay (eds.), *The Conservation of Georgian Edinburgh*, 1972

P Nuttgens, *Reginald Fairlie*, 1959

J Ockman, *Architecture Culture 1943-1968*, 1993

B Pentreath, 'Classical Modernism in Fifties Edinburgh', *Architectural Heritage* 5, 1995

A Reiach and R Hurd, *Building Scotland*, 1941 (first ed.)

R W K C Rogerson, *Jack Coia*, 1986

RIAS *Illustrated Architectural Guide* series (various areas)

RIAS Quarterly (various dates; between 1956 and 1960, *Architectural Prospect*)

G Scott-Moncrieff, *Living Traditions of Scotland*, 1951

Scottish Field, October 1968 (Changing Glasgow)

Scottish Review 8, 1971 (C McWilliam article)

T Spaven/RMJM, *The Early Years*, 1975

N Thomson, 'Building a New Scotland', *Scottish Field*, April-December 1967 (articles on Wheeler, Cocker, Coia, Matthew)

D M Walker, *St Andrew's House*, 1989

D M Walker, *Transactions of the Ancient Monuments Society*, 38, 1994 (article on 'listing')

P Willis, *New Architecture in Scotland*, 1977 (see also below for individual sites)

A McL Young and A M Doak, *Glasgow at a Glance*, 1965

PART THREE

(a) Cumbernauld Town Centre
(Copcutt papers: *AD* 5-1963; typescript 1995)

American Institute of Architects Journal 7-1967

ABN 5-12-1962

AJ 5-12-1962, 8-1-1964, 21-9-1966, 31-1-1968, 5-10-1977

AD 5-1963 (including Copcutt article)

Architectural Forum 8-1964, 11-1966

AR 12-1967

L'Architecture d'Aujourd'hui, 1-1963

R Banham, *Megastructure*, 1976, pp.10, 105, 167-72

Baumeister 10-1965

Bauwelt 1963, 99

B 13-11-1962, 8-5-1964

Concrete Quarterly 4/6-1963

Country Life 6-10-1966

P Johnson-Marshall, *Rebuilding Cities*, 1966, 371

Progressive Architecture 7-1968

Prospect Spring 1959

JRIBA 5-1964

(b) Basil Spence and Hutchesontown (Robertson lecture)

– *Spence, in general*:

    L Campbell, *RIBA Journal* 4-1993 (interwar Spence)

    B Edwards, *Basil Spence*, 1995

– *Hutchesontown*:

    AR 11-1967

    B 7-7-1961

    Surveyor 13-5-1961

– *Dunbar*:

    ABN 15-4-1949

    AJ 18-9-1952

    AR 12-1952

    B 2-11-1951, 7-11-1952

– *Edinburgh University Library*:

    Willis, 46-7

– *Mortonhall*:

    AR 4-1967

    B 11-5-1962, 2-6-1967

    Willis, 38-41

(c) Sam Bunton and Red Road (Glendinning lecture)

– *Bunton, in general*:

    AJ 14-10-1948, 18-1-1952

    B 25-4-1941, 22-1-1943, 14-1-1944, 31-3-1944

    Scottish Record Office, files DD6-269/1320-3/1326/ 1422/1515/2362, DD12-1156/1735

    R B White, Prefabrication, 1965, 221-2

– *Red Road*:

    AR 11-1967

    B 19-10-1962, 15-3-1963

    Glasgow Herald (Constructional Review), 31-10-1966

    Interbuild 1963, 27 *International Asbestos Cement Review* 10-1966

    Town and Country Planning 7/8-1982

(d) Dysart redevelopment (Wheeler lecture)

AJ 14-2-1962

AR 4-1967

Housing Review 7, 8-1967

Municipal Journal 20-12-1953 (Bowery development, Leslie) N Thomson, *Scottish Field*, April 1967

(e) Morris & Steedman's Houses (Page, Steedman lectures)

– *General*:

    S A F Macintosh, *The Private Houses of Morris & Steedman* (Honours Degree Thesis, Mackintosh School of Architecture), Glasgow University, 1995

– *Avisfield*:

    AD 1-1963

    AJ 18-12-1958, 1-1-1959

– *Wilson house*:

    AJff 28-1-1960, 1-1962

– *Principal's House, Morris house*:

    Willis, 18-21, 24-7

(f) Royal Commonwealth Pool (Richards lecture)

AD 1-1967

AJ 16-9-1970

J Richards, Edinburgh Architectural Association *Transactions* 1985

JRIBA 8-1970

Swimming Pool Review 12-1969

Willis, 76-9

(g) Gillespie, Kidd & Coia (Baines, Metzstein lectures)

– *General*:

    ABN, 13-2-1969, 42

    Mac Journal 1, 1994 (J Macaulay, C Hermansen eds.)

    RIBA Journal, 7-1969, 281-2

    R W K Rogerson, *Jack Coia*, 1986

    D M Watters, *Cardross Seminary*, 1997

– *Cardross*:
  Builder, 5-5-1967
  Clergy Review 3-1967
  CQ 1/3-1967
  Country Life 27-7-1967
  D M Watters, *Cardross Seminary*, 1997
  Willis, 56-9
– *Our Lady of Good Counsel*:
  Willis, 34-5
– *Robinson College*:
  AJ 5-8-1981
– *St Bride's Church*:
  B 23-7-1965

(h) Glasgow University Library (Whitfield lecture)
B 4-1-1963

PART FOUR

Borders
High Sunderland, Klein House and Studio:
  Architecture and Building, 7-1958
  Country Life, 15-9-1960
  RIBA Journal, 5-1969 and 5-1973
  Willis, 68-70

Central
Bannockburn:
  C McKean, *Stirling and the Trossachs*, 1985, 62
Falkirk Ward:
  SHHD, *The Falkirk Ward*, 1966
  Building, 26-1-1968
Stirling University:
  AJ 5-6-1968
  AR 6-1973
  Robert Matthew Johnson-Marshall & Partners,
    University of Stirling Development Plan Report,
    1968
  Willis, 52-5.

Fife
Dysart:
  See ref. above (Wheeler lecture).
Kincardine Power Station:
  AD 1-1962
  Prospect 1957
Kirkcaldy Town House:
  J Gifford, *Fife*, 1988, 283
St Andrews residences:
  AD 7-1966, 12-1966, 9-1970
  Architectural Forum 9-1970

  Werk 5-1971
  Willis, 48-51

Grampian
Aberdeen, Gallowgate redevelopment:
  W Brogden, *Aberdeen*, 1986, 81
Aberdeen, Gray's School:
  Building, 8-3-1968

Highland
Dounreay:
  I Sutherland, *Dounreay, an Experimental Research
    Establishment*, 1990

Lothian
Dunbar:
  See ref. above (Robertson)
Edinburgh, 'Avisfield':
  See ref. above (Page, Steedman)
Edinburgh, Chessels Court:
  RIBA Journal, 1-1967
Edinburgh, Leith Fort:
  AJ 6-2-1958, 7-4-1965
  AR 1-1961, 3-1965
  B 31-1-1958
  P. Whiting, *New Single-Storey Houses*, 1966, 166-9
Edinburgh, Moredun scheme:
  DOCOMOMO Scottish National Working-Party,
    Moredun Housing Area, 1993 (reproduced
    DOCOMOMO International *Journal* 12, 11-1994)
  Edinburgh Central Library, Edinburgh Room,
    Corporation Minutes (e.g. Housing Committee
    4/30-11-1948 and Progress Reports)
Edinburgh, Mortonhall Crematorium:
  See ref. above (Robertson)
Edinburgh, National Library of Scotland:
  B 10-7-1936, 5-8-1956
  P Nuttgens, *Reginald Fairlie*, 1959
Edinburgh, New Club:
  AR 11-1970
  B 14-5-1971
  Willis, 84-7
Edinburgh, Pollock Halls:
  Builder 4-7-1952
Edinburgh, Plant Houses:
  B 1-12-1967
  E E Kemp, *Royal Botanical Garden 1946-70:
    The New Plant Houses*, 1992
  D M Whitham, DOCOMOMO Register fiche on RBG,
    1994
  Willis, 72-3

Edinburgh, Royal Commonwealth Pool:
  See ref. above (Richards)
Edinburgh, Scottish Provident Institution:
  J Gifford, C McWilliam, D Walker, *Edinburgh*, 1984, 323
Edinburgh, Sighthill Health Centre:
  AJ, 6-8-1953
  Builder 12-6-1953
  Lancet, 23-5-1953
  Municipal Journal 3-7-1953
Edinburgh, Turnhouse Airport:
  ABN 7-3-1957
  AJ 5-7-1956
  AD 10-1956
  Bauen & Wohnen 4-1959
University of Edinburgh Redevelopment:
  AJ 19-6-1968 (Library)
  AR 6-1968 (departmental buildings)
  Percy Johnson-Marshall, *University of Edinburgh CDA*,
    1962
  Willis, 46-7 (Library)
Edinburgh, Nuffield Transplantation Surgery Unit:
  AD 4-1968
  L'Architecture d'Aujourd'hui, 10-1969
  Baumeister, 7-1968
  Progressive Architecture, 9-1968
  Werk, 5-1968
  Willis, 88-9
Forth Road Bridge:
  B 4-9-1964
  ACD Bridge Company, *Forth Road Bridge*, 1964
Monktonhall Colliery:
  National Monuments Record, record sheet of June
    1989 by Miles Oglethorpe

Shetland
Lerwick, Heddell's Park:
  M Finnie, *Shetland*, 1990, 25

Strathclyde
Alexandria, Vale of Leven Hospital:
  ABN, 29-9-1955
Awe Hydro-Electric Project:
  Electrical Review 6-1971
  Engineering News-Record 2-7-1964
  P L Payne, *The Hydro*, 1988
  Water Power 1-1966
St Peter's College:
  See ref. above (Baines, Metzstein)
Cumbernauld New Town, Housing Areas (General):
  ABN 29-3-1961
  AJ 5-12-1962, 31-1-1968

AR 2-1964
Cumbernauld Architects' Department,
  Cumbernauld Housing, 30 Years, c.1982
JRIBA 5-1964
(Seafar 2)
AR 1-1961
Cumbernauld, Kildrum Primary School:
  R W K Rogerson, *Jack Coia*, 1986
Cumbernauld Town Centre:
  See ref. above (Copcutt)
East Kilbride, Dollan Baths:
  B 14-6-1968
East Kilbride, St Bride's Church:
  See ref. above (Baines)
Glasgow, Anderston Cross Industrial Zone:
  E Williamson, A Riches, M Higgs, *Glasgow*,
    1990, 292
Glasgow, Crathie Drive:
  Scottish Georgian Society, Bulletin 1982
  Strathclyde Regional Archive, Dean of Guild ref.
    1949/273
  Strathclyde Regional Archive, file D.TC.H.5
    (multi-storey)
Glasgow Inner Ring Road:
  Planning History Group Bulletin v.14 no.3 1992
  Proceedings of the Inst. of Civil Engineers 10-1968, 2-
    1994
  Scott & Wilson, Kirkpatrick & Partners, *A Highway
    Plan for Glasgow*, 1965
  Structural Engineer 1-1961
Glasgow, Heron House:
  Building 19-4-1968
  Strathclyde Regional Archive, Dean of Guild ref.
    1967/322
Glasgow, Hutchesontown/Gorbals Area 'C':
  See ref. above (Robertson).
Glasgow, Lourdes School:
  Williamson et al. 603
Glasgow, Meadowside Granary:
  Williamson et al. 374-5
Glasgow, Notre Dame School:
  Williamson et al. 358
Glasgow, Red Road:
  See ref. above (Glendinning)
Glasgow, St Teresa's Church:
  Strathclyde Regional Archive, Dean of Guild
    ref. 1956/401
Glasgow, Smithycroft Road School:
  Strathclyde Regional Archive, Dean of Guild ref.
    1964/382
Glasgow, Stow Colleges:

Williamson et al. 143-4

Glasgow University Library:
    See ref. above (Whitfield)

Greenock, St Lawrence's Church:
    R W K Rogerson, *Jack Coia*, 1986

Hamilton, Lanark County Buildings:
    B 4-9-1964

Hunterston 'A' Power Station:
    B 18-6-1965
    Nuclear News 4-1989

Motherwell, Ravenscraig Works:
    P L Payne, *Colvilles and the Scottish Steel Industry*,
        1979, Chapter 13

Paisley Civic Centre:
    B 10-1-1961
    B 10-2-1967

Tayside

Dundee, Queen's College Arts Tower:
    C McKean, D Walker, *Dundee*, 1933 (new edition), 77

Western Isles

Eaglais Mathair nan Dorainn:
    The Clergy Review, 5-1966

ABBREVIATIONS

ABN	*Architect and Building News*
AD	*Architectural Design*
AJ	*Architects' Journal*
AR	*Architectural Review*
ARU	Architecture Research Unit (Edinburgh University)
B	*The Builder/Building*
CDA	Comprehensive Development Area
CIAM	Congrès Internationaux d'Architecture Moderne
DHS	Department of Health for Scotland
DLO	direct labour organisation
DOCOMOMO	Documentation and Conservation of the Modern Movement
EAAYB	*Edinburgh Architectural Association Year Book*
GIA	Glasgow Institute of Architects
ILP	Independent Labour Party
LCC	London County Council
MW	megawatts
NMRS	National Monuments Record of Scotland
NOSHEB	North of Scotland Hydro-Electric Board
QRIAS	*Quarterly of the RIAS*
RFACS	Royal Fine Art Commission for Scotland
(J)RIBA	(Journal of the) Royal Institute of British Architects
RIAS	Royal Incorporation of Architects in Scotland
RMJM	Robert Matthew, Johnson-Marshall & Partners
SBCEY	*Scottish Building and Civil Engineering Yearbook*
SDD	Scottish Development Department
SED	Scottish Education Department
SHAC	Scottish Housing Advisory Committee
SHHD	Scottish Home & Health Department
SNBR	Scottish National Buildings Record
SSHA	Scottish Special Housing Association
UIA	International Union of Architects

INDEX